Gil Walker

The
Compact History
of the
United States
Marine Corps

New and
Revised Edition

Lt. Col. PHILIP N. PIERCE, USMC (Ret.)
and
Lt. Col. FRANK O. HOUGH, USMCR

Illustrations by GIL WALKER

HAWTHORN BOOKS, INC. ★ *Publishers* ★ NEW YORK and LONDON

THE

COMPACT HISTORY

OF THE

UNITED STATES

MARINE CORPS

★ ★ ★ ★ ★ ★ ★

First Edition, May, 1960
New and Revised Edition, March, 1964

Preface

The intent of this book is to compress almost two centuries of United States Marine Corps history into one brief volume. To whatever degree this goal has been realized, a large measure of credit belongs to the late Lieutenant Colonel Frank O. Hough, USMCR, whose name appears as co-author. Colonel Hough accomplished much of the necessary research, and organized much of the material included before his untimely death on May 15, 1958.

The author is particularly indebted to Mr. Michael O'Quinlivan, Head, Records and Research Section, Marine Corps Headquarters; Major James C. Gasser, USMC, and Captain George E. Morrison, USMC, for their extremely valuable advice and generous assistance in the preparation of the manuscript.

The opinions expressed herein are those of the author, and his alone. They are not to be construed as reflecting those of the Department of Defense, the Department of the Navy, nor the United States Marine Corps.

Philip N. Pierce
Lieutenant Colonel
U.S. Marine Corps Retired

Arlington, Va.
January 20, 1964

Contents

The
Compact History
of the
United States
Marine Corps

★ ★ ★ ★ ★

Origins of a Mission

THE YOUNG SON of a Marine was once asked by his ancient history teacher to name the most important contributions to civilization made by the Phoenicians. After thinking for a moment, he answered, "The alphabet—and the United States Marines."

Presumably the young man's national identification of the "soldiers of the sea" was prompted by filial pride, an understandable reason for a chronological error of some thirty-two centuries. There is, however, ample historical evidence to support the lad's answer, in part.

Phoenician ships were indeed manned by Marines, though hardly of the United States variety. Subsequently, the galleys of Greece and Rome carried complements of men whose sole function was to fight, in contrast to the crews who navigated them and the oarsmen who were the human engines. The chronicles of Herodotus include a battle between Athenian Marines and seamen of the Persian fleet, just prior to the classic battle of Marathon. Thus Marines, *Epibatae,* as the Athenians called them, can claim participation in one of the first sea battles of history.

Our contemporary Marines date from the seventeenth cen-

tury. In 1664 a regiment was raised in England expressly for
duty with the fleet and the mission of fighting ashore. This organization bore the rather ponderous title: "Duke of York and
Albany's Maritime Regiment of Foot." Over a period of many
decades of evolution, during which no one knew for certain
whether they belonged to the Army or the Navy, this basic unit
developed into the corps known today as the Royal Marines.

Legend has it that an officer of this regiment was responsible
for the origin of the well-known phrase, "Tell it to the Marines."
It seems that Charles II had granted audience to the captain of
the ship *Defyance,* which had recently returned from a cruise
in the Indies. The ship's master embellished the account of his
cruise with tales of many strange and wonderful things. The
king accepted as much as he could, but when the captain told
of seeing fish that flew through the air, it was too much for the
royal ears.

"Fish that fly through the air!" exclaimed the monarch. "Sir,
such a thing is beyond our believing."

He turned to Sir William Killigren, a member of his court,
and colonel of the newly formed maritime regiment.

"What say you, Sir, to a man who tells for truth that he has
seen fish that fly like birds?"

"I should say, Your Majesty," replied the colonel, "that he
hath sailed in southern waters. When Your Majesty's business
carried me thither of late I did frequently see such a sight."

The king turned to Samuel Pepys, his Secretary of the
Admiralty.

"Mr. Pepys, from the very nature of their calling, no class
of our subjects has as wide a knowledge of the seas and lands
as the officers and men of our loyal maritime regiment. Henceforth, whenever we cast doubt upon a tale that lacketh likelihood
we will tell it to the Marines. If they believe it, it is safe to say
that it is true."

That the Marine Corps is well known and generally popular
today tends to obscure the fact that such was not always the
case. For the first century of its existence the tiny organization

was virtually unknown outside the other services, and often imperfectly understood within them. The average citizen lacked the most remote conception of what constituted a Marine. Very few had ever heard the term—and probably cared less. In a very real sense the Corps won recognition by dint of its own achievements—spectacularly in war, but substantially between wars—as will be subsequently related.

Marines have fought in every official war of the United States; and scores of obscure affairs that lacked official blessing but in which, to quote an eminent Marine writer, Colonel John W. Thomason, Jr., ". . . a man can be killed as dead as ever a chap was in the Argonne." Yet so closely were they tied up with naval operations throughout the age of sail, and beyond, that their history, with the exception of a few notable incidents, is essentially that of the Navy. Thus their emergence from obscurity is a comparatively recent development, dating from around the turn of the twentieth century.

The spectacular war correspondent of that era, Richard Harding Davis, is generally credited with originating the news catch line, "The Marines have landed and the situation is well in hand." When and where the phrase first appeared is obscure and unimportant. However, it appeared so often during the early 1900s that it lodged in the public mind as a sort of trade mark. Then, with World War I, the Corps burst full armed, as it were, upon the public consciousness, largely due to the miscensoring of a dispatch by an equally spectacular correspondent —the late Floyd Gibbons.

Gibbons, who was with the Fourth Marine Brigade during the first week of bitter fighting at Belleau Wood, wrote a story of the heroic action and sent it, via messenger, to A.E.F. Headquarters for transmission to the United States. Contrary to strict censorship regulations, Gibbons boldly named the Marine unit in his dispatch, in the hope that it might slip through the censors by mistake. Since all roads were choked with troops and equipment moving up to the front, it was long after nightfall when the messenger arrived with the dispatch.

In the meantime, Gibbons had been severely wounded in the day's action. Thus the daily casualty list, reporting that he had been shot through the head, arrived simultaneously with his news dispatch. The censor, a close personal friend of the correspondent's, thinking it would be the last story ever filed by Gibbons, failed, probably out of sentiment, to delete the forbidden mention of a specific unit. It was the only time that the name of a fighting unit got by the censor. Gibbons recovered from his wounds, with the loss of an eye, and lived to file many another exciting story.

But it was through no accident that the Marine Corps emerged from World War II generally regarded as the greatest fighting organization this nation has ever seen.

Behind lies the heritage of a proud band of men—a long chronicle of uneven evolution.

★ **2** ★

★　　★　　★　　★　　★

Marines and the Revolution

MARINES OF SEVERAL VARIETIES served the cause during the War for Independence. Or, perhaps more accurately, men performed the duties of Marines in various categories. It could hardly have been otherwise in a war which often saw things done in a strange manner. Most of the revolting colonies, soon to become states, commissioned their own navies. Many of them issued letters of marque and reprisal which permitted hordes of privateers to roam the seas. A fleet was improvised far inland from the coast to meet the British on Lake Champlain. And, in the latter stages of the war, American naval vessels, based in French ports, kept their crews up to strength by recruiting among the many nationalities to be found on foreign waterfronts.

Little is known about the Marines who were a part of this strange hodgepodge of naval forces. Most of the state navies included Marines of one sort or another. Applicants who wished to join the Massachusetts Navy were required to have, "a good effective Fire Arm, Cartouch Box, Cutlass and Blanket." It is evident that other states were not as specific in their arms requirements. Early accounts show that Marines' weapons included bayonets, pikes, spears, lances, hatchets and Indian tomahawks.

The oldest known record of American Marines is the payroll of the sloop *Enterprize,* which was a part of the improvised navy Benedict Arnold sailed against the British on Lake Champlain. Dated May 3, 1775, it bears the names of James Watson, a lieutenant of Marines, and seventeen enlisted men who drew pay accruing from that date.

The war in general, and the armed forces in particular, did not begin to make much sense on a national basis until the establishment of the Continental service. The Continentals derived their title from the fact that they were authorized by the Continental Congress, in contrast to the militia organizations of the states and their naval equivalents. They were, in short, the regulars of their time.

The present day Marine Corps celebrates its birthday on the 10th of November, that being the date in the year 1775 that Congress passed the following resolution:

> "That two battalions of Marines be raised consisting of one colonel, two lieutenant colonels, two majors, and other officers, as usual in other regiments; that they consist of an equal number of privates with other battalions; that particular care be taken that no persons be appointed to offices or enlisted into said battalions but such are good seamen or so acquainted with maritime affairs as to be able to serve with advantage by sea when required; that they be enlisted and commissioned to serve for and during the present war between Great Britain and the colonies, unless dismissed by order of Congress; that they be distinguished by the names of the First and Second Battalions of American Marines."

Like so many resolutions of those brave young days, this one looked and sounded a lot more impressive than it proved in actuality. In the scanty records extant, there is nothing to indicate that the two battalions were ever raised. Nor is there any evidence that any Marine officers ever attained a rank above that of major during the war. However, Marine guard detachments were recruited and assigned aboard the ships of the new Navy almost as fast as they were put in commission. Samuel

Nicholas and Robert Mullan are credited for this; two men about whom modern Marine historians wish they knew more.

Nicholas, a well-known Philadelphia clubman, was commissioned a captain of Marines on November 28, 1775. Exactly why he was selected for a commission remains obscure. It might have been the results of political influence. His uncle, Atwood Shute, a former mayor of Philadelphia, was prominent in both military and political affairs. By one of those legislative accidents so frequent during the times, Nicholas' commission pre-dated, by twenty-four days, that of Esek Hopkins, senior officer of the Navy. Although he had been selected earlier than Nicholas, Hopkins' commission was not confirmed until December 22. This fact has lent dubious weight to the later claims of over-zealous Marines that theirs is the older service. There is no doubt, however, that Samuel Nicholas was the senior Marine officer of his time. Later in the war he was promoted to major and served in a capacity analogous to the modern Commandant. The official numerical lineage of the Commandants of the Marine Corps dates from Nicholas.

Mullan's qualifications for his post were less obscure. This robust gentleman was the proprietor of Tun Tavern, a popular rendezvous for seafaring gentry. In the days when patriotism occasionally needed stimulation of a more tangible sort, having a taverner on your side could be a great help. So, Mullan, too, received a captain's commission and was placed in charge of recruiting. The fact that Mullan established his recruiting headquarters in his barroom undoubtedly accounted for some of his success. It is just as probable that the glib promises of bounty, a pension and ample grog and rations contributed their share in luring recruits into signing up.

The problem of procuring individual firearms for Marines was one which remained acute throughout the Revolution. The Committee of Public Safety of Pennsylvania helped to solve the problem partially. The Committee made donations of muskets and equipment to several Marine detachments formed in Philadelphia. During the course of the war, Marines' firearms included muskets from practically all the armies of Europe. The most common to be found were the celebrated "Brown Bess" tower muskets captured from the British, and the Charleville muskets obtained from the French.

By the time the nation's first naval expedition got under way early in February 1776, Nicholas and Mullan had succeeded in their recruiting efforts to the extent that Commodore Esek Hopkins' fleet included a complement of 268 Marines. Nicholas commanded the Marine detachment on board the flagship *Alfred,* a ship of the line which boasted 30 guns and a first lieutenant, later to be heard from, named John Paul Jones. Mullan sailed as commanding officer of the 60-man detachment aboard the *Columbus.*

The destination of this expedition was the island of New Providence in the Bahamas. The object was to capture what was believed to be a large quantity of powder and military stores maintained there by the British under inadequate guard. The small squadron, consisting of two ships, two brigs, two schooners and two sloops, arrived off the target area on the first day of March. The capitol city, Old Nassau, was situated on a high hill and protected by two forts, Fort Montague to the east and Fort Nassau to the west. Hopkins elected to initiate hostilities by a surprise attack on Fort Nassau. A landing party, consisting of 220 Marines and 50 sailors, was organized under command of Nicholas. The landing force was placed on board two innocent appearing sloops, recently captured from New Providence. All hands received orders to keep themselves concealed. Hopkins hoped to achieve tactical surprise by this ruse. The supporting ships of the squadron were to approach the island far enough astern of the sloops to avoid detection by lookouts ashore. The plan might have worked if Hopkins' navigator hadn't miscalculated the slow sailing speed of the captured sloops. As it happened, the supporting ships of the squadron loomed above the horizon before the landing force reached shore. The suspicious British immediately fired warning shots from the fort's cannons, nullifying any hopes of a surprise landing.

The two sloops then proceeded to the eastern end of the island where Nicholas landed his force without opposition. Establishing himself ashore, Nicholas sent a dispatch to the Governor announcing that his only object was to seize the military stores. His message further stated that he would respect the private property of citizens, and urged immediate surrender to avoid unnecessary bloodshed.

He then marched on Fort Montague, which stood about a mile east of town. His approach was greeted by three 12-pounder shots, fired as a token resistance. Upon his deployment for assault, the garrison spiked their guns and withdrew. A thorough search of the fort failed to produce the cache of munitions. Nicholas therefore concluded that they were stored in the second fort to the west of town. Since the hour was late, he decided to quarter his men for the night and continue the attack the following day—a decision which turned out to be a grave tactical error.

In a letter, written on April 10, 1776, Captain Nicholas described the course of action by which he captured the remaining fort.

"The next morning by daylight we marched forward to take possession of the Governor's house. On our march I met an express from the Governor. . . . The messenger then told me I might march into town, and if I thought it proper, into the fort, without interruption; on which I marched into town. I then drafted a guard and went up to the Governor's and demanded the keys to the fort, which were given to me immediately, and then took possession of Fort Nassau. In it there were forty cannon mounted and well loaded for our reception with round, langridge, and cannister shot. All this was accomplished without firing a single shot from our side. We found in this fort a great quantity of shot and shells, with fifteen brass mortars, but the grand article, powder, the Governor sent off the night before, viz. 150 casks."

While Nicholas and his men were spending the night at Fort Montague, the wily Governor had loaded 150 casks of powder aboard a merchant vessel. At three o'clock in the morning the ship quietly slipped through the eastern channel which Hopkins had conveniently left unguarded. The powder eventually arrived in St. Augustine, Florida where it was presumably put to good use by the British.

Thus what was probably the most successful American naval operation of the Revolutionary War netted seventy-one cannon, fifteen brass mortars and twenty-four casks of powder. Owing to lapses on the part of Commodore Hopkins and his landing force commander, it proved to be somewhat less than the grand *coup* envisioned by the planners.

Hopkins' fleet remained in the area for two weeks without further incident, then returned to New London with the captured naval stores. Shortly thereafter Nicholas and Mullan returned to Philadelphia, then capitol of the new nation and headquarters of the Continental forces. They continued recruiting to such good effect that Nicholas was able to muster a battalion of Marines when the eventful winter of 1776-1777 drew on.

It was during the summer and fall of 1776 that the British ousted Washington's forces from New York, badly defeated them at the battle of White Plains and chased them all the way across New Jersey. Fair-weather soldiers deserted in droves as Thomas Paine penned for posterity his bitter words, "These are the times that try men's souls. . . ."

The Commander-in-Chief was scraping the bottom of the manpower barrel as he withdrew across the Delaware into Pennsylvania. But he was already planning the counter-stroke that would turn the tide—the surprise attack upon the Hessian garrison at Trenton. Washington conceived this operation as a double envelopment. The Marines, brigaded with the Pennsylvania militia under General Cadwalader, were to cross the Delaware below the town of Burlington, while Washington crossed above with the main body. Cadwalader succeeded in crossing the ice-choked river on that historic Christmas night, but being unable to land his artillery was forced to return to the Pennsylvania side. However, the swift decisiveness of Washing-

ton's own attack proved quite sufficient to overpower the be-
fuddled Hessians and kill or capture the entire garrison.

The Marines rejoined Washington the following day. They
were with him as the British swooped down in force with the
intention of pinning the Continentals against the river bank
and destroying the entire force with a single stroke. They participated in the Second Battle of Trenton and the brilliant sweep
that carried Washington around the flank of the British main
body to rout their reinforcing elements at Princeton. They shared
with the Continental Line, as the Army was then called, that
dreadful winter in the encampment at Morristown.

With the coming of spring, 1777, Nicholas and his battalion
were recalled to Philadelphia, where the unit was split up into
ship's detachments. Thereafter Nicholas found himself so involved in recruiting and administrative duties that he was not
able to take to the field again, or to the sea. This is the presently
accepted accounts of Marine Corps history. Nothing could be
further from the truth!

For a great number of years scholars of Marine history have
been at a loss to explain an apparent void in the career of
Samuel Nicholas. During the latter part of the Revolution he
apparently dropped from sight for several months. This disappearance has been explained in various ways, but the officially
accepted explanation is that which relegates his activities to
administering the affairs of his widely dispersed Corps. These
attempts to explain the gap in the documentary evidence of his
career are based on pure guesswork. They are not only grossly
in error, but they do Major Nicholas a grave injustice.

It is true that Nicholas virtually disappeared from the scene
for approximately five months during the year 1781. But his
activities were a far cry from the prosaic duties of administration and recruiting. Not only was he very much in the field, but
the fate of the nation may very well have rested in his hands,
during what was undoubtedly the most important mission of
his lifetime.

Credit for the discovery of the long missing information belongs to the contemporary writer and historian Lynn Montross. Mr. Montross discovered the account of Samuel Nicholas' "disappearance" among the letters of Robert Morris, the Colonial Superintendent of Finance.

On September 11, 1781, Robert Morris, by special authority granted by Congress, assigned Major Nicholas to a special mission. The extreme secrecy which surrounded the planning and execution of the mission is well attested by the fact that it remained unknown to Marine historians for more than 175 years.

Nicholas' secret mission was to transport more than a million crowns in silver from Boston to Philadelphia by oxcart. The money, badly needed by the impoverished colonies, had been obtained as a loan from Louis XVI of France by Benjamin Franklin. Transported to America on board the French frigate *La Resolue,* it was to be delivered in Philadelphia. Due to severe storms encountered en route, the ship was blown off course and forced to make port in Boston. The new Superintendent of Colonial Finance thus found himself faced with the problem of transporting the money safely to its final destination. Because of the great number of British ships which roamed the off-shore sea lanes, he decided that shipping the money overland involved less risk.

We still do not know why Morris chose the 37-year-old Marine major for the job. Certainly there was no dearth of heroes from which to choose in a war now in its sixth year. There were others whose brilliant records of bravery and resourcefulness apparently qualified them more fully for the job than Samuel Nicholas. But Robert Morris was a cautious man, and perhaps this trait led him to his choice of Nicholas. Just what attributes he sought in the man to accomplish the task was recorded by Morris in one of his letters. It was vitally necessary, he wrote, ". . . to have a Gentleman of approved honour and honesty . . . of such an active indefatigable disposition as will be able to surmount difficulties and guard against dangers on the road. In short, a person with resources in himself to surmount all obstacles."

There is the remote possibility that Morris chose Nicholas for the job purely out of friendship. As fellow citizens and members of two of Philadelphia's most exclusive clubs, they had been friends for many years. The most logical assumption is that he chose Nicholas on the strength of his success in the Bahamas landing of 1776. Few indeed were the records which could boast of the capture of cannon, mortars and gunpowder from enemy shores without a single drop of blood. So, perhaps Morris sought a man of demonstrated ability who would fight if need be, but whose judgment dictated the avoidance of a scrap when it wasn't necessary. Conjecture notwithstanding, Samuel Nicholas was chosen for the task, and history has long since vindicated the judgment of Robert Morris.

For a mission upon which hung the financial salvation of a destitute country, the entire affair was singularly unspectacular. The 350-mile trek from Boston, through Worcester and across the Hudson at Newberg, was a tiring trip. Nicholas arrived in Philadelphia on November 6, without incident. On January 7, 1782, Morris opened the Bank of North America with capital assets of $250,000, secured by the silver delivered to him by the major of Marines. Within two weeks the bank made a loan of $100,000 to the Government—the initial step toward the country's eventual financial recovery.

Unfortunately, historians in general are patriotic souls, strongly inclined toward glorifying their country's victories and minimizing its defeats. For this reason, one of the highlights of the Marines' participation in the War of the Revolution is seldom mentioned in popular, patriotic histories. From this viewpoint, the ill-fated Penobscot Expedition of 1779 was an abject failure, about which the less said the better. Although it was probably the most completely bungled amphibious operation in the nation's history, from a Marine's viewpoint, the conduct of his Continental forebears in the proceedings has always been something to be remembered with pride. Of the Marines' part in the expedition, a participating Militia officer wrote, "There was not a more brilliant exploit than this during the war."

Since the early days of the war, American privateers had
been successfully operating from the coast of New England
against British supply ships. To defend their shipping against
these attacks, the British began construction of a fortified naval
base on Penobscot Bay on June 17, 1779, at the present location of Castine, Maine. Massachusetts, which then included the
Province of Maine, became aware of this intrusion of its domain
when the British dispatched some 700 soldiers from Halifax,
under command of Brigadier General Francis McLean, military
commander of Nova Scotia, to garrison the base. The normal
procedure at this point would have been for Massachusetts to request aid from the Continental Government in driving out the
British forces. But the Massachusetts Fathers, extremely jealous
of the new government in Philadelphia, decided, with typical
Yankee independence, to do the job themselves.

The State Board of War laid plans for an expedition which
called for a land force of 1,500 militia. Under the persuasive
urging of patriot Samuel Adams, they finally swallowed sufficient pride to accept the offer of three Continental vessels lying
in Boston harbor. Combined with the three brigs of the State
Navy, 19 transports and provision ships, and 12 privateers, the
federal ships rounded out an impressive naval flotilla. The land
forces, on the other hand, presented a less imposing picture.
Of the required 1,500 militiamen, all but 900 eluded the draft.
Hence, the 300 Marines, mostly combat veterans, which comprised the various ship's detachments were a welcome addition
to the meager landing force.

Captain Dudley Saltonstall of the Continental frigate *Warren*
was placed in command of the naval forces. Brigadier General
Solomon Lovell, of the Massachusetts Militia, commanded the
landing force, with Lieutenant Colonel Paul Revere, hero of the
famous night ride, as chief of artillery.

As events soon proved, a more inexperienced and inept group
of leaders have seldom been called upon to lead a battle force.
Their personal contributions to the sad fate of the operation
appear to have been a unanimous lack of leadership, and a col-

lective inability to reach a decision. Yet the causes of the failure
of the mission were not theirs alone. A full share of the blame
belongs to the misguided patriots of the Massachusetts Board
of War, who sired the heterogeneous mixture of troops and ships
that made up the attack force, then compounded their error
by failing to charge a single individual with the responsibility
of over-all command. Thus, on July 19, 1779, an expedition
of state, federal and privately owned ships, transporting a landing force of untrained militia and combat veteran Marines,
cleared Boston harbor, predestined for failure by the nature of
its composition.

On the evening of July 24, the fleet arrived off its objective,
Bagaduce Peninsula, twenty miles upstream from the mouth
of Penobscot Bay. Under cover of darkness, a Marine raiding
party, led by Lieutenant William Downe, slipped ashore on
nearby Fox Island and returned with several local inhabitants.
From them it was learned that the British were well along on
the construction of Fort George which occupied the key terrain
in the center of the mile-and-a-half long peninsula.

The following day the militia troops attempted a landing on
the peninsula, but were unsuccessful. The captain of the *Active*
noted in the ship's log, ". . . the troops made an attempt to
land, but left shore in a very short time, the reason is unknown
to me." An Indian scout was the only casualty suffered in the
abortive attempt.

Following the failure of the initial landing, a council of war
was held aboard Saltonstall's flagship, the *Warren*. After a considerably heated discussion, during which every frustrated tac-
tician in the expedition had his say, it was decided that the
Marines would attack nearby Banks Island. The island lay some
nine hundred yards offshore, and dominated the anchorage of
the three British sloops of war which were positioned to reinforce
the artillery fires of the fort.

The attack, led by the fleet's Senior Marine Officer, Captain
John Welsh, was launched just before sunset and proved highly
successful. According to Private George Brown, a participant,

the Marines ". . . drove the enemy off the island and took four pieces of artillery and a small quantity of ammunition, and without loss."

With the flanking Banks Isand safely in friendly hands, a second attack was launched against the southwestern side of the peninsula at sunrise on July 28. The assault force was organized into three landing divisions, the Marine unit being assigned to the right flank against the enemy's main defensive position. For reasons unknown, the Marines were the only division to land on schedule and found themselves facing an assault up a two hundred-foot precipice, without protection on either flank. Captain Welsh wisely held his small beachhead position, awaiting the arrival of the remainder of the landing force, before proceeding with the assault against a precipice, called Bagaduce Heights.

Bugler Philbrick, a member of the Marine detachment of the *Providence* recorded the following account of the battle: "When the Marines were all landed and about half of the militia, we began our ascent, which was indeed a very difficult one; had it not been for the shrubs growing on the side of the hill, we might have lost half our men before we gained the heights. . . . When we had ascended about one-third of the distance, the British from the brow began a brisk fire upon us, which they kept up until we were within a few rods of the top; they then courageously fled and left the ground to us. In this ascent we had forty men killed and twenty wounded. Among the killed was Captain Welsh of the Marines on board the *Warren* frigate, a very amiable young man and a brave officer. Our brave general did not lead the van in the ascent, neither did he bring up the rear, probably he and the commodore were walking the *Warren's* quarterdeck with their spy-glasses to see the fun. I saw him two hours afterward on the hill, giving orders about building huts, for which he was probably well calculated . . . Our general is said to be a very good man, but these [sic] good sort of men seldom make good generals. The place selected for landing was very injudiciously chosen, being a high bank covered with small trees and shrubs, with an ascent of at least 45 degrees,

whereas about a mile distant was a fine, level, clear spot, sufficiently large to hold the whole army, where we might have
landed under cover of the guns of one or two of our ships without the loss of a man."

The attack moved rapidly toward the fort which Paul Revere
described as, ". . . high as a man's chin and built of square
logs." One wag among the troops remarked that he could, "jump
over the walls with a musket in each hand." Unfortunately, he
was never given the opportunity to make good his boast. With
the leading element of the Marines within five hundred yards of
the fort, General Lovell suddenly issued orders to halt the advance. He then sent for Revere and his artillery to support the
final assault on the fort. With that decision, Lovell imparted
the kiss of death to what undoubtedly would have been a successful attack, had it been allowed to maintain the momentum
already gained. At least there was no doubt in the minds of the
British defenders about the outcome of the advance. Brigadier
McLean, the British commander, wrote, "I was in no situation
to defend myself, I meant only to give them one or two guns,
so as not to be called a coward, and then to have struck my
colours, which I stood by for some time to do, as I did not wish
to throw away the lives of my men for nothing."

Somehow the final assault never came. For sixteen long days
the Americans lay siege to the fort, while the puzzled British
defenders, daily expecting an attack, continued to improve their
defenses. The Marine officers repeatedly asked General Lovell
for permission to attack, pointing out that the delay only increased the possibility of the Royal Navy coming to the rescue
of the defenders. Their entreaties meant nothing.

Afloat, Commodore Saltonstall, fearing for the safety of his
ships, which greatly outnumbered and outgunned the three British ships, refused to attack until the militia ashore had silenced
Fort George's cannon. "I am not going to risk my shipping in that
damned hole," Saltonstall said. Ashore Lovell was fearful of
pressing the attack until the supporting British ships were driven
out of their defensive positions.

The stalemate ended abruptly on August 13 with the sighting of seven British warships quietly slipping up the bay through the whispy fog of the late afternoon. Fortunately for the Americans, a sudden heavy rain began falling at dusk which afforded concealment during their hasty night withdrawal from the peninsula. With escape to the open sea cut off by the Royal Navy squadron, Commodore Saltonstall abandoned any pretense of command. At first light the following morning he signalled all ships to fend for themselves as best they were able, and led the catastrophic retreat up the Penobscot River. The rout, during which every American ship was either run ashore and burned by their crews or sunk or captured by the British, provided a spectacle which was described for many generations around the camp fires of the Penobscot Indians who witnessed the sight. General Lovell later wrote, "An attempt to give a description to this terrible day is out of my Power, it would be a fit subject for some masterly hand to describe its true colours . . ."

Marines, militiamen and seamen found themselves in the deep Maine wilderness, 270 miles from the nearest settlements on the Kennebec River. Fortunately, the Indians who inhabited the area were friendly, and most of the members of the expedition found their way back to Boston.

Long before the last straggler was accounted for, charges and countercharges of cowardice and dereliction of duty began to fly. A Board of Inquiry was formed to investigate the charges. The findings of the board resulted in Commodore Saltonstall being court-martialled and cashiered from the Navy, and severe reprimands for several others.

The Penobscot Expedition cost the State Treasury $8,500,000, destroyed most of the State Navy, and completely discouraged the state's appetite for any further retaliatory forays. As one of the Marine officers later wrote, "Although I was indeed proud of the manner in which the Marines acquitted themselves throughout, it was in the overall view a most disheartening affair."

The final engagement in which the Marines took part in the

Revolution as a land force also ended in disaster. This was the defense of Charlestown, South Carolina, in the spring of 1780.

With operations in the north at a virtual stalemate, the British hit upon a plan to conquer the colonies by taking Georgia, and then working their way north. Georgia was selected as the first objective because it was still largely loyal to the Crown, in addition to being far from the seat of the Continental Government and peculiarly exposed to attack. Having captured Savannah in December, 1778, and successfully defending it against a combined sea and land counterattack in September of the following year, the British advanced on Charlestown, South Carolina.

The city was defended by a naval force of eight ships under Commodore Abraham Whipple, and an army of four thousand men under General Benjamin Lincoln. Whipple's fleet, consisting of four Continental frigates and four vessels of the Carolina State Navy, included a large force of Marines, commanded by Colonel John Laurens.

On February 11, 1780, General Sir Henry Clinton landed a force of ten thousand British troops south of the city and advanced against the defenders. At sea, Whipple's ships, hard pressed by a superior British naval force, retreated into Charlestown Harbor. This move was calculated to provide the best sea defense for the city, since the ships were positioned to reinforce the fires of Fort Moultrie which guarded the entrance to the harbor. Commodore Whipple transferred all Marines and some of the ship's cannon ashore to augment General Lincoln's land defenses.

The beleaguered city successfully defended itself for three wearisome months, but finally fell to the British on May 11, 1780.

The Marines, as a unit, took no further part in the land campaigns of the war after the defense of Charlestown. Thereafter their story is that of the Continental Navy.

As with other Continental services, uniform regulations described in meticulous detail the clothing and accoutrement of Marines. The enlisted men wore green cutaway coats, faced with white and decorated with many pewter buttons. Green shirts, light-colored breeches, woolen stockings and a round black leather hat bound with white tape completed their uniform.

The officers were also dressed in green coats faced with white, over a white waistcoat. The coats were decorated with silver buttons and carried a single silver epaulet on the right shoulder. Their white breeches were edged with green, below which they wore knee-length black gaiters and black shoes. The prescribed headpiece was a cocked hat.

The significance of the predominance of green in these uniforms remains unknown. However, through no orderly evolution, it has become the color most associated with the Corps. Since Congress lacked the funds, or the means to raise them through taxation, it is doubtful that many Marines ever wore such uniforms, other than the officers who possessed the means for outfitting themselves.

The Marines under the redoubtable John Paul Jones, who had a penchant for doing things his own way, managed somewhat better. Following the alliance with France, he based in French ports and operated in the English Channel and the Irish Sea with devastating effect on British commerce and men-of-war alike. With no superior to say him nay at that distance, he outfitted his Marines in gaudy red coats. It is generally believed the coats were obtained from a captured enemy vessel carrying a large stock of British uniforms.

Regardless of how incongruous their coats may have appeared aboard a U.S. warship, the performance of Jones' Marines left little to be desired. When his frigate *Bonhomme Richard*, a worm-eaten old tub, engaged HMS *Serapis* off Famborough Head, small arms fire from Jones' fighting tops so effectively cleared the Britisher's weather deck that her crew was able to man only the lower tier of guns. Finally a Marine crept over to a yardarm of the *Serapis* and lobbed a hand grenade down an open hatch where it blew up a powder chest—an incident generally regarded as the turning point of the battle. The action ended with Jones quickly transferring his crew to the captured British frigate just in time to escape his sinking ship.

As our War for Independence dragged wearily toward its close the Navy began to shrink. After the surrender of Cornwallis in 1781, the number of vessels in commission steadily decreased, and with them the number of Marines on active duty. Most of the ships were sold to private owners for commercial use. A sentimental, but unsuccessful, effort was made to retain the *Alliance* because of her gallant record. The Congress, faced with a rigid economy problem, finally presented her to the French who had contributed so much toward bringing the war to a successful conclusion. And with her passing in 1784, the Continental naval establishment, and its component, the Continental Marines, simply ceased to exist.

The Army followed the same trend, but was prevented from vanishing altogether because it had to maintain a small garrison to guard military stores at West Point. Thus the newest member of the family of nations stood defenseless on the threshold of a highly dubious future.

★   ★   ★   ★   ★

3

To the Shores of Tripoli—and Beyond

Foreign interference with U.S. seaborne commerce was mainly responsible for restoring the Navy to a somewhat effective footing. This interference stemmed from two sources. One was France. The other was a string of North African countries bordering on the Mediterranean, loosely and collectively known as the Barbary States.

The French Revolutionary government resented our refusal to abide by the treaty of alliance we had made with its royal predecessor in 1778. In retaliation, it began issuing letters of marque to privateers to prey on our ships at sea. These outrages finally reached the point where Congress was spurred to appropriate funds for armed vessels. As a result the Navy Department was established on May 1, 1798. France and the United States then entered into a "quasi-war" at sea, which was none the less real for being officially undeclared by either nation. Some of the ships were simply merchantmen, purchased and converted to war needs. More important was the fact that keels were laid for several frigates of advanced design which were destined to make U.S. naval history.

Recruitment of Marines to serve on board began as soon as the first ship was commissioned. However, the U.S. Marine Corps did not come into existence under law until July 11, 1798. The following day John Adams, acting on authority specifically granted to the President by the Congressional act establishing the Corps, appointed William Ward Burrows Commandant with the rank of major. Within a short time this rank was raised to lieutenant colonel, where it would remain for several decades to come.

On paper the new organization was unimpressive. Total authorized strength stood at one lone major, 4 captains, 28 lieutenants and 848 enlisted men of all categories, including 32 fifers and drummers. The total strength was augmented the following year by an additional four officers and 196 enlisted. Many years were to pass before the Corps' total effective strength would much exceed 1,000, and there would be times of peace when the strength would fall below 500.

Philadelphia was still serving as the nation's capital, and it was there that Burrows, like his predecessor, Samuel Nicholas, set up his headquarters and concentrated his initial recruiting efforts. When a sufficient number of recruits had been signed on, he established a Marine camp on the outskirts of the city. But the new Marine Corps was so hard put to provide for the Navy's burgeoning expansion program that the camp never reached any respectable size.

The "war" with France covered a period of about two years. Since it was fought entirely at sea, mostly in Caribbean waters, the Marines' story was again essentially that of the Navy. There were no fleet actions. Individual vessels of both nations fought ship-to-ship duels, with the advantage almost entirely on our side. The same may be said of the raiding operations against commerce. Many a poorly paid Marine was happy to participate in the prize money awarded for the capture of a richly laden merchantman engaged in the West Indies trade.

As in the case of all hostilities in which the Marines have been engaged, the end of the French affair saw a material reduction in the Corps' strength. That Thomas Jefferson was a great man in the history of this nation is a statement that would brook little argument today. However, it was a point on which it would have been extremely difficult to convince naval men of his time. Jefferson arbitrarily cut the Marine Corps to less than five hundred. He rendered the Navy virtually impotent by placing most of its capital ships in the 1800 equivalent of mothballs— "laid up in ordinary" was the term then. Jefferson did not approve of war. All of our naval efforts, he decided, should be strictly defensive. Instead of maintaining a seagoing fleet, he issued orders which confined our efforts to the construction of gunboats to operate in our harbors.

These decisions by Jefferson saved the taxpayers a lot of money. They also reduced the country's naval might to a few gunboats, so unseaworthy that they proved to be absolutely useless. But these and the mothball fleet were all we had when an irate monarch chopped down the flagstaff on the American consulate in his capital and declared war on us in 1801.

The monarch was the Pasha of Tripoli, which, together with Algeria and Tunis, made up the so-called Barbary States. This coalition controlled the Mediterranean so completely that they were able to levy tribute on nations whose ships traded in that sea. Such nations, including the United States, found it more expedient to pay the tribute than risk seizure of their ships and enslavement of their crews. Their only other choice involved the war effort necessary to suppress these "pirates" or "corsairs."

Such was the situation in 1801 when the Pasha decided that the United States was not paying enough tribute and demanded an increase. When this was refused, he declared war, began seizing American ships, and demanding ransom for their captured crews. All of which left the peaceable Mr. Jefferson with little choice but to accept the challenge.

The Navy began putting its laid-up warships into fighting condition. Ten ships were dispatched to the Mediterranean. This fleet destroyed a few of Tripoli's ships, bombarded a few of the Pasha's shore installations and clamped a blockade on his principal ports. However, the squadron lacked the strength to make the blockade wholly effective. The desultory fighting might have dragged on indefinitely had not a man named William Eaton come up with what seemed like a good idea at the time. With the backing of the U.S. Government, his scheme was to result in one of the most fantastic incidents in U.S. history—and, incidentally, to contribute the second line to the Marines' Hymn.

Eaton, an Army captain during the Revolution, had served as U.S. Consul to Tripoli's neighbor, Tunis. Familiar with Barbary politics, he knew that Yusuf Karamanli, the current Pasha of Tripoli, was a usurper who had murdered one older brother and exiled another in order to seize power. Eaton reasoned that if he could find the surviving brother, Hamid, and afford him some U.S. backing, they might well embroil Tripoli in a first rate civil war that would simplify the Navy's problems. He gained the Administration's authorization for the venture and arrived on the scene in 1804.

Hamid Karamanli was believed to be in Egypt. Eaton proceeded there with an escort of seven Marines, under a young lieutenant named Presley N. O'Bannon, assigned to him by Commodore Barron, commander of the U.S. Mediterranean Squadron. They found Hamid taking refuge some distance up the Nile with about ninety personal followers, which included a party of Arabian cavalry. With considerable difficulty Eaton persuaded him and his entourage to take the field against his brother.

Returning to Alexandria, notorious hangout for adventurous characters, Eaton recruited thirty-eight Greek soldiers of fortune, reinforced them with two light artillery pieces, and assumed the title of "General." He then hired a number of Arab camel drivers to transport the gear of this motley array and set off on a march of six hundred miles across the Libyan desert. His objective was Derna, Tripoli's second largest city. Prior to his departure, he arranged with the U.S. fleet to meet his force with supplies when they reached the coast.

The journal of this expedition reads like a protracted nightmare. At every critical juncture the camel drivers went on strike, demanding pay in advance on the threat of turning back. Hamid himself turned out to be a most unwilling warrior, and it took the combined persuasive powers of Eaton and O'Bannon to keep him going. Fortunately the Greek adventurers proved loyal and excellent fighting men. On several occasions force was needed to prevent mutiny, when the Christian and Arab contingents had a falling out and wound up facing each other with swords in hand. Only the timely arrival of Eaton's prearranged supplies saved the enterprise from complete disintegration once they reached the coast.

The zealous adherents to Hamid's cause, so optimistically prophesied by Eaton, failed to materialize as the force approached Derna. And, when the Governor of that city refused a demand to surrender it, "General" Eaton's command shaped up as a most improbable force to capture a fortified city.

Yet capture it they did, with the aid of naval gunfire support from the fleet. O'Bannon, at the head of his Marines and the Greek mercenaries, broke into the town and stormed a fort on the high ground dominating it. With his own hands, O'Bannon hoisted the American flag for the first time over a captured position in the Old World. He then turned the guns of the fort on the Governor's palace and bombarded that dignitary out of the city. With that, as often happens in such cases, the population came over to Hamid's side en masse. With their aid Eaton was able to repulse a strong expeditionary force that Pasha Yusuf had sent to recapture Derna.

The remainder of the story constitutes sheer anticlimax—and a double-cross of epic proportions. With Derna in the hands of Americans, Yusuf's position had been rendered extremely critical. Eaton was preparing to advance on the city of Tripoli, the Pasha's stronghold, when he received orders from Commodore Barron to evacuate Derna at once, and embark his force upon such vessels of the fleet as were available.

It seems that President Jefferson, reluctant to rely solely on what he thought from the beginning was a mad scheme, sent a special emissary of his own to treat directly with Yusuf. This gentleman, Tobias Lear, whose sole claim to distinction seems to have been a striking resemblance to the late George Washington, had abjectly yielded on nearly every Tripolitan demand that had caused the war in the first place.

Thus Hamid's cause came to naught, despite all the fine promises Eaton had made him, presumably with the approbation of the U.S. Government. Eaton was able to evacuate Hamid and the Greeks to Malta, but Hamid's native supporters had to be left to the tender mercies of Yusuf. It was at Malta, according to tradition that cannot be wholly documented, that Hamid presented O'Bannon with the sword he had carried while a refugee with the Mamelukes. This scimitar-like blade, known as the Mameluke sword, is worn by Marine officers today. It also happens to be the oldest weapon in continuous use in the Armed Forces of the United States.

Of O'Bannon himself, there is little more to record. He returned home with the fleet to be presented with a ceremonial sword by his native state of Virginia. But when the Marine Corps failed to reward his achievements with promotion, he resigned his commission and moved to the West, an embittered man. Eaton spent years lobbying Congress for reimbursement of private funds advanced in his venture. He was finally granted a year's pay as a captain, his previous rank in the Continental Army during the Revolution.

So passed into history "The Shores of Tripoli."

While O'Bannon and Eaton had been busying themselves in Tripoli, Marine Corps Headquarters had followed the National Government from Philadelphia to the new capital city of Washington. For the first couple of years, after their arrival in 1800, the Marines were quartered during the summer months in a tent camp on what was known as Camp Hill. This site today is occupied by the headquarters of the Navy Department Bureau of Medicine and Surgery. During the winter they were moved into rented buildings.

However, Commandant Burrows was a personal friend of President Jefferson and, in 1801, managed to get an appropriation from Congress for construction of permanent barracks.

Jefferson helped the Commandant to select the site, the two riding about the city together to survey the situation. The site finally selected lay in the southeast section of the city conveniently located close to the Washington Navy Yard.

It soon became apparent, however, that the Congressional appropriation, while sufficient to purchase the land and some materials, could not be stretched to include the cost of civilian labor. So the Marines, as they were to do many times again in their long history, stacked arms, laid aside their fancy uniforms and set about to take care of their own needs. Carpenters and masons were found among them and the construction proceeded. In addition to the ordinary skills, they were forced to burn their own bricks, which were made from clay taken from a pit lying between the barracks site and the Navy Yard. That these bricks may not have been very well burned is perhaps understandable under the circumstances. Their quality has since been described by a critical, and obviously unsentimental, inspector as being "very soft salmon."

The barracks and a house for the Commandant, situated at the northern end of the compound, were completed in 1805, and the Marines moved in. They have been there ever since. Hence, the Marine Barracks, Washington, D.C. is the oldest military post in the United States from the standpoint of continuous occupancy, with the sole exception of the Army's West Point.

However, William Ward Burrows, who had done so much to stamp his own personality on the Corps he commanded, never occupied the fine house he was largely responsible for getting built. Failing health brought about his retirement on February 7, 1804. His successor, Lieutenant Colonel Franklin Wharton, became the first to occupy the quarters which has housed every Commandant of the Corps since that time. As far as can be determined, the house is the oldest Government building in Washington to be continuously occupied.

Another national institution within the Marine Corps which also owes its origin to the energetic leadership of Lieutenant Colonel Burrows is the Marine Band. Burrows was quick to appreciate the unique position occupied by his small Corps. As the only regular military unit permanently stationed in the nation's capital, it was responsible for the city's security. But Burrows conceived the idea that it might also serve the more welcome function of contributing to the city's entertainment. The fact that he had no authority to organize a band, and no funds with which to purchase instruments, didn't appear to bother him. He solved the money problem by personally writing to every officer in the Marine Corps, indicating that each was to contribute a certain percentage of his pay—or else. It is a matter of record that he officially reprimanded one officer who was either delinquent or reluctant to donate.

To the accompaniment of many groans, the money came in and the instruments were bought. By this time Burrows had enlisted enough men to play them. On New Year's Day, 1800, he marched his new organization across the city to the Presidential Mansion and staged a concert for President John Adams— and anybody else interested in listening.

How good this band actually was, even by the standards of its time and place, is problematical. The important point was that it had no competition. The President was delighted. The local citizens gave it an ovation, and its White House concerts became a Washington institution. By the time competition did appear, the Marine Band was so firmly entrenched as the "President's Own" that it retains that status to this day. That it subsequently came under the directorship of such leaders as John Philip Sousa is reason enough that it enjoys a position which it richly merits.

Lieutenant Colonel Burrows, however, carried his musical zeal still further, a step which was to give rise to certain complications. In the crude, sprawling United States at the turn of the nineteenth century, competent native musicians were few and far between. Europe was the home of this sort of culture— and the Navy had a squadron operating in the Mediterranean. So Burrows wrote to Captain John Hall, one of his officers stationed with the fleet, pointedly suggesting that he give some attention to enlisting Italian musicians who might be interested in coming to the Land of Opportunity. Captain Hall applied himself so energetically to the problem that in a short time he had enlisted eighteen assorted musicians, two of whom turned out to be age nine and ten respectively. By the time Hall was able to arrange transportation for his charges to the United States, Burrows had retired, neglecting to mention this particular brainstorm to his successor. The next Commandant, Franklin Wharton, was more surprised than pleased to find himself saddled with a sizable group of temperamental foreigners.

Under Wharton, its third Commandant, the Marine Corps was to take part in a war which was extremely unpopular in many parts of the country. The French and Tripoli affairs had provided fine training for a much more serious struggle that had been long in the offing. This was our second war with Great Britain —the War of 1812.

The underlying causes of this war were many and varied. The ostensible causes were completely obvious. The British Royal Navy had achieved complete dominance at sea. But she ruled so arrogantly, and with such contempt for the rights of neutral nations, that an unbearable situation was created. The British issued a series of edicts called the Orders of Council which prohibited neutral nations from trading with the continent of Europe—meaning Napoleonic France. These Orders in Council also provided for the seizure of any vessels engaged in such commerce. British men-of-war also began intercepting American vessels on the high seas and screening their crews for deserters from the Royal Navy. There were many of these, conditions being what they were in the Royal Navy. If the British had contented themselves with impressing only the guilty culprits, all might have been well. But they showed no scruples whatever in impressing any likely looking seamen, including legal citizens of the United States.

As far as American national policy was concerned, there was still another aspect to the picture. Britain might be supreme at sea, but she was something less than invulnerable on land. On the continent of Europe, the British Army was locked in a life-and-death struggle with Napoleon. On the North American continent, the British colony of Canada lay just north of the United States across an ill-defined border. So, in June 1812, President James Madison's administration declared war on Great Britain on charges relating to impressment and the Orders in Council—and ordered an immediate invasion of Canada, with whom we had no quarrel.

The naval outcome of the war was inevitable. It ended with our war vessels either sunk, captured, or blockaded in home ports. But before this came to pass, His Majesty's Royal Navy sustained the most shocking experience of its royal existence.

The U.S. Navy had no ships-of-the-line which, in an era of sail, were the equivalent of today's battleships. The British had more than twenty on the North American station alone. But the United States did possess a type of frigate that outclassed their opposite numbers in anybody's navy. The British regarded these ships with nothing short of complete scorn. Although they had a high respect for French shipbuilders, and adapted to their own use such French men-of-war as they could capture, they had only contempt for American ships. "Built of pine," they scornfully said of them at the outset of the war. Before the war was over, they were accusing America of sending ships-of-the-line to sea disguised as frigates to trap their own.

The simple fact was that the new U.S. frigates were expressly designed to outsail anything they could not outfight. They were larger, faster, more heavily gunned and more strongly manned than other ships of their class in any navy of their day, particularly those of the Royal Navy of Britain.

An example of their superiority was provided very early in the war by the exploits of the USS *Constitution*, destined to become affectionately known to the whole nation as "Old Ironsides."

En route from Annapolis to New York, she encountered a British squadron of five ships off the coast of New Jersey. In three days of complicated and ingenious maneuvering she managed to evade them all, Then, not far from Boston, she came upon HMS *Guerriere*.

The *Guerriere,* although originally French, was more or less typical of British men-of-war of her class. She mounted 49 guns to the *Constitution's* 56. The *Constitution* carried thirty long 24-pounders and twenty-four 32-pound carronades to the Britisher's thirty long 18-pounders and sixteen 32-pound carronades. The British crew, including Marines, numbered 272 against the *Constitution's* 456, including a Marine detachment of 58.

These were formidable odds, and the *Guerriere's* captain must have been aware of them since squadrons of the two navies had operated together in the Mediterranean. His only chance lay in keeping as far away as possible in order to take advantage of the longer range of his lighter guns. It is doubtful that he could have done so for long in view of the *Constitution's* superior sailing qualities. But Captain Dacres did not even try. With the arrogance typical of the British Navy of that period, he bore straight in and the two ships closed each other like a couple of strange wildcats.

The *Constitution's* material advantages cannot fully account for what ensued. American gunnery proved as superior as the sheer weight of shot thrown. In thirty minutes the *Guerriere* was a foundering shambles, the *Constitution* virtually unscarred. Desperately the British closed to attempt boarding, only to find the *Constitution* all set to board them. Young Lieutenant William Bush, commanding Old Ironsides' Marine detachment, was shot dead as he leaped to the rail to lead a boarding party, but the *Guerriere* fell off in dismay.

The Marines in the fighting tops had swept the *Guerriere's* weather deck with such a volume of small arms fire that no one remained topside to man her guns, or even strike her colors. Silent, she wallowed in the trough of the sea, a hopeless wreck. Captain Isaac Hull of the *Constitution* sent a small boat over to inquire politely if her commander desired to surrender.

With fifteen of his crew dead and sixty-three wounded, with two of his three masts shot away and his ship in a sinking condition, Captain Dacres had little choice in the matter. The *Constitution's* casualties numbered seven killed and seven wounded.

She sustained no serious material damage, whereas the *Guerriere* was so far beyond salvage that Captain Hull ordered her burned after taking her crew off as prisoners.

An interesting participant in this engagement, according to her own account, was one Lucy Brewer, the original Woman Marine. Lucy, as she tells it, was working in Boston when the *Constitution* put in at that port of call en route to her rendezvous with destiny. One of Lucy's Marine friends, it seems, so imbued her with the Marine Corps *esprit de corps* that she promptly donned men's clothing and enlisted onboard. Her account of the battle is detailed and accurate; in fact, it is almost a verbatim transcript of Captain Hull's official report. Regrettable though it may be, it must be recorded that there is not one scrap of evidence, save that from her own pen, to support the legend of Lucy Brewer.

But no figment of an active imagination and a prolific pen was Lieutenant John Marshall Gamble, the only Marine officer in history to command a U.S. naval vessel in combat. And certainly no chronicle of Marine participation in the War of 1812 could properly be set down without relating the epic of the *Essex*.

Commanded by thirty-two-year-old Captain David Porter, the USS *Essex* was one of the smallest ships afloat to be classed as a frigate. She mounted only thirty-two guns. Her Marine detachment, commanded by Lieutenant Gamble, numbered thirty-one. With all sails set before a spanking breeze, she cleared the mouth of the Delaware on the bright morning of October 27, 1812. Her orders were to rendezvous with a small U.S. squadron off the coast of Brazil to operate against British commerce in the South Atlantic. When this rendezvous failed to materialize, Porter sailed off on his own, rounded Cape Horn and cruised up the west coast of South America. At the Galapagos Islands, headquarters of the British whaling fleet in the Pacific, he found rich pickings. Two of the ships he captured there were armed. Porter strengthened their armaments, put detachments of his crew aboard both and commissioned them as warships in the U.S. Navy.

One he renamed the *Essex Junior* and placed under the command of his first lieutenant. The second, renamed the USS *Greenwich,* he entrusted to Gamble, who not long thereafter captured the armed whaler *Seringapatam* in a brisk engagement, marked by the Marine officer's skillful ship handling and maneuvering.

After a year of being constantly at sea, Porter found his men becoming restive. He also had reason to presume that word of his activities had reached England and that he could expect an avenging squadron to descend upon him shortly. So he headed west with the object of setting up an out-of-the-way base where he could refit his ships preparatory to returning to the United States. He told his crews that their destination was a place where "the maidens of the South Sea Isles will assuage your loneliness."

On the last count he proved only too right. He set up his base at Nukuhiva, in the Marquesas Islands. The "maidens" took up their assuagement so enthusiastically that it became apparent he would have some difficulty getting his men to put to sea again. He also became embroiled in a native civil war, during which he claimed the island group in the name of the United States, an action to which no one paid any particular attention.

Finally, on December 12, 1813, Porter put to sea with the *Essex* and the *Essex Junior* and headed for the west coast of South America. He left Gamble with the *Greenwich* and a couple of other prizes, twenty-one sailors and Marines, and six captured British crewmen to hold the base for five and a half months against his possible return.

But David Porter had played his luck to the limit, and time was running out on him. He made it to Valparaiso, Chile, on February 3, 1814, where two British men-of-war bottled him up in the harbor. At the first opportunity he made a desperate attempt to gain the open sea. But when the two Britishers cornered him against the coast, and in an engagement in which he sustained more than fifty per cent casualties, he was forced to surrender.

At the base in Nukuhiva, Gamble found himself in hot water almost as soon as the *Essex* was hull down on the horizon. The "maidens" began swimming out to his ships at night to see their men—and, incidentally, to plunder the few remaining stores. The native men became increasingly hostile as they realized the small size of Gamble's force. Finally the British prisoners revolted, wounded and overpowered Gamble and his one remaining officer, seized the *Seringapatam* and set sail for home. Gamble managed to regain his two remaining prize ships, one of which he burned. The natives took the revolt of the prisoners as a cue to attack him. He beat them off but lost his only officer and four men in doing it. Finally he cut the anchor cable and managed to put to sea in his last ship. With only seven men left, most of whom were either sick or wounded, he could not sail the ship properly but was forced to coast along with the trade winds in hopes of reaching the Hawaiian Islands.

This he finally accomplished. Island natives and white traders received him cordially, reviving his hopes of being able to outfit the ship properly and eventually reach home. His hopes were short lived. HMS *Cherub,* one of the ships which had captured Porter, suddenly appeared on the scene. Then and there the war ended abruptly for John Marshall Gamble, outstanding Marine of his particular era. He remained a prisoner of the British until the end of the war, finally making his way back to the United States after an absence of two and a half years.

By early 1813, British might had swept all effective U.S. naval strength from the high seas. However, from the naval viewpoint, a more important field of operations lay in the inland waterways which both separated and penetrated the United States and Canada. These were Lakes Ontario, Erie and Champlain, and the St. Lawrence and Niagara Rivers.

The most important was Lake Ontario. The navy which controlled this body of water held the key to invasion of its enemy's territory. The ensuing struggle to gain this control led to one of the most inept and futile contests ever recorded in the annals of naval warfare.

The American naval commander on Lake Ontario was Captain Isaac Chauncey, holding the temporary rank of Commodore for the occasion. Chauncey was based at Sacketts Harbor, New York. His opponent was Sir James Yeo, who operated out of Kingston, Ontario. Chauncey and Yeo apparently learned their naval tactics from the same book. Both were past masters at continually maneuvering their squadrons about the lake without ever meeting each other in a decisive engagement.

During the winter of 1813-1814 they became involved in a ship building race which resulted in probably the most fantastic naval fleet ever assembled, considering its area of operations. By the end of the war, Yeo's fleet included a 102-gun ship-of-the-line and Chauncey had a 75-gun monstrosity named the *New Orleans* on the ways.

From the standpoint of Marine Corps history, the entire farce is worthy of mention only because of the demands placed on the Corps' meager strength to furnish Marines for Chauncey's futile fleet. The barracks detachment at Charlestown, South Carolina, simply closed up that post and marched northward. Along the way, they picked up such increments as could be spared from Marine posts at Washington, Baltimore and New York. And, in April 1813, a rather pathetically small force of three officers and 121 enlisted Marines reached Sacketts Harbor.

From any standpoint, the Lake Ontario story is one of utter futility. Perhaps its most distinguishing characteristic is the fact that history fails to disclose any instance when two more reluctant warriors than Chauncey and Yeo were ever pitted against each other.

Fortunately the story of Lake Erie was dramatically different. The Navy sent brilliant twenty-eight-year-old Oliver Hazard Perry to assume command there.

Detailed as Perry's Marine officer was even younger Lieutenant John Brooks, son of a former Governor of Massachusetts. He proceeded overland from Washington, via Pittsburgh, to join Perry at Presque Isle, now the city of Erie, Pennsylvania. Brooks had authority to recruit men for the Marine Corps along the way. But people in those backwoods regions had never heard of Marines, and apparently had no desire to correct this deficiency in their education by personal experience. Consequently the Lieutenant arrived with only the twelve Marines with whom he had started his journey. Brooks had to fill out his Marine complement by drawing picked men from General William Henry Harrison's army forces, and accepting volunteers from among the shipyard workers.

Perry was confronted with a number of serious problems. In the first place, he had to build his fleet before he could fight. This he had to accomplish under the eyes of Commander R. H. Barclay's British squadron which controlled the lake. Secondly, he was nominally under command of Chauncey who was supposed to furnish him with skilled naval personnel for at least the key positions. Chauncey was so frightened of his own position that he failed to do so. In addition to all this, Perry faced a difficult command situation. The original officer assigned to Lake Erie was Lieutenant Jesse D. Elliott. His signal failure to accomplish anything of importance had caused the Navy Department to send Perry, his junior in age but senior in rank, to supersede him. Elliott, however, remained second in command, and deeply resented the whole business.

Perry drove his workers hard to get his little fleet built, then recruited many of the same workers to man it. Brooks drew the personnel for his Marine force from the army and trained them for service afloat. By August 12, when they put to sea, they had developed between them one of the tautest little forces in the history of the U.S. Navy.

They met the British in Put-in-Bay on September 9, 1813. As far as armament was concerned, Barclay's fleet mounted long guns against Perry's large caliber carronades. Perry had to close quickly, which he proceeded to do with his flagship, the little 20-gun brig *Lawrence*. For half an hour Perry's small ship sustained the full fury of the British fire. Then Perry, realizing that his second in command, Elliott, had not even maneuvered within firing range, performed one of the most unusual moves in naval history. Via small boat, he transferred himself and his flag from the shambles of the *Lawrence* to Elliott's untouched *Niagara*. There he relieved Elliott of command and waded in on the British again. Half an hour later, his legs spraddled against the roll of the deck, he wrote his historic dispatch to General Harrison: "We have met the enemy and they are ours. . . ."

Thus Oliver Hazard Perry sent a dispatch which so thrilled a nation that it became immortalized on the hallowed pages of its history. But Lieutenant John Brooks filed no dispatches. Along with half of his small band of Marines, he lay dead on the fire-swept deck of the *Lawrence*.

As the year 1814 progressed, a sinister tactical trend became increasingly evident. Until then the British had been unable to conduct the American war with much vigor because of the commitment of a large portion of their military forces to the struggle with Napoleon. Now with Napoleon safely disposed of—for the time being—veteran British troops from Europe began appearing in increasing numbers in the American theater of operations. The picture appeared exceedingly grim. Only British ineptness at high level kept the crushing defeat which appeared inevitable from becoming an actuality.

In the spring of 1814 the British embarked several thousand of the Duke of Wellington's Peninsular veterans under Major General Robert Ross in transport ships. Under convoy of a fleet commanded by Admiral Sir George Cockburn, the transports crossed the Atlantic to Bermuda, where the force set up an advanced base preparatory to descent upon the U.S. coast.

The target selected was the Chesapeake Bay area. The fleet entered the Bay on August 17. The British chased their only naval opposition, Commodore Joshua Barney's small flotilla of Mr. Jefferson's ineffectual gunboats, up the Patuxent River and raided the shores at leisure. On the 20th, British troops landed in force at the town of Benedict on the west bank of the Patuxent, and it became apparent that they were preparing to attack

Washington. Thereupon Barney destroyed his gunboats, assembled his sailors on shore and set out for the capital, dragging his salvaged naval guns with him.

With Barney's arrival, the small garrison at the Washington Marine Barracks marched out under Captain Samuel Miller, the Corps adjutant, to join forces. Altogether the combined force numbered only some five hundred officers and men.

Overall command of the force defending Washington had been entrusted to Brigadier General George Winder, mainly for political reasons. He was a nephew of the Governor of Maryland, and the Maryland militia would have to bear the brunt of the forthcoming campaign. Winder was not a professional soldier. He had distinguished himself on the Niagara the previous summer by managing to be taken prisoner by the British. Few generals in history, professional or otherwise, ever handled a campaign more ineptly than he handled the defense of his country's capital. However, in all fairness, it must be said that few generals ever received less support or more harassment from their superiors. The superiors in this case consisting of the President, the Secretary of State and the Secretary of War. On paper, at least, Winder had an adequate number of troops. But adequacy of numbers seldom compensates for the deficiencies of militia and volunteers, short on training and shorter still on morale.

After much futile marching and counter marching, Winder established his main line of resistance at Bladensburg, only a short distance beyond the District of Columbia's northeastern boundary. There on the morning of August 24, he set up in two lines; the first along the bank of a small stream, the second on higher ground behind. A more than casual observer might have been appalled at the distance separating Winder's secondary line from his initial line. It was well beyond the range of the weapons of its defenders, far beyond immediate supporting distance. Thus they waited, their thin lines deployed in flagrant disregard of the most elemental principle of defensive warfare. In the stifling humidity of midday, the British advance came upon them.

The first American line, strongly reinforced with artillery, repulsed two enemy attacks. With the third it began to fade away in the face of the awesome precision and determination of the British veteran regulars. Presently there was no longer any first line. The British, pausing only to regroup, started up the road toward the center of the second line, occupied by Barney's sailors and Miller's Marines.

Barney's salvaged naval guns quickly swept them from the road and caused them to deploy more widely than they had intended. But this over-extended deployment proved no unmixed blessing. As the troops on the flanks realized they were going to get their share of the oncoming assault, they began to get jittery. And, as it had happened on the river bank, presently there were troops neither to the right nor left of center. Five hundred sailors and Marines found themselves pitted against more than 3,000 of the best troops in the world. Behind them Winder's withdrawal to Washington developed into a panic-stricken rout.

Three times Barney and Miller repulsed the British assault. But it was only a matter of time and blood in the face of such odds. The red-coated tide lapped around both flanks of the defenders in a double envelopment. Barney and Captain Miller fell severely wounded. The outflanked survivors were finally forced to withdraw, leaving their wounded, including Barney and Miller, on the field. With true British sportsmanship, General Ross treated the only Americans to furnish him serious resistance that day as honored guests. He had them cared for in a field hospital set up in Bladensburg, and left them there to fall again into friendly hands upon his retirement.

The British reached Washington with no further resistance. But when they sought to demand the surrender of the city, they were nonplussed to find no one there to receive the demand. The President, the Cabinet and Congress had found pressing business elsewhere and had hurriedly ridden off in all directions.

At their leisure the British set fire to all public buildings they could identify as such, and a few others they did not bother to be sure about. They declared then, and later, that they did this

in retaliation for the Americans having done the same thing
during the capture of York (Toronto), capital of Upper Canada,
the previous summer. So the Capitol, Presidential Mansion,
Treasury and Arsenal, among others, went up in flames. The
Commandant of the Washington Navy Yard saved them the
trouble by destroying his own installation and the vessels in it
to prevent them from falling into enemy hands.

Why did the British spare the Marine Barracks and the Commandant's house? That question aroused much speculation at
the time, and has since given rise to a number of versions, more
legend than provable fact.

One logical presumption is that General Ross and Admiral
Cockburn found the house to their liking as a headquarters,
and spared it for that purpose. Since these two gentlemen subsequently found it expedient to leave town so hurriedly that they
left their wounded behind, they perhaps forgot to put the torch
to the place in the haste of withdrawal.

A much more colorful version of what happened has been
told, with slight variations, in Marine barracks rooms for over
a century. This tale has to do with two sergeants who were assigned by the Commandant to hide some Marine Corps funds
in the house to prevent them from falling into British hands. The
early stories set the amount at $2,500, while the latter day ac-
counts have inflated the amount to $75,000. In keeping with
such yarns, the two sergeants met an untimely end, carrying with
them the secret location of the hidden treasure. Some say that
they were killed at Bladensburg, while others stoutly maintain
that they made the supreme sacrifice in a desperate defense of
the Commandant's house.

But the version most often told by proud Marines is that
General Ross was so impressed by the magnificent stand made
by the Marines at Bladensburg that he ordered the Barracks and
the Commandant's house spared as a gesture of soldierly respect.

The last action of the War of 1812, actually occuring after
the peace treaty was signed, also involved Marines. Captain
Daniel Carmick gathered all the Marines from the New Orleans

Navy Yard and joined Andrew Jackson in his historic defense of that city. During the fighting they manned a sector in the center of the line. In the final assault the British lost 700 killed, 1,300 wounded and 500 prisoners. The American casualties were 8 killed and 13 wounded. As for the conduct of the Marines, Congress passed a resolution expressing, "the high sense of valor and good conduct of Major Daniel Carmick, of the officers, non-commissioned officers, and Marines under his command, in the defense of said city."

All in all the fledgling Marine Corps had acquitted itself well in the second war with Britain. All hands emerged from the war with a feeling of pride and unity. Marines had invariably fought well when the opportunity had occurred. Where it had not occurred, as on Lake Ontario, the blame was hardly theirs. Several officers had achieved individual distinction. But, unfortunately, one had not. This was the one sore spot.

It has been noted that the Marines marched off to fight at Bladensburg under the command of Captain Miller, the headquarters adjutant. Where, then, was Lieutenant Colonel Franklin Wharton, the Commandant?

"I was," he said sheepishly in his subsequent report, "at Frederick with the paymaster."

And that was the literal truth. Upon the approach of the British the thrifty Wharton had hired a wagon, loaded aboard valuables and the payroll the two unnamed sergeants were supposed to have buried, and had taken off at a fast gallop for the small town in Maryland. This incident provoked some pointed jibes from the other services and some heavy handed kidding that embarrassed the Marines.

Among those who saw nothing funny in the situation was young Archibald Henderson, who had commanded the Marines on the *Constitution* where he had been cited for conspicuous gallantry. Henderson already realized that the tiny new Corps of which he was a part was destined to owe its very existence to the conduct of its members in combat. That its ranking officer should have had his mind on the payroll when his troops went forth to battle struck him as nothing short of disgraceful. In an effort to wipe the escutcheon clean, he preferred charges of cowardice against his superior officer.

To the young captain's disgust, the ensuing court-martial cleared Wharton. He remained inconspicuously at his post until his death in office in 1818. In Marine Corps annals he remains a shadowy figure whose one positive act most Marines of his own and subsequent generations would prefer to forget.

Archibald Henderson, however, was a man long to be remembered.

★　　★　　★　　★　　★

4

Archibald Henderson—an Era

FOLLOWING THE DEATH OF WHARTON, the Marine Corps was without a Commandant for six months. This unusual situation was rectified by the appointment of Lieutenant Colonel Anthony Gale, a most unfortunate choice.

Most of the people concerned did not want Irish-born Anthony Gale as Commandant of the Marine Corps. On numerous occasions he had been reported for personal misconduct. He had also managed to incur the wrath of Commandant Wharton over his handling of a construction contract while commanding the Marine Barracks in Philadelphia. The fact that a Board of Inquiry absolved him of all blame in the matter did nothing to decrease Wharton's enmity. The Commandant's displeasure eventually resulted in Gale being transferred to a less desirable post in New Orleans. It also resulted in considerable unfavorable opinion concerning his professional ability.

These facts were well known to the Secretary of the Navy, and they were apparently the reason why the Secretary took six months to get around to submitting Gale's name for approval as the next Commandant. Nevertheless, under the inviolate rule of seniority, Anthony Gale became the fourth Commandant of the Marine Corps on March 3, 1819.

His tour of duty as Commandant was a most unhappy one and lasted only eighteen months. Much of the unhappiness was caused by the Secretary of the Navy, Smith Thompson. Either out of lack of confidence, or a strong tendency to meddle, Thompson continually countermanded Gale's orders. On one occasion, he revoked the Commandant's orders to one of his officers to report to a new duty station, and granted the officer eight months leave. Three months before this, he had sent Gale sharply worded instructions to grant no more than sixty days leave to his officers under any circumstances. To add to Gale's humiliation, the news of having his orders countermanded came not from the Secretary, but from the officers themselves. Some of these officers were not above flaunting their influence with the Secretary in Gale's face.

In desperation Gale wrote a brilliantly reasoned letter in which he analyzed the proper division of functions between himself and the Secretary. He concluded the letter by respectfully pointing out the impossibility of his position under the circumstances. Having officially entered his reaction to the infringements of his authority, Gale took to drinking. Three weeks later he was placed under arrest charged, among other things, with ". . . being intoxicated in common dram shops and other places of low repute in the City of Washington. . . ."

The records of the ensuing court-martial, although extremely sketchy, reveal some rather curious facts. The prosecutor in the case was the hero of Bladensburg, Major Samuel Miller, who had never been a friend of Gale's. In addition, Miller not only prepared the charges and specifications against Gale, but also executed the Secretary's arrest order. Perhaps most curious of all, upon the day of Gale's arrest, he became acting Commandant of the Marine Corps.

As a defense against the charges, Gale pleaded temporary insanity. He properly petitioned the court for permission to present defense witnesses in support of his plea. The court informed him that such permission must be obtained from the Secretary of the Navy, since that official had ordered his arrest.

The Secretary, on the other hand, bluntly told him that the court was competent to handle such matters. It can not be categorically stated that Gale was denied his rights in the matter. If he was successful in obtaining his witnesses, the record of trial is in error for failing to mention their appearance in court.

On October 17, 1820, the court found Gale guilty as charged, and the President approved the sentence. Seven months later Gale managed to obtain a copy of the court-martial proceedings. And, although it took him fifteen years to do it, he evidently managed to establish his case of temporary mental derangement. In 1835 he was granted a pension of $15.00 per month, which he continued to receive until his death in 1843. Thus did Anthony Gale achieve the unfortunate distinction of being the only Commandant of the Marine Corps ever to be cashiered from the service.

Coincident with Gale's dismissal, the responsibility of conducting the affairs of the Marine Corps passed to the hands of a Virginia gentleman who was to guide its destiny for thirty-nine years. On October 17, 1820, Major Archibald Henderson was promoted to the rank of lieutenant colonel and at thirty-seven became the fifth Commandant of the Marine Corps.

Under the blunt, outspoken Henderson, the Marine Corps underwent some profound charges. The long span of years of his command were eventful ones and, through a series of dramatic events which commanded wide attention, the Corps established a high reputation with the people of the nation. The man who was to become known as "the grand old man of the Marine Corps" was largely responsible.

Morale was low in the Armed Forces of the 1820's. As usual after each war, the military had been shunted aside. The War of 1812 was rapidly passing into the limbo of forgotten things. It had been an unpopular war to begin with, as far as Americans were concerned. The war-torn era of Napoleon had ended at Waterloo, and the great powers of Russia, England, Austria and Prussia had combined in the Quadruple Alliance to "preserve the tranquillity of Europe" against a revival of revolution. The danger of being drawn into a European war appeared very remote. The United States Congress was much too occupied with internal expansion to pay any attention to the relatively few people it hired for the defense of the nation. The strength of the Marine Corps stood at 49 officers and 865 enlisted men.

A Marine private during this period was paid between $6.00 and $10.00 per month, depending upon the length of his previous service. If he was on his first enlistment, the chances of him drawing a full month's pay were pretty slim. In order to discourage desertions, it was the general practice for the paymaster to withhold part of each month's pay until the expiration of the man's enlistment. Pay for non-commissioned officers began at $8.00 a month for corporals and increased, according to rate, to a high of $17.00 which was the pay of a sergeant major. Each man received an allowance of three rations a day, supplemented by a gill of grog. Fifteen to twenty cents a day were allowed for rations and the annual clothing allowance amounted to $30.00 a year.

Officer's pay began at $25.00 per month for second lieutenants and gradually increased with rank to the Commandant's pay, which was slightly less than $75.00. Officers were allowed from four to twelve rations per day, according to their rank. The Commandant received additional allowances for travel. He was also allowed $12.00 a month for forage, and $10.00 for cord wood to supply the heat for his house.

Immediately upon assuming command, Henderson, who had evidentally given the matter considerable thought, set about improving the morale and efficiency of his Corps. He began by personally inspecting every shore station which included Marines, and many of the ship's detachments. He was a stickler for detail, and continually gave evidence of knowing thoroughly the job of every one of his Marines. He insisted on the strictest economy in the expenditure of funds, and personally handled most of the Corps' legal affairs. Although he had the reputation of being a martinet, he went to great lengths to insure that his officers and men were properly accorded their every right.

In the matter of training he was almost a fanatic. He had long realized that the key to the efficiency of any fighting organization lay in two inseparable and basic fundamentals—training and spirit. He ordered all newly commissioned officers to duty at Marine Corps Headquarters, in order to supervise personally their indoctrination and training. During most of his tour of duty, the Army was unable to absorb all of the graduates of West Point. Henderson obtained as many of these officers as possible for the Marine Corps. To assist in the training of the new officers, and to act as a nucleus for a landing force, he kept a skeletonized battalion at Headquarters. This battalion was thoroughly trained in the latest developments of military weapons and tactics.

Henderson demanded, and received, the strict subordination of all his officers. He took no nonsense from anyone, including his superiors in the U.S. Navy. On one occasion, when the Navy Department countermanded his orders to a Marine captain to go to sea, Henderson went directly to the President. He respectfully, and probably vigorously, explained that it was imperative that his orders be carried out in order to vindicate his position and authority. Four days later the captain in question reported for sea duty, and the Secretary of the Navy reported to the President for a dressing down.

The agencies for maintaining law and order in the United States during the first half of the nineteenth century were few and far between. Those which did exist were poorly organized, and even more poorly trained. During this era the Marines were often called upon to lend a hand in local disturbances.

In the great Boston fire of 1824, they performed both rescue work and police functions in helping to stamp out the wave of pilfering and looting which followed the holocaust.

A short time later, Major Robert D. Wainwright earned prominent mention in the classic school books of the era, *McGuffey's Readers*. And, for the next seventy-five years, the nation's school children received a lesson dealing with the heroic conduct of Marines.

The scene of the action was the Massachusetts State Prison at Boston. Having become thoroughly dissatisfied with their lot in life, some 283 prisoners staged a riot which rapidly got beyond control of the prison authorities. With the situation out of hand, the warden sent a frantic call for help to the Boston Marine Barracks.

Major Wainwright, with a detachment of thirty Marines, soon arrived at the prison area. Making a hasty estimate of what was apparently a bad situation, Wainwright came up with a simple solution. Hastily forming a single rank facing the prisoners, he ordered his Marines to fire a warning volley into the air. The shots had the desired effect and the clamor of the riot subsided. As his Marines reloaded their muskets, the Major addressed the rebellious prisoners, "These men are United States Marines," he said. "They follow my orders to the letter."

Turning to face the Marines, Wainwright consulted his watch, and then issued his orders in a loud, parade ground voice. "Exactly three minutes from now I shall raise my hand over my head," he bellowed. "When I drop my hand you will commence firing. You will continue to fire until you have killed every prisoner who has not returned to his cell."

For three long minutes not a word was spoken. The only sound was the shuffle of the inmates' feet as they dejectedly returned to their cells.

With the advent of the 1830's, the traditional isolationism of America underwent an abrupt change. It had become apparent to the United States that many areas of commercial advantage lay beyond its own boundaries. This change in policy had a pronounced effect on the functions performed by Marines. As a result of it, the Marines, under the energetic leadership of their fifth Commandant, ranged far and wide to protect the interests of their country.

Late in 1831 the natives of Sumatra seized and robbed an American merchantman in the harbor of Quallah Battoo. This act of piracy resulted in the murder of several members of the crew. In retaliation the United States sent the frigate *Potomac*, especially outfitted for the job, on a punitive expedition against the Sumatran pirates. Arriving in February, 1832, the *Potomac* put a landing force of over 250 Marines and sailors ashore. In two days of bloody warfare, the force captured four pirate forts and reduced the town of Quallah Battoo to a heap of smoldering ruins.

At the same time, on the other side of the Southern Hemisphere, Marines were having some difficulties in South America. Argentina was attempting to establish claim over the Falkland Islands. In pursuit of this claim, that country looked with extreme disfavor on American vessels conducting trade with the Islands. In an effort to discourage this practice, the Argentineans proceeded to impound three American schooners and jail their crews. Marines from the sloop *Lexington* waded ashore and, through dint of considerable small arms fire, succeeded in impressing the Argentine officials that the United States did not look kindly upon such treatment of its ships and citizens.

But, as far as the Marine Corps was concerned, the most far-reaching effect of the new anti-isolation policy of the United States was reflected in the Act of 1834. Passed by Congress on June 30, the legislation authorized a substantial increase in the strength of the Marine Corps. It also settled the question of its control, by placing it in the hands of the Secretary of the Navy. In addition, it authorized the President to order the Marines into whatever action his judgment dictated, including duty with the Army. Within the the year the President was to make good use of his newly-granted powers.

In the Everglades of Florida a bad situation of long standing was rapidly coming to a head.

Over a period of many years runaway Negro slaves had found refuge with the Seminole Indians and many of the slaves and members of the tribe had intermarried. The southern planters, aware of this refuge for their escaped slaves, had made repeated petitions to the Crown of Spain, without avail. Unhappy with the refusal of Charles IV to take the necessary steps to return their slaves, the southern land owners began to petition their

own government for the annexation of Florida. In 1819 a portion of Florida was purchased from Spain for $5,000,000. Im-
mediately the slave owners renewed their demands to the government that their slaves be returned. Inasmuch as some seventy-five
years had passed since their ancestors had taken refuge in
Florida, it was a little difficult for the Seminoles to understand
the claims of the planters. As a result, such demands met with
a particularly unenthusiastic response by the Seminoles.

Under the political pressure eventually brought to bear by
the slave owners, the Administration completed a treaty with
the Indians, under which the government would take the tribe
under its protection and assign the Indians to reservations. Perhaps things might have worked out if certain enterprising souls
hadn't become aware of the lucrative possibilities in the profession of slave catching. The "slave-hunters," in direct violation
of the terms of the treaty, entered Florida in organized bands
to catch runaway slaves who brought high prices on the slave
markets. There is no evidence to indicate that the government
made any attempts to stop this practice, although the Indians
continually demanded redress.

In 1828 the proposal was made to the Seminoles to move to
a reservation in the area now occupied by the state of Arkansas.
Tribal chiefs made a reconnaissance of the area and returned
with the report that "snow covers the ground, and frosts chill the
bodies of men." Their objections notwithstanding, the Seminoles were ordered to emigrate west. At which point things got
rapidly out of hand.

Determined to force the emigration, the government sent
troops into Florida. Just as determined to remain where they
were, the Seminoles made preparations for war. In December,
1835 the hostilities began in earnest, and in a short time the
horrors of the Seminole War were being chronicled throughout
the land.

Brigadier General D. L. Clinch, who was commanding the
U.S. troops in Florida, was charged with the responsibility of the
removal of the Indians. The end of the year found the well-armed

Indians, under the leadership of a colorful half-breed named Osceola, assembled in the almost inaccessible swamps of the Withlacoochee River.

Clinch, whose immediate problem was to protect the white settlers, decided to attack the Indians. Since his own force, which occupied Fort King near the present town of Ocala, was too small for the job, he sent to Fort Brooke on Tampa Bay for reinforcements.

The reinforcements, numbering 110 and under the command of a Major Dade, answered the call of General Clinch with colors flying and bugles blaring across the swamps. With the possible exception of Custer's debacle at Little Big Horn, the fate of this force is without parallel in the history of Indian warfare.

Shortly after Dade's force crossed the Withlacoochee, they were met with an ambush so effective that only two survivors remained to crawl through the wire grass to safety. One was Private Clark of the 2nd Artillery who, although badly wounded, is reputed to have crawled to Fort Brooke, a distance of sixty miles. The other was Louis Pacheo, a Negro slave who acted as guide for the force. There is reason to suspect that the escape of Pacheo from the ambush was something more than blind luck. Be that as it may, the only man to survive without a scratch lived to the venerable age of ninety-five without being taken to task for his supposed treachery.

On the same day as the Dade Massacre, Osceola and a small band invaded a dinner party being given by General Wiley Thompson, who had been sent from Washington to oversee removal of the Indians, and murdered the General and his five guests. If there had been any doubts about the earnestness of the war in Florida, the Dade Massacre and the murder of General Thompson clinched the argument.

By the spring of 1836, the Army in central Florida found themselves in difficulty. One thousand soldiers were trying to round up and deport over three thousand Indians. The state militias, which had originally augmented the Army of the South, soon had their fill of poor food, swamp fever and general discomfort. And, with the coming of spring, they left Florida for healthier climes.

To add to the general misery, the Creek Indians of southern Alabama and Georgia decided to go on the warpath. The results of this uprising were severe enough to cause the Army to shift its main effort from the Seminole country to the area occupied by the Creeks.

At this juncture Archibald Henderson volunteered the services of a regiment of Marines for duty with the Army. The offer was promptly accepted. On May 23, 1836, President Jackson, under the recently enacted law, ordered all available Marines to report to the Army. Henderson, never one to sit on the sidelines, insisted on leading the regiment personally. By taking practically all officers, reducing shore station detachments to sergeant's guard, and leaving behind only those who were unfit for duty in the field, Henderson was able to mobilize more than half the total strength of the Corps.

There is a tale, often related by Marines, that Colonel Henderson closed Marine Corps Headquarters during this period. It is said that he locked the door to his office, placed the key under the mat, and tacked a neatly-lettered sign to the door which read:

> *Have gone to Florida to fight Indians.*
> *Will be back when the war is over.*
>
> > *A. Henderson*
> > *Col. Commandant*

More reliable accounts indicate that the Commandant left the Headquarters in charge of Lieutenant Colonel Wainwright, with the Band to provide the guard. Among those deemed unfit for duty in the field was one Sergeant Triguet, whom Henderson commended to Wainright in a letter of instruction which began: "Sergeant Triguet is left to assist in attending to the duties at Headquarters. He is a respectable old man, and has not other failing than that which but too often attends an old soldier. . ."

Henderson, with a force of 38 officers and 424 enlisted men, reported to General Winfield Scott at Columbus, Georgia. Since the Commandant was under direct orders of the Secretary of War, he technically became an Army officer and was placed in command of a brigade composed of Marines, Army Infantry and Artillery, and friendly Creeks.

Presaging the modern Marine battle garb of dungarees, the troops wore white fatigues, rather than the green and white uniforms of the period. Armed mostly with muskets, they also carried some of the new-fangled Colt rifles which had a disconcerting tendency to explode spontaneously when carried loaded for any length of time in the hot sun.

Both the Marine commander and General Scott took an optimistic view of the final outcome of the campaign. In a letter to the Secretary of the Navy, Henderson wrote: "It is now expected that the Campaign will be closed in the course of ten days or two weeks. . . ." On the same day General Scott went on record to the effect that "war against the hostile Creeks is supposed to be virtually over." One may well speculate as to the thoughts of General Scott a month later when he was recalled to Washington for an investigation of his conduct of the war against the Creeks and Seminoles. After a long, drawn-out investigation, Scott was exonerated and restored to his command.

The end of summer brought with it the termination of the Creek Campaign. The Creeks were removed to a reservation in what is now the state of Oklahoma, and the Army of the South again turned its attention to the Seminoles in Florida.

On June 24 a battalion of Marines under Lieutenant Colonel W. H. Freeman reached Milledgeville, Georgia, and moved on into Florida. In October, Freeman's battalion was consolidated with the one Henderson had been leading into a six-company regiment and moved to Apalachicola, to garrison Fort Brooke. The Marines were augmented by a regiment of Creek Indians, some 750 strong, who had been mustered and were paid as militia. The regiment was officered mainly by Marines, and wore white turbans to distinguish them from the enemy during battle. The Seminoles were rather unhappy about being pursued by their blood relatives, and showed their dislike by scalping all Creeks who fell into their hands.

On November 21 the Creeks, under the command of First Lieutenant Andrew H. Ross, fought an advanced guard action at Wahoo Swamp. From Wahoo a four-pronged advance, two columns of Army troops and two of Marines, pushed the Seminoles back to the Hatchee-Lustee River. Six days later the main body of Indians was located in the area of the Great Cypress Swamp, and was promptly attacked. The attackers managed to capture the horses of the enemy and twenty-five prisoners, most of whom were women and children. The braves slipped back into the swamp. Henderson left a detachment to guard the prisoners and horses, while the regiment pressed on after the warriors who had taken up positions on the opposite bank of the Hatchee-Lustee. The troops extended along the river bank and took up a cross fire, in an effort to dislodge the enemy. As soon as the Indians' fire slackened, the troops crossed the river by swimming and on logs. According to Henderson's report, ". . . we pursued the enemy as rapidly as the deep swamp and their mode of warfare permitted."

The chase continued until nightfall when Henderson was forced to withdraw his troops from the dense undergrowth. The result of the day's operations was the capture of the Indian women and children already mentioned, twenty-three Negroes, a few horses and some clothes and blankets. The battle report states that one Indian and two Negroes were seen dead by the troops.

As a result of his routing of the Indian forces, Henderson was brevetted a brigadier general and several Marines were promoted for "gallantry." Four days later, Abaham, a Seminole Chief, appeared at Henderson's camp under a flag of truce. This marked the beginning of several days of negotiations between Major General T. H. Jesup, to whom General Scott had relinquished command upon being recalled to Washington, and the Indian leaders at Fort Dade. These meetings finally resulted in an agreement by the chiefs to assemble their people for transportation to their new reservation. The peace treaty was formally signed on March 6. Jesup, believing the war to be over, began to discharge his volunteers.

On May 22, 1837, Henderson received orders to proceed to Washington. Taking with him all Marines except two companies, which totalled 189 officers and men, Henderson left Florida the next day.

On the night of June 2, Micanopy, grand chief of the Seminoles, and several of his lesser chiefs who had encamped with their followers near Tampa Bay, the port of embarkation, were abducted and taken to the interior. The next day a report was received from the troops south of Hillsboro that the Seminoles encamped in that vicinity had disappeared. These two incidents were the signal for the renewal of hostilities. General Jesup reported, "This campaign, so far as relates to Indian emigration, has entirely failed," and requested to be "immediately relieved from the command of the Army." The Seminole War was far from over.

For the next five years Archibald Henderson vainly tried to get the remaining Marines recalled from Florida. His appeals were refused by the Secretary of War who felt that the need for Marines in Florida was more pressing than the need for their return.

Jesup was finally relieved and realized what had been his burning desire since the beginning of the campaign—to join his family and spend the rest of his life on his farm. He was replaced by Colonel Zachary Taylor, who was soon promoted to the rank of brigadier general.

The campaign wore on and the possibility of success appeared more remote with each passing day. Osceola, who had been arrested while conferring with General Jesup, died in prison at Fort Moultrie in October 1837. The next year some 4,000 Seminoles made the move to Oklahoma, though many of them slipped away from the New Orleans concentration camps and returned to the Everglades.

The two remaining companies of Marines put in four more

years of duty along the coast and around the keys of Florida with the Mosquito Fleet. From June 1838 to the summer of 1842, this array of half a dozen small vessels, two barges and 140 canoes was manned by 68 officers and 600 men. The Marines of the fleet numbered about 130, and for the first two years of operation were commanded by First Lieutenant George H. Terrett who, seven years later, was to lead the way into Mexico City.

The object of the Mosquito Fleet was twofold, to intercept communications between the Indians and small boats operating off the Florida coast, and to conduct amphibious sorties into the interior of the Everglades. The fleet operated successfully throughout the remainder of the campaign, and the Indians came to have great respect for the "sailor boats" as they called them.

In the summer of 1842, the Seminole War gradually waned, without formal cessation of hostilities and with neither side clearly victorious. The Marines returned north in July, well pleased to be relieved of what had been six long years of extremely dreary duty. In the final accounting, sixty-one Marines had given their lives in the Seminole Campaign. More than half of them had died from disease, and one unfortunate had departed the scene, dispatched by a friendly musket ball—"discharged by accident." In analyzing the success of the campaign, one need only reflect upon the fact that the Seminoles still occupy the Everglades of Florida.

With the Seminole War a matter for the record books, Henderson again turned his attention to strengthening and developing the Corps. His efforts were aimed at keeping the Marines in a state of readiness for any emergency, domestic or foreign. The remainder of his career was distinguished by such important events as the Mexican War and Perry's Expedition to Japan. Under his direction Marines virtually covered the globe. To protect Americans and their commerce with China, they stormed the forts of Canton during the great Taiping Rebellion. In the South Seas they splashed ashore to bring the rampaging Fiji Islanders to heel. In the jungles of Central America they made their first contact with the Republic of Nicaragua, which was to see the repeated return of Marines over the next three quarters of a century. Along the Gold Coast of Africa the slave traders, on more than one occasion, felt the bite of a Marine's bayonet.

For the fifty years he wore the uniform of a Marine, Archibald Henderson preached the gospel of strong leadership and constant readiness. At the age of seventy-four he dramatically demonstrated that advanced age was no deterrent to practicing what he preached. The issues of the elections of 1857 were particularly bitter ones. In an effort to control the election in Washington, the "Know Nothing" Party imported a gang of hired thugs, known as the "Plug-Uglies," from Baltimore. The gang commenced activities by physically threatening the voters, and finally put a complete halt to the elections by taking possession of the polling places throughout the city. Civil authorities, unable to cope with the situation, appealed to the President who ordered two companies of Marines from the Marine barracks to restore order to the city.

The Marines met the "Plug-Uglies" on Pennsylvania Avenue, in the vicinity of City Hall. The rioting thugs, who were armed with every conceivable weapon, dragged up a brass cannon, aimed it at the Marine formation and demanded that they return to their barracks. Captain Tyler, commanding the Marines, ordered a detachment forward to capture the cannon. At that moment, General Henderson, who had been mingling with the mob and was dressed in civilian clothing, walked calmly up to the muzzle of the cannon and forced the weapon around. Henderson addressed the "Plug-Uglies," warning them of the seriousness of their acts and telling them that the Marines would fire if it became necessary. In the hectic few minutes that followed, a number of rioters, who fortunately were very bad marksmen, fired their pistols at Henderson. A platoon of Marines charged in to protect the Commandant and capture the cannon. One of the rioters, at point-blank range, aimed his pistol at Henderson's head. A Marine knocked the pistol to the ground with a butt stroke of his musket. The General promptly grabbed the culprit

by the collar and the seat of his pants and marched him off to
jail. With the riot getting out of control, the Marines opened fire.
The rioters, suddenly convinced that the Marines meant business,
retreated and order was restored to the city.

On January 6, 1859, the "grand old man of the Marine
Corps," who had served as Commandant under eleven Presidents, died in office at the age of seventy-six. The impact of his
strong personality and zealous devotion to duty remains to this
day, indelibly engraved on the Corps to which he devoted over
fifty years of his life.

On the bleak winter's night of February 13, 1943, General
Thomas Holcomb was entertaining dinner guests in the house
which had been home to Archibald Henderson for so many years.
Among the other duties he had attended to that day, Commandant Holcomb signed an order establishing the Women's
Reserve. During the course of the dinner conversation, he remarked to his guests, "Old Archibald would turn over in his
grave if he ever found out that females could become commissioned officers in his beloved Marine Corps." The words had
hardly left his lips when Henderson's portrait, which hung over
the sideboard, came crashing to the floor.

The era of Archibald Henderson had encompassed two wars
worthy of examination from the standpoint of the nation's history. One, which had been purely internal, was the protracted
campaign against the Creek and Seminole Indians. The other,
which took place on foreign soil, provided the Marines with the
first line to their hymn, and the nation with something it had long
wanted—a western boundary that bordered the blue Pacific.

5 ★

★　★　★　★　★

The Halls of Montezuma—
and Points West

IT HAS OFTEN BEEN SAID, by many authorities, that the fighting spirit of American troops reached an all-time high during our war with Mexico. This may be true. If it is, it helps to explain one peculiar aspect of this particular conflict. Never in the history of warfare between civilized nations has victory been achieved so consistently against such numerical odds.

Yet few American fighting men who met the Mexicans in combat have ever disparaged the physical bravery of the individual Mexican soldier. Individual bravery seems to have comprised the whole Mexican concept of war. You marched bravely into battle, and you fought bravely. Whether you fought skillfully and in accordance with fundamentally sound tactical concepts was purely incidental. The Mexicans of that era were the worst-led soldiers in history.

As a comanding general, Antonio Lopez de Santa Anna was a politician—and not a particularly good one at that. He had been ousted from the Presidency of Mexico no less than three times. The Texans had trounced him soundly and taken him prisoner at San Jacinto, when the Lone Star State had revolted against Mexican rule in 1836. Apparently the only opponents he had been able to defeat in the field were political, and these not too consistently.

Many generations after the event, it has become popular to characterize our war with Mexico as a big bully picking on a weak neighbor. This was not really the case at the time. The two nations had approximately equal manpower resources, and the Mexican armed forces were considerably larger than ours. Many European observers regarded our chances of success as highly dubious. No less than that dean of military authorities, the Duke of Wellington, just wrote the whole thing off when General Winfield Scott abandoned his line of communications in order to stage the climactic campaign that won the war. "Scott is lost," Wellington said, and let it go at that.

The Marine Corps played no major part in the Mexican War, but the part it did play had some interesting aspects.

By the first half of the nineteenth century, Mexico had become an over-expanded country, threatened with disintegration through centrifugal force. Its northern provinces included what are now the states of Texas and California, largely inhabited by immigrants from the United States. Also included was the sparsely populated territory lying between, the present states of New Mexico, Arizona, Utah and Nevada. All of this territory lay far distant from the seat of government, making efficient administration practically impossible.

Texas revolted and established her independence after decisively defeating General-President Santa Anna in the spring of 1836. The Mexicans had excellent reason to suspect the United States of complicity in the revolt. So, when Texas was annexed to the United States in 1845, at her own application, the Mexican Government was unhappy about the whole procedure.

The big bone of contention which existed was the southern boundary of the new state. Texas claimed that it extended to the Rio Grande River. Mexico claimed that it reached only to the Neuces River, one hundred miles to the north. Upon the opening of negotiations dealing with the boundary dispute, a U.S. Army force of regulars and volunteers under Major General Zachary Taylor was sent to the border, in February, 1846, with orders to defend Texas. Taylor fortified Point Isabel on the Gulf coast, a terrain feature which comprised the northern bank of the mouth of the Rio Grande. He then moved westward to consolidate the boundary assigned him. In doing so, he failed to maintain physical contact with his fortified position on the coast, which protected his eastern flank. This tactical mistake, which proved to be of little consequence, brought about the first participation of the Marines in the Mexican War.

This did not amount to much, actually. Across the river, Taylor faced a force of six thousand Mexican troops under General Avista. When Taylor moved westward, Avista crossed the Rio Grande into the disputed territory and interposed his force between Taylor and the weakly garrisoned Point Isabel.

Taylor, who scorned wearing a uniform and gloried in his nickname of "Old Rough and Ready," was a fighting man, if not much else. He promptly turned his two thousand three hundred men around and fought his way back to Point Isabel. This action required two days and two battles, which are recorded as Palo Alto and Resaco de la Palma. But in accomplishing this feat he greatly alarmed the squadron the Navy had sent down to support him, and which was lying off Point Isabel.

The two battles took place so close to the coast that the men aboard the ships could hear the musketry and see the columns of black smoke rising in the still air. As the ground action continued, Captain R. H. Gregory, the squadron commander, became increasingly concerned for the security of Point Isabel. On May 8, he sent a landing party of about five hundred men ashore, spearheaded by 145 Marines, to reinforce the Isabel garrison. Gregory might just as well have saved himself the trouble. General Taylor fought his way through the Mexicans with no particular difficulty, and secured his seaward flank.

Taylor continued his advance westward along the northern bank of the Rio Grande. In his support a landing force of two hundred Marines and seamen moved fifteen miles upriver to seize Barita on the south bank, to cover the flank of the invading army. This force proved to be actually the first to occupy Mexican soil, as Taylor's troops did not begin their crossing until more than an hour after the landing.

But this dubious distinction was about all it did accomplish. Taylor marched on to a thoroughly victorious, and equally inconclusive, campaign in northern Mexico, while personnel of the naval force returned to their respective ships.

From this point on, the principle task of the Navy on the east coast became the blockade of Mexican ports. Such ports were neither very numerous nor, with the exceptions of Vera Cruz and Tampico, very important. The blockade proved pretty much of a routine operation, since the Mexicans possessed no navy capable of opposing it. However, American attempts to capture the ports can hardly be considered as brilliantly successful. The town of Alvarado repulsed two attempted landing attacks decisively enough to force Commodore David Connor into a humiliating withdrawal. Thus the harassed Mexicans had something to cheer about for the first time since the sorry struggle had started. San Juan Bautista, seventy miles up the Tobasco River, did much the same thing to Connor's second in command, Commodore Matthew C. Perry. But the more important port of Tampico surrendered on November 15. Not long thereafter the war entered a new phase.

It was becoming apparent in Washington that General Taylor, for all his local successes in northern Mexico, was in no position to force a decisive decision. Hundreds of miles of arid, mountainous terrain separated him from the heart of the country. So plans were drawn up for a stroke at the vital spot, Mexico City. The first step in the grand strategy called for the capture of the port of Vera Cruz.

The Vera Cruz expedition under General Winfield Scott, Commander-in-Chief of the U.S. Army, arrived off the target area early in March, 1847. On March 9 the transports and the warships of the convoy took position about three miles south of the port and prepared to assault.

The landing that followed bore a remarkable similarity to the amphibious tactics developed nearly a hundred years later, and practiced in World War II. The troops debarked into landing craft supplied by the Navy. These approached the beach under cover of heavy fire by the naval vessels. The flanks of the landing waves were protected by gunboats, standing close inshore. When the personnel of the first wave reached shore, fortunately without opposition, they rushed inland and formed a defensive perimeter to cover the landing of the succeeding waves. Thus establishing what would be defined in World War II as a "beachhead."

The squadron Marines, numbering 180 and under the command of Captain Alvin Edson were among the first units to land. They were attached to the First Division under Brigadier General W. J. Worth, and continued to operate with that unit throughout the siege that followed. On March 29 Vera Cruz capitulated.

During the course of the operation an important change took place in the naval command. Commodore Perry, on order of the Secretary of the Navy, relieved Commodore Connor as commander of the Home Squadron.

Matthew Calbraith Perry was the younger brother of Oliver Hazard Perry, the distinguished victor on Lake Erie in the War of 1812. Justin Smith, one of the leading historians of the Mexican War, has described the younger Perry as ". . . that ambitious, coarse-grained, willful man." But whatever his characteristics in those respects, he was a vigorous and skillful naval officer. Under his direction things began to happen more rapidly and decisively than they had under Connor. Perry sailed up rivers, seized coastal points regardless of their importance, and generally raised hob along Mexico's east coast.

The capture of Alvarado, the invincible town of the previous fall, came as an anticlimax. Perry got together with the Army and planned a joint expedition against the town. The objective was to capture a large number of horses and beef cattle known to be in the region. The plan called for a division of Army Volunteers, under General John A. Quitman, to march overland and attack the town from the inland side. Perry was to conduct a simultaneous naval attack. Since it would take several days to get the troops into position for the attack, Perry sent the USS *Scourge* to blockade the port until the attack forces arrived.

The *Scourge* was commanded by C. G. Hunter, a young lieutenant with very little taste for the dull assignment of blockade duty. Hunter arrived on the scene and promptly began bombarding the fort that protected the town. His ship's fire drew little reaction from the fort, since the military were already in the process of evacuating, following the fall of Vera Cruz. Carried away by his own enthusiasm, Hunter sent a landing party ashore and captured the place.

Learning that the enemy was withdrawing inland, he left a token garrison behind and sailed up river with all possible speed, in an effort to intercept them. Thus, Perry's fleet and Quitman's army arrived with all the panoply of war, to find their objective in full possession of five sailors commanded by a fuzzy-cheeked midshipman.

Quitman saw the humor of the situation, but "Old Bruin," as the sailors called Perry, flew into a rage. Actually Hunter's impetuosity was a big factor in foiling the main objective of the expedition. His attack had accelerated the withdrawal of the troops and livestock Quitman had hoped to cut off. Perry added nothing to his own popularity by ordering Hunter court-martialled for disobedience of orders. As a result of the trial, Hunter was cashiered from the Navy.

Perry held his Marines in high regard, and employed them extensively throughout his operations. This, eventually, was to have a result which some students of Marine Corps history have considered unfortunate.

It will be recalled that Commandant Archibald Henderson had fought extensively on land with the Army during the Indian wars of the thirties. In Scott's expedition into Mexico, Henderson saw an opportunity to repeat that exploit. Why not send a regiment of Marines to Scott's support again, just as he had done eleven years earlier?

With authorization of the Secretary of the Navy, Henderson set about organizing such a regiment. Again he stripped all posts and stations of all available personnel. He also incorporated all the new recruits which had been enlisted under a recent authorization to increase Marine Corps strength. The best of these recruits were no more than half trained. And there was no opportunity for further training, since the regiment boarded ship and sailed three days after its formation.

It was a regiment in name only; a skeleton regiment at best. Henderson expected to bring it up to strength by drawing on the ship's detachments of the squadron already on the scene. His plan, however, hit a snag in the person of Commodore Perry. Not only did Perry feel that he needed the Marines himself, but he considered an extensive land campaign no proper employment for seagoing troops. As a result, he refused to part with any of his Marines. At length, under prodding by the Navy Department, he grudgingly released one officer and twenty-eight men. So the regimental commander was obliged to reorganize his Marines as a battalion after reaching Vera Cruz, and demote himself to a battalion commander.

This officer was Lieutenant Colonel Samuel Watson, a veteran of the War of 1812 and somewhat past his prime. Major Levi Twiggs, another 1812 veteran, served as second in command. Many people concerned assumed that Twiggs got his post through the influence of his Army brother, General D. E. Twiggs, who commanded one of Scott's divisions. As a matter of fact, the Marine Corps had drawn on most of its officers in the effort to field the regiment.

The unit arrived at Vera Cruz on July 1. On the 16th, the reorganized battalion set out to join the main army, attached to a newly arrived Army contingent commanded by Brigadier General Franklin Pierce, later to become U.S. President. The soldiers were as green as the recruits which made up much too large a proportion of Watson's Marine battalion.

On August 8, Scott set in motion one of the most daring offensive campaigns in the history of warfare. Knowing that he could expect no further reinforcements, he abondoned his line of communications, left his Puebla base garrisoned by invalids and walking wounded, and set out to capture Mexico City. To do this he would have to destroy an army nearly three times the size of his own, fighting on its own territory. As some contemporary put it, "He drew the sword and threw away the scabbard."

But daring was one of the more admirable traits of Winfield Scott, known to his troops as "Old Fuss and Feathers." A hero of the War of 1812, he was now past sixty but retained an amazing amount of energy and stamina in his enormous frame. Scott stood six feet, four and one-quarter inches in height, and he insisted on including the one-quarter. His lateral measurements were also ample, having been rounded out by many years practice as a gourmet. One of his colleagues has said of him, "In great matters he is one of the greatest men I know, in petty matters the most petty." Vain, pompous, and with sublime confidence in his own genius, he aspired to the presidency. On the battlefield of politics he was destined to be soundly defeated by one of his present brigadiers, Franklin Pierce. In spite of characteristics which might well be considered serious shortcomings, Winfield Scott also happened to be one of the greatest military figures in the history of the United States.

Watson's brigade played no part in the several battles that punctuated Scott's advance on Mexico City. To its collective disgust, it was held in reserve to guard the baggage train. Not until the Battle of Chapultepec, before the gates of the city itself, did the Marines see any action worth mentioning. And even there, though it was quite roughly handled, the Marine battalion can not be said to have played a decisive role. In truth it had no chance to do so.

The great Castle of Chapultepec, home of Mexico's military academy, stood atop a formidable height which rose two hundred feet above the surrounding countryside, dominating the approaches to Mexico City. The castle gardens, which were heavily fortified, were surrounded by a high wall, broken only by two massive gates. To even the greenest recruit, it was evident that Chapultepec would have to be disposed of before the advance could proceed. It was just as evident that the capture of those frowning heights would be a difficult and bloody job.

The attack plan called for two coordinated assaults, one from the west, the other from the south. Major General John A. Quitman's division was assigned to the more difficult southern sector. The division commanded by Major General Gideon J. Pillow was to make the attack from the west. For tactical purposes Quitman organized six special storming and pioneer groups to perform special functions along the line of advance. Some were made up of Marines, some of soldiers, some of a combination of the two. Each was led by a hand-picked officer. Major Twiggs commanded one of the storming parties of 120 men.

As dawn broke on the morning of September 13, the American artillery blasted the castle heights with everything available. But the defenders of Chapultepec replied with heavy artillery and small arms fire. The fire of the defenders was so heavy that the Americans in the advanced positions on the south were pinned down. In an attempt to get the attack rolling, Major Twiggs leaped to his feet and ordered his storming party forward. He was killed almost instantly. The southern attackers were unable to advance until the assault from the west carried the top of the height, and succeeded in silencing the Mexican artillery.

Being pinned down by enemy fire is a galling and frustrating experience. After a certain amount of it most men cease to care particularly whether they live or not. Following the death of Major Twiggs, the Marines and Volunteers of Watson's brigade grew impatient to end this unpleasant business, regardless of the cost. But Watson ordered them to stand fast until orders for a concerted attack were passed by General Quitman. Thus, with the exception of one unit, they did not get into the fight until the main issue had been decided elsewhere.

In order to get into position, the brigade had been obliged to traverse a road that was squarely flanked by the height of Chapultepec. To make matters worse, an enemy artillery battery had been positioned to fire straight down the road, forcing the Americans to take cover in the deep drainage ditches which bordered it.

Marine Captain George H. Terrett commanded the forward element of the advancing brigade. An experienced and resourceful officer, he saw as his immediate mission the silencing of the enemy battery that interdicted the route of approach. Advancing along the drainage ditches, he made a combined frontal and flanking attack which was successful in capturing the guns and routing the cannoneers. In doing so, he lost contact with the main body and was thus unaware of Watson's order to stand fast. Seeing the enemy to his front in full flight, Terrett obeyed the natural impulse of a good soldier and set out in pursuit. Although his force numbered only forty-three officers and men, he pressed on, deeper and deeper into enemy territory.

Accounts differ in detail as to just what followed. Somewhere along the line of his advance he picked up a wandering battery of artillery, just in time to use it to break up an attempted charge by Mexican cavalry. Still farther on, he came upon an entrenched enemy position held by a disorganized group estimated to number about a thousand.

Despite the absurd numerical odds, Terrett attacked immediately. Repulsed frontally, he launched another attack and turned the flank of the enemy position. The Mexicans, apparently little more than a mob, fled in panic with the Marines in hot pursuit.

By this time casualties had reduced Terrett's small force to about twenty men. He was able to replace some of his losses by gathering individual soldiers and small groups which had become separated from their units in the confusion of battle. With this assortment of troops, he pressed on to clear the final approaches to the city.

As he neared San Cosme Gate, he was joined by a force of twenty-six Army regulars commanded by a young lieutenant named Ulysses S. Grant. Like Terrett, Grant had lost contact with his main body. Combining the two groups into a single unit, Terrett and Grant continued the advance. At the San Cosme Gate they launched a swift attack, seized the position and entered Mexico City, the first Americans to reach the final objective.

Terrett's idea was to hold the gate to permit the unopposed entry of the main army, not realizing how far ahead his advance had taken him. Within an hour a runner appeared with orders from General Worth, Grant's division commander, to withdraw all troops from this exposed position and rejoin the main body at once. As a result, Terrett and his Marines became separated from their own brigade and fought the remainder of the campaign attached to the 11th Infantry, U.S. Army. Thus they were not on hand to take part in General Quitman's "capture" of Mexico City the following morning.

Throughout the campaign there had been considerable rivalry between the regular Army troops and the Volunteers. Major General Quitman was a Volunteer officer, commanding a division made up entirely of short-term Volunteer troops, with the exception of the Marine battalion. For some time he had suspected that the high brass of the regulars had been discriminating against himself and his troops. When his division failed, for whatever reason, to gain distinction in the storming of Chapultepec, he became convinced of this and determined to do something about it.

General Scott had ordered Quitman to make only a serious threat against the southwestern gate of the city, while the regular Army division under Major General William J. Worth made the main attack. But the disgruntled Quitman had some entirely different ideas on the subject. Borrowing a part of General Pillow's troops, he hastily reorganized his division and set out in vigorous pursuit of the enemy.

All went well until he launched an attack against the gates of the city. There heavy enfilade fire from both flanks, as well as from the front, stalled his attack. Four times Quitman personally led the assault, and each time was forced to turn back in the face of the withering fire of the defenders. Finally weariness, casualties, and a shortage of ammunition forced the determined Quitman to consolidate his position just short of the gate and to dig in for the night.

The American attack however had a telling effect on the Mexicans. Under the cover of darkness, Santa Anna withdrew his troops from the capital, realizing the futility of further defense. At daylight, on the morning of September 14, Quitman was just about to renew his attack when an enemy soldier emerged from the gate of the city under a white flag. He informed Quitman that Santa Anna had withdrawn his forces during the night, and there were no troops to deny his entry into the city. Cautiously the General led his troops into the capital city of Mexico. The column that moved through the rubble-strewn streets looked like anything but an army of conquest. At its head hobbled the bone-weary Quitman, one of his shoes missing. Strung out behind him was a ragged, blood-smeared mob of regulars, volunteers and Marines. At the central plaza the troops formed ranks to render honors to General Scott upon his entry into the city. Thus, with appropriate ceremony, the American flag rose triumphantly over the fabled "Halls of Montezuma."

But the conquest of Mexico City was only a part of the story of the War with Mexico. While Scott and Taylor fought their victorious armies across the heart of the country, another drama was taking place far to the northwest.

By 1845, after a series of rebellions, Mexico had recognized the government of California as independent, although she still claimed the territory. Both Mexico and the United States were well aware that the province was too weak to defend itself, and would be an easy conquest for any foreign power interested in making the effort. This fact was of particular concern to the United States. Obviously the possession of the area by another country would be a serious deterrent to U.S. expansion westward. Consequently plans were afoot in Washington to insure that such a thing didn't happen. Thereby hangs a tale.

The Marine Corps' claim to major participation in the events which led to the annexation of California, rests on the exploits of a single individual. This gentleman was Lieutenant Archibald Gillespie, perhaps as improbable a pawn as the hand of destiny ever moved across the chess board of history.

How did Gillespie come by the assignment that was to afford

him his brief place in the Far Western sun? No one really knows. Probably it was due to two factors—he spoke Spanish fluently, and happened to be available.

Gillespie had served a routine career as a Marine officer. He held the rank of first lieutenant at the age of thirty-three when President James K. Polk handed him the most unique assignment of his undistinguished career. His mission was to carry secret dispatches to the three top U.S. officials in the Mexican territory of California. Perhaps "agents" might be a more accurate term for the individuals concerned.

To reach his destination, Gillespie traveled through Mexico in the guise of a Scotch whiskey salesman. As a safety precaution, he memorized the contents of the dispatches and then destroyed them. Exactly what information was contained in the dispatches has never been revealed. One thing is certain, not long after their delivery in mid-April of 1846 things began to happen in California.

The situation in California in 1846 was similar to that which had existed in Texas a decade earlier, but with some significant differences. The total strength of the Mexican Army force stationed in California was two officers and seventy enlisted men. The possibility of reasonably prompt reinforcement for the garrison, in case of emergency, simply did not exist. Either for that reason, or because of natural inclination, the inhabitants of California were seldom bothered by the Mexican military.

Successive generations of native-born Californians of Mexican origin grew increasingly apart from their home government, with little respect or affection for it. They were a poor but carefree people, noted for their hospitality and happy in an easy way of life that included as little work as possible. They asked only to be left alone to enjoy it. When their nominal government was tactless enough to appoint a governor, or *commandante general,* in an attempt to take them in hand, they simply threw him out and went on about their business. After several attempts, all with the same result, the Mexican government stopped appointing officials and allowed the Californians to select their own.

Many Americans had moved in during recent years. Most of them were located in the northern part of the province where they got along well enough with their native-born neighbors, whom they regarded with a sort of tolerant contempt. Unlike the Texans, they did not become actively resentful under Mexican rule because it was non-existent. But, like the Texans, they had a latent desire for separation and eventual annexation to the United States.

The United States had been thinking of extending her boundaries from coast to coast. In the case of California, an extraneous factor had begun to add compulsion. For some time Washington had been engaged in a controversy with Great Britain over the Oregon Territory immediately to the north. This brought about the fear that the British would take advantage of the chaotic conditions in Mexico to seize this outlying province. This, in turn, led the U.S. to reinforce its Pacific Squadron, and to issue it orders to keep a sharp eye on the situation in California.

The first of the three addressees to whom Lieutenant Gillespie delivered the President's messages was the commander of the Pacific Squadron, Commodore John D. Sloat. The second was Thomas O. Larkin, U.S. Consul at Monterey, then capital of California—at least by courtesy. The third was a young man about Gillespie's own age, who occupied a somewhat ambiguous position which has never been fully defined. Officially, he was Captain John C. Frémont, Topographical Engineers, U.S. Army. Ostensibly, he was an explorer under government auspices, seeking the most practical overland route to the Pacific. He had with him a party of 60-odd men, hired for the job, but not regularly enlisted in the U.S. Army. It is also apparent that he had an extra-curricular mission confidentially assigned by the President. Frémont's activities were viewed with extreme suspicion by the Mexican commander in California, who was convinced that he was attempting to foster a revolution against the Mexican government.

Frémont was audacious, impetuous and ambitious, with a burning desire to achieve personal distinction. It appeared that he was in a good position to do so, since his wife happened to be the daughter of Thomas Hart Benton, Chairman of the Senate Military Affairs Committee. Among other messages, Gillespie brought Frémont a personal letter from his eminent father-in-law. Reading between the lines, the 32-year-old Captain interpreted this missive as a subtle mandate to seize California for the United States at the first promising opportunity.

Such opportunity was not long in materializing. Another of Mexico's perennial revolutions had overthrown the government of President Jose Joaquin de Herrera in December, 1845, and brought in that of General Mariano Paredes. Native leaders of California immediately took sides, with the *Commandante General,* Jose Castro, in support of Paredes and Governor Pio Pico for Herrera. The political issues involved were not particularly profound, being concerned principally with jurisdiction over the collection of customs, and proportionate division of the revenue. So Castro at Monterey in the north, and Pico at Los Angeles began gathering men and supplies for what promised to be a leisurely little civil war.

Fremont declared himself an interested party on June 10, 1846, by stealing 170 horses which had been rounded up to be sent to the camp of General Castro. He then seized the village of Sonoma, the northernmost Mexican settlement in California. Immediately upon taking possession of the town, Fremont raised a crude flag, depicting something that was supposed to be a bear, and declared California an independent republic. This action so alarmed Castro and Pico that they agreed to forget their own differences and unite forces against this interloper whom they suspected was acting with the backing of the United States.

Operating from his Sonoma headquarters, Fremont set about recruiting the settlers in the north to undertake the conquest of the entire province under the Bear Flag. Evidently he found a kindred spirit in Gillespie, whom he appointed as his second in command.

The Bear Republic was destined to be short lived, however.

For some time the aged and ailing Naval Commander, Commodore Sloat, had been vacillating as unverified rumors arrived concerning a state of war between the U.S. and Mexico. Finally the combination of Fremont's warlike moves and the threat of British intervention spurred him to action. He sailed for Monterey and, on July 7, put ashore 85 Marines and 165 sailors, under the command of his Marine officer, Captain Ward Marston. The landing party seized the undefended port and raised the American flag over the Customs House, to the accompaniment of cheers and a 21-gun salute.

Sloat then issued a proclamation which he had drawn up with the collaboration of Consul Larkin, taking possession of the entire province in the name of the United States. In doing so, he went far beyond any orders he had received, but tempered his actions with generous promises, "to greatly increase the value of real estate and the products of California."

Learning of Sloat's success, Fremont and Gillespie hauled down the Bear Flag at Sonoma and rode off to Monterey, with their California Battalion of Mounted Riflemen, 160 strong, to offer their services to the Navy.

Many native Californians welcomed their changed status, and the majority at least accepted it. But Castro and Pico, angered and alarmed by what they considered the lawless depredations of Fremont, refused all offers of conciliation. Collecting eight hundred followers at Los Angeles, they declared for Mexico and prepared to fight.

In the meanwhile, Sloat, who had been reinforced by another small squadron under the command of Commodore Robert F. Stockton, decided that his physical condition called for his immediate return to the East and retirement. So he turned over his command, his squadron and his problems to the new arrival and sailed majestically out of the California picture.

Stockton and Fremont were singularly alike in temperament and outlook. Neither could see much chance of achieving the personal glory they sought under the conciliatory attitude advocated by Sloat and Larkin. Stockton's first act upon assuming command was to issue an abusive proclamation denouncing Castro for all the troubles in the province. He then sailed for San Diego where he landed with a party of 360 Marines and sailors. On August 7, reinforced by Fremont's band of horsemen, he set out for Los Angeles.

En route he was met by a delegation of Californians, asking for suspension of hostilities to permit negotiation. This request Stockton brusquely brushed aside, declaring that he would negotiate only after Castro raised the American flag.

Castro's cause had never been popular with the majority of his fellow Californians. As Stockton and his force continued to advance, the *Commandante General's* followers disappeared, and the Commodore entered Los Angeles, on August 12, to find that Castro had departed for other regions.

For all practical purposes, the California problem had been resolved at small cost of either blood or treasure. It might have remained so if Stockton and Fremont had seen fit to follow the peaceable advice of Consul Larkin, who knew the nature of the Californians. But they did not choose to follow the Consul's good advice, and the individual who fell heir to the role of scapegoat was none other than Lieutenant Archibald Gillespie, U.S. Marine Corps.

On August 17, Stockton learned definitely that a state of war existed between the U.S. and Mexico. He issued his own proclamation annexing the province of California to the United States, and appointed Archibald Gillespie military governor of Los Angeles. Among other things, the proclamation stated that military law should prevail until civil law could be placed in effect. This required approval from Washington, many weeks' journey away—too many weeks, as events proved. The Californians soon became restless under military government, especially resenting the 10:00 P.M. curfew imposed on all civilians, and the ban against carrying weapons.

Martial law is harsh at best, and there is little evidence that Gillespie did much to mitigate it. He has been described as having "a short, pointed beard and a temper to match it." He was a professional military man with a mission to perform. His means for performing his mission were extremely limited. His entire detachment numbered only fifty-four men, a ridiculously small force for potentially the most hostile area in the province. In his position as a combination governor, mayor, sheriff and judge he could afford to display no weakness, and Gillespie displayed none. But the net result of his performance of duty was to precipitate all of Southern California into a revolt against the new order.

The resentment of the inhabitants of Los Angeles against Gillespie's martial law enforcement finally boiled over. In the early morning hours of September 23rd an armed mob of about 150, led by Don Cerulvo Varela, attacked the small garrison. Gillespie beat off the attack with little difficulty, but it proved only the beginning. Two days later he found himself under siege by over five hundred aroused citizens, organized and commanded by Captain Jose Flores, an officer of the Mexican Army.

Since Stockton had returned to San Francisco with his squadron, Gillespie had no source of reinforcements. The garrison resisted as best they could, but, after a week's diet of dried beef and water, decided to surrender. Gillespie readily acceded to the generous surrender terms which allowed his whole detachment to march to San Pedro, the port for Los Angeles, with their arms and personal possessions. Flores expected the released Americans to get out of the province altogether, but Gillespie chose not to interpret the terms of his capitulation as such. He took his men aboard the American merchantman *Vandalia* which lay at anchor in the harbor of San Pedro and prepared for further operations.

The revolt spread throughout Southern California. Stockton sent Navy Captain William Mervine south with the *Savannah* in an effort to halt the Californians. Mervine put a landing party of three hundred Marines and sailors, including Gillespie's detachment, ashore. After advancing about five miles inland, they were unable to come to grips with Flores, whose horsemen constantly harassed their flanks and rear.

This obvious success against American arms greatly encouraged the spirit of revolt. On October 29 something passing for the legislature of California elected Flores to the joint post of Governor and *Commandante General*. Southern California was once again in the hands of its native sons.

It was a different picture in the north. Stockton and Fremont were organizing to put down the rebellion, and a new factor was about to be added to the situation, on the side of the United States. Colonel Stephen W. Kearney of the U.S. Army, having secured the territory now comprising the states of New Mexico and Arizona, was crossing the Sierra Nevada. He had with him only about one hundred men of the 1st U.S. Dragoons. En route he had received a message to the effect that California was safely under the control of the U.S. Navy. As a result, he had sent two-thirds of his command back to Santa Fe, an act which he soon had cause to regret.

Kearney received word of the revolt on November 22 while encamped at the junction of the Gila and Colorado Rivers. Ordering a forced march, Kearney and his Dragoons made contact with Gillespie and thirty-five of his survivors at the Santa Maria Ranch on December 5th. Gillespie told Colonel Kearney that the enemy was massed in some strength about nine miles away. Kearney, who had no experience in fighting Californians, decided to attack at once.

Kearney met the enemy at the Indian village of San Pasqual on the following day, and received a lesson in Californian tactics. Luring the Dragoons into a headlong charge, the California horsemen feigned panic and fled. They continued their flight until the American formation had become well disrupted. Suddenly the Californians turned against their pursuers in a well organized counter charge, killing and wounding many of them. While trying to rally his disorganized men, Gillespie was attacked by seven lancers. Receiving severe chest wounds, he was knocked from his horse, and, while trying to rise, was felled by the blow of another lance. The action ended with the retirement of the Californians from the field, leaving Kearney grounds on which to declare the so-called Battle of San Pasqual a victory. But it was a victory of the most hollow sort. His small force had sustained crippling casualties, and both he and Lieutenant Gillespie nursed severe wounds.

Realizing that his force was in wretched shape, burdened with wounded, and short of provisions, Kearney pitched camp. He then dispatched a messenger to San Diego, the one port in Southern California held by Americans, calling for reinforcements. Don Andres Pico, leader of the Californians and an acquaintance of Gillespie, took advantage of the lull to send medicine to the wounded Marine. On December 10, a relief column of one hundred sailors and eighty Marines arrived in response to Kearney's call for help. Two days later the combined force fought its way through to San Diego.

Navy forces were holding San Diego as a potential base of operations. Fremont was supposedly raising volunteers in the north for reconquest of Southern California. Commodore Stockton joined Kearney in San Diego, and, after waiting three weeks without receiving word from Fremont, decided to march on Los Angeles.

The composition of the force that sortied from San Diego on December 29, 1846, is indicative of the strange assortment of people who brought about the annexation of California. As an "army" it appeared pretty ridiculous. There were 397 sailors and sea-going Marines acting as infantry; 57 of Kearney's Dragoons, 45 additional sailors acting as artillerymen to man the six small cannon, and 60 civilian volunteers. Against well organized opposition its fate would have been problematical. But, as the entire scope of operations has clearly indicated, the revolt of the Californians had been inspired more by personal pride than patriotic fervor.

On the 4th of January, 1847, the leisurely advancing Americans met an enemy party carrying a flag of truce. Captain Jose Flores, who led the party, proposed that all fighting be stopped and the fate of California be decided on the outcome of the war between the United States and Mexico. Stockton refused to treat with Flores on the grounds that he had broken his parole—as indeed he had—and resumed his advance.

Flores made a stand to dispute Kearney's crossing of the San Gabriel River four days later. But his faint-hearted force failed to stand up against a determined advance by the sailor-Marine infantry and Dragoon-volunteer cavalry, supported by the sailor artillery. After a little desultory fighting the following day, the Americans entered Los Angeles in triumph on January 10. The revolt was over. Archibald Gillespie, who had made the march despite his wounds, was given the satisfaction of raising the flag he had been obliged to lower more than three months earlier.

While Stockton had been marching from the south, Fremont had been approaching the scene from the other direction at the head of four hundred horsemen he had succeeded in recruiting in northern California. On January 13, he encountered a group of Flores' routed rebels under Andreas Pico. Fremont rose to unexpected heights and accomplished what was probably the most constructive achievement of his entire career. He accepted the rebels' surrender terms which allowed them to go where they pleased, guaranteed them the same protection, privileges and property rights as U.S. citizens—and conveniently overlooked the broken paroles of their leaders.

This put Stockton in a somewhat awkward position, since he had refused to treat with Flores only a few days earlier. Stockton eventually acceded to the terms made by his subordinate. This generosity on the part of the victors put an end once and for all to any ideas of revolt in California.

History reserved no brilliant futures for the four men mainly responsible for the annexation of California. Stephen Kearney, promoted to brigadier general, died the following year at the age of fifty-four. Stockton, a year his junior, resigned from the Navy in 1850, served a term as U.S. Senator from Delaware, and retired to well-to-do obscurity. Fremont also resigned from the Army and remained in California to amass a sizeable fortune. With the advent of the Civil War, his father-in-law's influence obtained for him a commission as major general of Volunteers, but his ineptness soon caused him to be relieved of command.

Archibald Gillespie returned to the East, where the Marine Corps rewarded his service with successive brevets to captain and major. But, he too, had been bitten by the California bug. In 1854, he resigned and emigrated to the state he had helped to create. There he sank back into the obscurity from which he had been so abruptly precipitated—because he spoke Spanish and happened to be in Washington in the autumn of 1845. Of the four, only he failed to make the not-too-exclusive pages of the *Encyclopaedia Britannica*.

The War with Mexico had settled the status of the southern boundary of Texas, and provided the addition of a great state to the nation. According to the best information available, it also provided the Marine Corps with a song which has since become one of the world's best known pieces of martial music. The first verse of the Marines Hymn was written shortly after the occupation of Mexico City. History, which is often guilty of such regrettable oversight, failed to record the identity of the author.

Prior to the War with Mexico, the Marine Corps Colors bore the inscription: "To the Shores of Tripoli." With the capture of Mexico City and the National Palace, which was also known as "The Halls of the Montezumas," the inscription was changed to read: "From the Shores of Tripoli to the Halls of the Montezumas." More interested in the niceties of euphony than chronological accuracy, the author reversed the phrases when he set them to music.

As far as the music itself is concerned, there is a difference of opinion which has never been fully resolved. According to Walter F. Smith, second leader of the Marine Band, "the aria of the Marine Hymn is certainly to be found in the opera, *Genevieve de Brabant*. The melody is not in the exact form of the Marine Hymn, but is undoubtedly the aria from which it was taken." In a letter to Major Richard Wallach, in 1878, he wrote, "I am informed by one of the members of the Band, who has a Spanish wife, that the aria was one familiar to her childhood and it may, therefore, be a Spanish folk song."

The famous band leader and composer, John Philip Sousa, stated, "The melody of the 'Halls of Montezuma' is taken from Offenbach's comic opera *Genevieve de Brabant*, and is sung by two gendarmes." Jacques Offenbach's *opéra-bouffe*, a farcical form of opera, generally referred to as musical comedy, was first presented in the *Théâtre de Bouffes Parisiens*, in Paris, on November 19, 1859.

Whether the melody is the original product of the German-born composer, or owes its origin to the folk music of Spain, will probably remain an unanswered question. But for those who lustily sang the stirring refrain in the brief interlude of peace which followed the War with Mexico, the forces of destiny were framing a question which demanded an unequivocal answer by all who bore the arms of the United States.

6 ★

Uneasy Interlude

T HE FOURTEEN YEARS between the end of the War with Mexico and the outbreak of the Civil War found the Marine Corps involved in a number of far-flung activities. The Navy was actively engaged during this period in "showing the flag," a euphemism for displaying strength. International Law was interpreted in direct ratio to the power of any country to enforce its will. It was, on the surface, an interlude of peace—an uneasy interlude.

The Latin-American countries had been free from Spanish domination for only a short time. They had yet to become fully organized as responsible nations. In most of these areas lay golden opportunities for enterprising individuals. Among the adventurers who flocked to these territories were many Americans. As always happens in such instances, inevitably some toes were trod upon.

This resulted in U.S. Navy interventions in Argentina, Brazil, Uruguay, Paraguay and Nicaragua. Panama, one of the main routes for Americans flocking to the newly discovered gold fields in California, became a constant source of trouble. When an American company built a railroad across the peninsula to expedite this traffic, Marine landing forces were obliged to intervene several times between 1856 and 1860.

For sheer pageantry probably the most interesting event of the era was the opening of Japan to foreign trade. The profitable commerce enjoyed by western nations with China had whetted their appetite for more. But the Japanese were not interested. They rudely rebuffed all overtures in this direction, indicating that they were content to mind their own business, and insisted that others do the same.

In 1852 the United States made up its mind to break this hard shell—by diplomacy if possible, by force if necessary. The method employed was a naval expedition led by Commodore Matthew C. Perry of Mexican War fame. With his Marine detachment of six officers and two hundred men, Perry proceeded to Japan. There he staged such an ostentatious display of showmanship that he completely captivated the Japanese. En route to Tokyo, the expedition stopped at the Ryukyu Islands to perfect last minute plans and hold a dress rehearsal ashore. Thus it was that the U.S. Marines made their first landing on Okinawa, an action which was to be repeated under considerably different circumstances many years later.

Perry accomplished what he had set out to do. As a result of his efforts, the door of the Empire of the Rising Sun was opened to mutually profitable trade. Japan emerged from medieval isolation to occupy a place among the modern nations of the world. The Marines had played an important part in the opening of this door. But the time would come when Marines, and countless thousands of other Americans, would come to regard this as anything but a blessing.

In the remote regions of the Pacific the Fiji Islanders got out of hand again and had to be taught another lesson. It was, evidently, a lesson well learned, since the Marines did not encounter the Fijians again until they turned up as their allies in World War II.

As the nineteenth century passed mid-point, the bloody Taiping religious rebellion flamed across the Chinese Empire. During the fifteen years of its course, over 20,000,000 people were to lose their lives in the holocaust of history's greatest insurrection. Then, in rapid succession, China made enemies of France and Great Britain.

The trouble with England arose over Chinese attempts to put a stop to the profitable British traffic in opium. France became an enemy when a Chinese court ordered the execution of a French missionary, without benefit of proper trial.

Thanks to the fanatical disciples of Hung Hsiu-Ch'aun, who were bent on replacing the paganism of China with a distorted form of Christianity, the Chinese soon came to regard all missionaries as spies. With hatred for foreigners growing day by day, O. H. Perry, the American Consul at Canton, called in the U.S. Navy to protect American nationals and interests.

By November 13, 1856, three American warships under Commodore James Armstrong stood at anchor in the Pearl River below Canton. Ashore, a landing force of 181 Marines and bluejackets, commanded by Marine Captain John D. Simms, manned hastily constructed fortifications around the American compound in the city. Based on both diplomatic and tactical considerations, the Americans were in a precarious position.

An American military force defiling the soil of the Empire could only be considered a gross insult by the over-sensitive Chinese. From a tactical standpoint, supplying the garrison in Canton involved great risk. Any craft carrying needed supplies would be forced to pass under the guns of four well-constructed fortresses, known as the "Barrier Forts," which guarded the winding, narrow channel of the Pearl River. While the Commodore was pondering the best course of action, the Chinese temporarily solved his problem by guaranteeing the safety of American interests in Canton. Much relieved, the Commodore began to withdraw the bulk of his landing force, leaving a small detachment of Marines at the American compound.

On the same day the assurance of protection was made by the Chinese government, one of the river forts opened fire on the American boats ferrying the landing force back to their ships. The following morning an unarmed boat making a reconnaissance of the channel was fired upon without warning.

Two of the three volleys failed to find their mark, but the third crashed into the boat, killing the coxswain.

Outraged by these breaches of faith, Armstrong determined to avenge the insult to the American flag. Moving the sloop-of-war *Portsmouth* upstream on the afternoon of November 16, the Commodore brought her into position and took the nearest fort under fire. According to his official report of the engagement, ". . . the *Portsmouth* (approached) within 500 yards of the nearest fort, at about 4:20 P.M., and got in a position for shelling the forts. The forts opened a brisk and well-directed fire upon her before she had come to anchor, which was at once returned by her with a rapid discharge of shells, and which was kept up with little intermission until dark. The Chinese fired exceedingly well and hulled the *Portsmouth* six times, but doing no material injury to her. . . . The largest of the forts, and the one nearest to us, was silenced early in the evening; and the fire of the others became very lanquid at the close of the action. . . ."

Having satisfied the honor of his country's flag, Armstrong requested a meeting with the Imperial Commissioner of Canton to seek an explanation of the unwarranted attack. Before leaving, he turned the command over to Captain Andrew H. Foote of the *Portsmouth,* advising him to hold his fire unless the Chinese attacked.

On November 19 Armstrong received a report that the Chinese were repairing and strengthening their defenses. He sent a message to Foote, ordering him to "take such measures as your judgment would dictate, if it were even the capture of the forts."

Andrew Foote belonged to the school of fighting men which believes that the best defense is a good offense. From the bridge of his ship he could see the four towering fortifications that commanded the river. From their massive granite walls jutted a total of 176 cannon, some of them of 10-inch caliber. Reports from various sources indicated there were between 5,000 and 15,000 Chinese troops in the Canton area. The number of troops was impressive, but Foote knew something of Chinese armies. For the most part they were poorly equipped and poorly trained. There were only two courses of action; fight a defensive duel with his small ships against the strongest forts in the Empire, or attack. As far as Foote was concerned, there was only one answer.

On the morning of November 20, the *Portsmouth* and the *Levant* went into action against two of the forts. Under cover of the ship's guns, the landing force troops lowered themselves into the small boats. An official report filed by Foote contains the following account: ". . . The storming party, consisting of 287 persons—officers, seamen and Marines—with four howitzers, commanded by myself, then left the ships, and pulled in three columns for the shore. The company of Marines was most efficiently led by Captain Simms. . . . The party formed, and marched towards the fort, dragging three howitzers with them across the rice-fields, and wading a creek waist deep. In order to attack the fort in the rear it was necessary to pass through a village, in which several shots were fired upon us, till the howitzers cleared the streets, and secured for us an unobstructed advance. When near the fort, the soldiers were seen fleeing from it, many of them swimming for the opposite shore. The Marines, being in advance, opened fire upon the fugitives with deadly effect, killing some 40 or 50. . . . The city of Canton being only four miles distant, a portion of its army, variously estimated at from 5,000 to 15,000, and which I believe to have numbered at least 3,000, was stationed near. This force twice advanced; but were both times repulsed by the Marines, with 10 or 12 killed. . . ."

Early the next morning the Marines and the sailors piled into their boats and began moving toward their next objective, the second Barrier Fort. The three remaining forts unleashed a hail of fire upon the landing boats and their supporting ships. A 64-pound shot smashed into one of the landing boats, killing three and wounding seven.

Once ashore, Captain Simms and his Marines waded across a deep creek and stormed the granite walls. The Chinese defenders poured volley after volley of musket fire into the attacking Marines, but were unable to halt their determined charge. As the Marines swarmed across the parapets, the defenders bolted, splashing across the rice paddies toward safety.

Reinforcing themselves with fresh troops from the main body in Canton, the Chinese launched a determined counterattack. Over 1,000 screaming Chinese swept across the rice paddies toward the Americans. Captain Simms ordered his men to hold their fire until the horde was within 200 yards of their position. As Simms bellowed the order, the Leathernecks sent volley after volley thudding into the enemy ranks. The sheer momentum of the attack carried the surging Chinese within 50 yards of the defenders. But the accuracy of the Marines' marksmanship was too much for the enemy who broke and ran. Two other counter-attacks were attempted but were beaten back.

With half the forts safely in American hands, Foote ordered Simms and his Marines to clear the Chinese from the river bank so that his boats would not be caught in a cross fire during the second phase of the operation. The next objective was the third fort, located on an island in the Pearl River. Hugging a steep embankment, Captain Simms led his men cautiously along the river shore. Suddenly they came upon a Chinese battery of seven guns. Caught completely by surprise, the Chinese fled the position amid a fusillade of musket fire. Leaving a handful of men behind to destroy the guns, Simms moved his force to the top of the embankment and began pouring a withering fire into the island fort across a narrow strip of river. Within a few minutes the guns of the fortress fell silent. Simms withdrew his company along the embankment to join Foote in the assault.

Directing the fire of the two captured citadels against the third fort, the Americans launched their attack. Charging through the swirling clouds of dust and smoke that enveloped the bastion, the assault wave surged over the battlements. For the second time that day, Corporal William McDougal, standard bearer of the Marines, planted the Stars and Stripes on the para-pet of an enemy fortress.

The final objective, Center Fort, lay on the Canton side of

the river, just beyond the eastern suburbs of the city. Preparations for the attack began in the pre-dawn darkness of the following morning. All captured artillery pieces which could not be used to advantage in supporting the attack had been destroyed. The best of the captured weapons were dragged into position and sighted on the massive hulk of the last fortress. At the first flush of dawn an American howitzer thundered across the water. There was no reply from the silent, frowning walls. Again and again the American cannons roared their challenge, but there was no answer.

Three waves of assault boats slowly pulled across the river toward the final objective, as the supporting fire of the howitzers and captured cannon screamed overhead. Still the guns of Center Fort were mute. With the first wave of boats only yards from shore, the fortress suddenly erupted with the crash of gunfire. Leaping from their boats into the waist-deep water of the muddy river, the storming party began wading toward the base of the walls. As they clambered relentlessly up the steep, sloping side of the fort, the fire of the defenders slackened. Finally reaching the parapet, the Marines found that the enemy had fled, leaving the fortress undefended, except for a crude booby trap of a loaded cannon with smoldering fuse aimed at the boats.

With all the forts in possession of the Americans, destruction of the fortresses began in earnest. All guns were torn from their mounts, spiked and rolled into the river. Demolition parties, moving from fort to fort, set off huge charges of gun powder which reduced the stone fortifications to rubble. All ammunition and supplies found in the forts were burned.

On November 23, Commodore Foote weighed anchor and moved his ships down stream to their normal anchorage, leaving behind him the smoldering ruins of the most formidable bastions in the Chinese Empire. In three days of furious fighting his command had captured four massive forts, killed more than 500 Chinese and routed an army that numbered in the thousands. His own casualties totalled 10 killed in action and 32 wounded. Included among those who were listed as dead was Marine Private William Cuddy who, "took sick and died."

If there was any doubt in Foote's mind that he had failed to teach the Chinese a much-needed lesson, it vanished the following day. An emissary of the Imperial Commissioner of Canton arrived at the flagship. With appropriate ceremony, he tendered a profuse apology for the unprovoked attack on the lone American reconnaissance boat on November 16. It had been, he assured Foote, a most regrettable mistake.

Meanwhile, back in the United States in this uneasy interlude potentially the most serious incident of the times was the attempted uprising headed by the Abolitionist fanatic, John Brown.

Brown had played a bloody part in the slave-state versus free-state struggle that had won the disputed area the sobriquet of "Bleeding Kansas." In 1859 he conceived the idea of abolishing slavery by force. His plan called for seizing an area in the rugged mountains of the South where runaway slaves could take refuge. Then, under his leadership, they could defend themselves against recapture. He obtained ample financial backing from wealthy abolitionists in the North, few of whom knew his real objective.

In the fall of that year, under an assumed name, he purchased a farm near Harper's Ferry in what was then Virginia, now West Virgina. Here a number of equally fanatical followers, both white and colored, gathered surreptitiously to plot the abolition of slavery. In order to obtain arms for the great mass of adherents he confidently expected would flock to the cause, Brown laid careful plans to capture the Federal Arsenal, located in the village of Harper's Ferry.

On the night of October 16 Brown and about twenty of his followers overpowered a lone sentry at the bridge which spanned the Shenandoah River, and quietly stole into the sleeping village. They captured another surprised sentinel at the main gate and took over the Arsenal without firing a shot. The band then rounded up a number of prominent local residents as hostages, and Brown issued a manifesto calling upon all slaves throughout the South to flee their masters and come to him.

The scheme didn't work out quite the way Brown had planned it. The slaves, with few exceptions, were not psychologically adaptable to seeking their freedom by violence. Brown's summons had little time to circulate very far afield before swift and violent reaction took place. Even locally, his call to arms elicited small response among the slaves. But the South, apprehensive of an uprising since the successful Haitian slave revolt of 1804, was thoroughly alarmed.

The governors of both Maryland and Virginia ordered their state militias to the scene to quell the uprising. The Secretary of War called out Federal soldiers from Fort Monroe, Virginia, and the Secretary of the Navy ordered out all available Marines from the Marine Barracks in Washington, D.C.

Brown committed the tactical error of separating his small band and stationing them at various vantage points throughout the village. As a result, militiamen and local residents had little difficulty in picking them off one by one. By nightfall his original force numbered only six or eight men. Brown moved what remained of his followers, and several of the more influential hostages, into a brick engine-house which stood within the Arsenal enclosure. Barricading the stout oak doors of the building, the band prepared to make a stand.

Eighty-six Marines, under the command of First Lieutenant Israel Greene, arrived on the scene about 11 P.M. on the night of October 17. They were accompanied by Army Lieutenant Colonel Robert E. Lee and his aide, Lieutenant J.E.B. Stuart, who had been sent from Washington by the War Department to take charge of operations.

Lieutenant Colonel Lee sent Stuart, under a flag of truce, to the engine-house to demand the surrender of Brown. The old raider refused. Lee decided to wait until daylight before making an attack against the stronghold.

At sunrise the following morning, as some two thousand spectators who had gathered to watch the show looked on, Lieutenant Stuart again approached the engine-house.

"Are you ready to surrender and trust to the mercy of the government?" Stuart shouted.

"Never," Brown answered. "I prefer to die here!"

Lieutenant Colonel Lee then approached Colonel Shriver who commanded the Maryland Volunteers and offered him the opportunity of making the attack. The colonel declined the honor. "My men have wives and children at home," he told Lee. "I will not expose them to such risks. You are paid for doing this kind of work."

Lee then approached Colonel Robert W. Baylor, commanding the Virginia Militia, with the same offer. Baylor refused. Pointing to the Marines, he said, "Let the mercenaries do it."

Hiding the chagrin he must have felt, Lee turned toward the Marine lieutenant who had quietly observed the militia officers' reactions. No words were necessary between these two professional soldiers. Lieutenant Greene called his Marines to attention, saluted Lieutenant Colonel Lee, and began to issue orders to his troops.

Forming a storming party of twelve Marines, Greene ordered that only bayonets would be used in the attack, to prevent accidental injury to the hostages. He then armed three Marines with sledge hammers to knock down the barricaded door of the engine-house. With these preparations made, he looked at Lee for the signal to attack. Colonel Lee once more ordered his aide forward to demand Brown's surrender. Again Brown refused. Lee nodded his head toward the Marine officer and the Marines swung into action.

After several lusty blows with the sledge hammers had failed to breach the door, the Marines discarded them in favor of a heavy ladder which they used as a battering ram. On the second smash they knocked a hole in the huge door, near the bottom. Lieutenant Greene, armed only with a light ceremonial sword, darted through the hole, with several Marines at his heels. In the semi-darkness inside, a tall, gaunt figure leaped toward him and fired twice almost in his face. Somehow both shots missed Greene. The first round killed Private Luke Quinn who was behind Greene, and the second seriously wounded the Marine immediately behind Quinn. Lieutenant Greene slashed viciously at his assailant, cutting him badly on the neck and shoulder. As he aimed a thrust at his adversary's heart, the Marine recognized him as John Brown. Greene's light dress sword struck Brown's ammunition belt, which was slung across his body, and bent double. The blow, however, was strong enough to knock Brown to the ground.

With the fall of the leader, all resistance in the engine-house ceased. Outside Lieutenant Colonel Lee looked at the gold watch in his hand. The Marine attack had lasted exactly three minutes. The man who, in a few short years, was to become one of the most famous generals in American history slowly pocketed his watch. The invasion of Harper's Ferry was over.

The Marines conducted the would-be rebels to Charlestown to be tried for treason. John Brown recovered from his wounds to be convicted and hanged. During his trial this strange and contradictory man, who had been known to slaughter his opponents in cold blood, conducted himself with such dignity and righteousness that he made himself a martyred hero in the eyes of Northern abolitionists.

Two years later Lieutenant Israel Greene was no longer an officer of the U.S. Marine Corps. Along with Lee and Stuart, he was fighting against the nation to which he had been bound by the highest oath of loyalty on that eventful October day in 1859.

★　　★　　★　　★　　★

7

National Tragedy

The AMERICAN CIVIL WAR differed from most internecine struggles by virtue of the fact that the political differences that engendered it divided the country geographically, rather than politically. The civilian Southerner had little difficulty in seeing that his loyalty lay with the Confederacy once the issue was joined. His sympathies were with his friends, neighbors and local leaders, whether or not he had ever owned a slave. Likewise, the Northerner who had never seen a slave, and never really understood the problem, felt a strong sense of devotion to the Union and outrage toward those who would disrupt it. Only in the border states did the situation of father against son and brother against brother arise in the literal sense.

Southerners in the armed services of the United States were confronted with some severe soul searching. They had sworn an oath of loyalty to the Union. They had made a career of defending it against all enemies. To carry out their oath now meant waging war against the people among whom they had grown up. It meant devastating the land of their birth. To all but a handful, this was the most important point.

Within the Marine Corps the question of the hour was what Archibald Henderson would have done had he still lived. Would he have gone over to the Confederacy, like his fellow Virginian, Robert E. Lee? Or, would he have remained loyal to the Union as did another prominent Virginian, Winfield Scott? The only certain thing is that his son, Captain Charles A. Henderson, did resign and accept a Confederate commission. So did Major George H. Terret of Mexican War fame, Israel Greene, captor of John Brown, and many others. Altogether, the Marine Corps lost nearly fifty per cent of its officer strength through such defection. Although the majority of those who resigned were Southerners, the records of the Confederate States Marine Corps indicate that at least five of those who served in that organization hailed from New England.

At the outset, such resignations were accepted as a matter of routine. But, beginning in March of 1861, the Marine Corps refused to accept any further resignations and summarily dismissed those who tendered them.

In a letter to the Secretary of the Navy, Virginia-born Captain Robert Tansill set forth the reasons which impelled him to offer his resignation.

U.S. Frigate 'Congress'
Monte Video, May 17, 1861

Sir:

I have read the inaugural address of President Lincoln, and it seems to me that if the policy therein announced is carried out, civil war must ensue.

In entering the public service I took an oath to support the Constitution, which necessarily gives me a right to interpret it. Our institutions, according to my understanding, are founded upon the principle and right of self-government.

The States, in forming the Confederacy, did not relinquish that right and I believe each State has a clear and unquestionable right to secede whenever the people thereof prefer, and the Federal Government has no right or moral authority to use physical force to keep them in the Union.

Entertaining these views, I cannot conscientiously join in a war against any of the States which have already seceded, or may hereafter secede, either North or South, for the purpose of coercing them back into the Union. Such a war, in my opinion, would not only certainly and permanently destroy the Confederacy, but if successful establish an unlimited despotism on the ruins of our liberty. No personal consideration or advantage however great can induce me to aid in a cause which my heart tells me is wrong, and I prefer to endure the most terrible hardships, rather than to prosper in the destruction of the freedom of my country, and believing, Sir, that it should be disingenuous in me to retain my commission until the Government might require my service in such a contest, and then decline to serve, I consider it but prudent and just to now tender my resignation as a Captain in the United States Marine Corps.

I am, Sir, respectfully,

> Your obedient servant,
> Robert Tansill,
> Capt. U.S. Marine Corps.

The letter accomplished its purpose of obtaining Tansill's separation from the U.S. Marine Corps, but hardly in the manner he had in mind when he wrote it. Mailed from South America, the letter was not received by the Secretary of the Navy until August 24, 1861, by which time the Civil War was well under way. Upon his return to the United States, Tansill was confined in a federal prison as a prisoner of war and notified of his dismissal from service. He remained in prison until January 10, 1862, when he was transferred to Confederate jurisdiction during a formal exchange of prisoners.

No brilliant careers awaited Marine officers who joined the Confederacy. The South, with not much of a Navy, had need for only a small Marine Corps, and many accepted Army commissions. Nor was there much opportunity for achieving distinction for those Marines who remained loyal. Most of the defectors had been younger men. As a result, many vacancies existed in the junior officer grades, but opportunities for promotion were limited. The Corps was cluttered with deadwood at the top. There were many elderly officers of field rank physically incapable of serving in the field. When the Union decided to fight the war with volunteer troops, expansion of the regular service was greatly curtailed. Regular Army officers could achieve high command over such volunteer units, but there were no volunteer troops in the Marine Corps.

A contributing factor to the unfortunate state of affairs in the Marine Corps lay in the nature of the Commandant. Gone was the dynamic leadership of Archibald Henderson. Promotion was strictly according to seniority, and upon Henderson's death, in 1859, John Harris succeeded to the position of Colonel Commandant after forty-five years of commissioned service. Harris was another relic of the War of 1812. Nearly as old as Henderson, he was infinitely less vigorous. He had a mediocre combat record in two wars and numerous expeditions, and had never demonstrated a particularly high order of executive or administrative ability.

There can be no doubt that the inevitable division of loyalty in the Corps had considerable effect upon Harris, although he was not a Southerner. When one of his officers tendered his resignation with the obvious intention of joining the Confederacy, Commandant Harris wrote him a letter of recommendation, highly commending him to any military organization in need of an experienced officer.

During the Civil War, the Marine Corps contributed relatively little to the nation in comparison to the usefulness it had demonstrated in previous wars. Just how much of this failure was due to the peculiar nature of the war itself, and how much to those individuals who charted the Corps' destiny, is difficult to ascertain. The Marine Corps records of the time, however, appear to indicate that the Commandant and his staff were content to confine the activities of the Corps to guarding shore installations and providing ship's detachments. If it ever occurred to anyone to utilize the Marine Corps as an expeditionary force in an attempt to extend the operations of the fleet ashore along the Confederate coast, the idea was never followed up. That such was never attempted, with one singular exception, leads one to the conclusion that the strategists of the Union forces never understood the full potentialities of sea power. The Marines acquitted themselves well as part of the crews of naval vessels and that was all.

As for Harris, it is apparent that he placed little trust in his officers. It is also apparent that there was much internal dissent within the Corps. Most of the older officers were continually at loggerheads with their Commandant who failed to sustain the Corps in the high esteem Henderson had earned for it. Harris made no attempt to increase its responsibilities, and his regime precipitated a decline in Marine Corps prestige and usefulness which lasted more than three decades.

For the Marine Corps, the Civil War started most inauspiciously some three months before the Confederates took Fort Sumter under fire. In January, 1861, several hundred Alabama militia under the leadership of Florida authorities marched against the Pensacola Navy Yard. The yard's commanding officer, Captain James Armstrong who had commanded the Navy squadron that destroyed the Great Barrier Forts at Canton, hastily summoned his small Marine detachment to defend the yard. It wasn't much of a contest, although the success of the attackers may well have depended more on fifth column activities than on the force of arms. According to a Washington, D.C. newspaper story, appearing in the *National Intelligencer* on January 24, "not more than one-twentieth of the employees of the Government and the Navy Yard remained true to the allegiance to the United States."

Marine Captain Josiah Watson was required to sign a pledge never to bear arms against the State of Florida and, with his Marines, departed from Pensacola on the first ship headed north. Upon his arrival in New York, Watson forwarded his parole to Colonel Harris, the Commandant. Harris acknowledged receipt of the parole with the biting comment that he was "not aware of the United States being at war with Florida."

By the first of February, 1861, South Carolina, Georgia, Alabama, Florida, Mississippi, Louisiana and Texas had seceded from the Union. Three days later, delegates from the seven states met at Montgomery, Alabama, and formed the Confederate

States of America. On March 4, Abraham Lincoln was inaugurated President of a United States no longer united. By this time all of the forts and navy yards in the seceded states, except Fort Pickens at Pensacola and Fort Sumter at Charlestown, South Carolina, were in control of Confederate authorities.

From the viewpoint of the Confederacy, the jurisdiction of such installations, upon secession, automatically passed to the state in which they were located. For the Federal Government to maintain garrisons in them was considered a hostile act. Consequently, Confederate representatives journeyed to Washington to negotiate for their surrender with Lincoln's Secretary of State, William H. Seward. The Secretary refused to receive the delegation, but indirectly gave them assurance that no supplies would be sent to such installations without formal notice. The representatives returned home feeling that they had been promised a speedy evacuation of the Federal garrisons.

The issue came rapidly into focus when the commanding officer of Fort Sumter informed the War Department that his supplies were running low. The Confederacy had made it plain that any attempt to supply Fort Sumter would be regarded as an overt act. The Federal Government refused to recognize the Confederate States of America. If the Government yielded to the Southern demands to evacuate federal troops from Sumter and Pickens, the principle of union would be fatally compromised. Against the advice of five of his seven Cabinet members, Lincoln ordered a relief expedition to Fort Sumter on April 6.

On the night of April 11, General Beauregard, the Confederate commander of the Charleston district, sent four of his officers to Fort Sumter to demand its surrender. Sumter's commanding officer, Major Robert Anderson, was a Kentuckian. The whole idea of civil war was extremely repugnant to him. He had no desire to achieve fame as the spark that kindled the flame of such a war. As yet there had been no word from the relief expedition. After considerable conversation with the Confederate staff officers, Anderson agreed to surrender the fort as soon as he might do so with honor. This appeared to be within two days time, when his food supply would be exhausted. Anderson's conditions were peremptorily refused by the Confederate officers. At 4:30 A.M., April 12, Confederate cannon thundered across Charleston harbor to send the first shell of the American Civil War crashing against the battlements of Fort Sumter. On the following day Major Anderson accepted the terms of surrender. On Monday, April 15, President Lincoln called for 75,000 volunteers to put down the secessionists who were "too powerful to be suppressed by the ordinary course of judicial proceedings."

The first action of the Marines in the "official" war was the destruction of the Norfolk Navy Yard. Although Virginia had not formally seceded from the Union, her troops were mobilizing. The Union command made a belated effort to reinforce the defenses of the Norfolk Navy Yard and, on April 19, Commandant Harris was ordered to provide one hundred Marines as a relief expedition. Sailing on a chartered steamer, the *Pawnee,* the Marines arrived at Norfolk just in time to take part in the destruction of the installation to prevent it from falling into Confederate hands. The Marines on the *Pawnee* joined the detachments aboard the *Pennsylvania* and the *Cumberland,* who were already in the yard. All official records and archives were transferred to the *Pawnee.* A large amount of gold from the Customs House in Norfolk was carried aboard the *Cumberland* and the destruction began. First to go were thousands of stands of arms. Carbines, their stocks broken by a blow from another rifle barrel, were thrown into the bay. Several tons of shot and shell were sent plunging to the bottom, and a large supply of revolvers suffered a similar fate. Over fifteen hundred artillery pieces, mostly Dahlgren guns and Columbaids, were spiked and many of them pushed off the piers.

According to a *New York Times* correspondent who witnessed the spectacle, the destruction went on until four o'clock in the morning. When the moon sank below the horizon, the Marines set fire to their own barracks to provide illumination for their work. Seven ships, including the *Merrimack,* were either scuttled or set ablaze. As the Marines withdrew to their waiting ships, pre-set powder trains fired the remaining buildings and the ship-houses.

Then came the first Battle of Bull Run. It would be a pleasure to record that the performance of the Marines stood as the one redeeming feature of an otherwise disgraceful military action, as it had at Bladensburg. But it would not be true. The fact is that the Marines ran just as fast as everyone else, once the rout began.

From the beginning there was considerable disagreement among the Union planners as to the proper strategy to be em-ployed in crushing the Confederacy. The commanding general of the Federal Armies, General Winfield Scott, was convinced that the best plan was to rely on Union seapower to strangle Confederate commerce, while Federal forces drove down the Mississippi. But Scott was an old man, as his detractors were quick to point out. His "Anaconda Plan," so-called because it en-visioned the encirclement and final crushing of the South, was derided as the product of a senile mind. Why waste time in what would obviously be a long, protracted campaign, Scott's critics demanded? The only sensible approach to the problem was one quick thrust at Richmond, the heart of the Confederacy. So, nurtured by the Northern business men, to whom profitable Southern markets were no longer available, the battle cry be-came, "On to Richmond!"

To a seasoned old campaigner like Scott, who was more in-clined to think of the science of war as a matter of tactics and logistics, rather than politics and economics, a quick thrust at Richmond had little chance of success. In the first place, to put Union forces in position for an assault on the Confederate capi-tal meant marching an army over winding roads halfway across the state of Virginia. The only army available to accomplish this considerable feat was, for the most part, composed of militia who had received less than ninety days of military training. Finally, somewhere along the route lurked a Southern army whose ability was unknown to the Northern command. But, politics being what they are, only a professional soldier would be concerned about such trifling considerations in the face of the

emotional fever which demanded immediate defeat of the sedi-
tionists. So Scott placed General Irving McDowell in charge of
a Union army which trudged southward out of Washington,
D.C. on a hot midsummer's day, bent on humbling the rebels.

Included in the Union army was a battalion of Marines commanded by Major John G. Reynolds. Very few officers would
have cared to be in Major Reynolds' shoes. Of the 12 officers
and 336 enlisted men who made up his battalion, only 5 officers
and 9 noncommissioned officers could be considered as having
had any experience. The remainder were the rawest of recruits,
none of whom had been in military service over three weeks. Because of their inexperience, the Marines were placed in support
of Captain Charles Griffin's "West Point Battery," a Regular
artillery unit which had trained at the Military Academy.

The long, dusty road to Richmond ended at Bull Run, 26
miles west of Washington. There, on the afternoon of July 16,
the First Division of the Union Army found the Confederate
Grays massed before them. The fate of the Marine battalion was
recorded by Major Reynolds in his battle report.

". . . On reaching the field, and for some hours previously,
the battery's accelerated march was such as to keep my command, more or less, in double-quick time; consequently the men
became fatigued or exhausted in strength. Being obliged at this
period to halt, in order to afford those in the rear an opportunity
of closing up and taking their proper place in the line, the battery
was lost to protection from the force under my command.

"Upon our arrival at the battlefield the position of the battery
was pointed out, and I was directed to afford the necessary support. In taking the position the battalion was exposed to a galling
fire. While holding it, General McDowell ordered the battalion
to cover or support the Fourteenth New York Regiment, which
was about to be engaged. The battalion, in consequence, took
the position indicated by the general, but was unable to hold it,
owing to the heavy fire which was opened upon them. They
broke several times, but were as frequently formed and urged
back to their position, when finally a general rout took place, in

which the Marines participated. . . . The abrupt and hasty retreat from the field of battle presents a deplorable deficiency in
both arms and equipment."

The Union Army, Marines and all, beat a hasty retreat back
to Washington to lick their wounds, and replenish the equipment
they had thrown away on the battlefield. Reynolds' battalion
counted its casualties as nine killed, nineteen wounded and sixteen missing.

As a result of Bull Run, it became obvious that the Union
forces needed considerable reorganization. As far as the Marine
Corps was concerned, the need for more efficient forces was reflected in an act passed by Congress in July, 1861. The act authorized an increase of 28 officers and 750 enlisted, which
brought the Corps' total strength to just over 3,000. It also attempted to provide younger officers for the Corps by specifying
that officers appointed under its provisions be between the ages
of twenty and twenty-five years. The increase, however, was not
sufficient to provide enough Marines to keep pace with the rapid
expansion of the Navy. As the war began to develop along the
lines prophesied by "senile" old General Scott, there were ever-
increasing calls for Marines to man the detachments of the larger
Union ships. During the entire war, the Marine Corps was severely handicapped by insufficient personnel. As a result, they
were able to field only a single amphibious battalion.

The first naval expedition against a Confederate port took
place in August, 1861, at Hatteras Inlet, North Carolina. Large
quantities of war materials were being smuggled into the South
by British blockade runners through that port. To put a halt to
this operation, General Benjamin F. Butler organized an expedition of about 1,000 army troops and several naval vessels at
Hampton Roads and set sail for the North Carolina coast.
Rounding Hatteras shoals on August 28, the expedition found
that both sides of the entrance to the inlet had been fortified. The
original plan, which called for a full-scale landing, was postponed
when a suddenly rising storm began to lash the coast. But the
Marines had come to make a landing, and finally succeeded in

convincing General Butler that they should be allowed to make an attempt. The Marine detachments from the *Minnesota, Cumberland* and the *Wabash* were combined under Captain William L. Shuttleworth, along with 250 army troops, and successfully made the landing through boiling surf. Although relatively few men were lost in the hazardous landing, almost all of the specially constructed landing boats were destroyed in beaching.

With naval gunfire support, the landing force, in a four-hour engagement, captured Fort Clark which guarded the eastern shore of the inlet. It was late in the afternoon by the time Fort Clark had been taken, and the landing force was not anxious to make a night attack against Fort Hatteras on the other side of the inlet. Marines and soldiers spent a miserable night seeking shelter from the driving rain. General Butler was fearful that the Confederates would march out of their works and capture his small landing force. But the defenders evidently cared as little about waging battle on a wet night as the attackers, and chose to wait until daylight. The following morning the issue was speedily decided by a lucky hit on the fort's magazine during the naval bombardment, and Fort Hatteras surrendered. With the loss of Hatteras Inlet, Confederate morale was badly shaken. The Union had established a foothold on the coast of Carolina which it was to hold throughout the remainder of the war.

The single amphibious battalion of the Marine Corps during the Civil War was organized to take part in the expedition against Port Royal, South Carolina. Flag Officer S. F. DuPont, who commanded the South Atlantic Blockading Squadron, had considerable experience with Marine landing forces during the War with Mexico. As commander of the naval forces for the forthcoming expedition, he was anxious to have a specially trained battalion of Marines as a part of his fleet. The battalion was organized and placed under the command of the same Major Reynolds who had led the ill-fated battalion at Bull Run. For the second time within the short period of three months Reynolds' command was doomed to failure, although this time the

enemy at whose hands it was to suffer defeat were the forces of
nature, rather than those of the Confederacy.

Due to the shortage of transports which continually plagued
the Union command, Reynolds embarked his battalion aboard
the *Governor,* a chartered sidewheeler. The expedition left
Hampton Roads on October 29, with the troop-carrying ships
following the fighting vessels. Two days later off Cape Hatteras a
severe storm lashed the Federal flotilla, scattering the ships. Battered by heavy seas, the *Governor* soon became separated from
the other ships, and sustained heavy damage. Reynolds formed
his Marines into damage control parties to shore up sagging
bulkheads and bail out flooded compartments. On Saturday, November 2, the storm reached the peak of its fury. The *Governor's*
stack carried away, a steampipe burst and a crashing wave
wrenched away her rudder, leaving her to wallow helplessly in
the mountainous seas.

Answering the *Governor's* call for help, the frigate *Sabine*
took her under tow but the plunging ships' towing cables soon
parted. The *Sabine* then came alongside and attempted to take
off the Marines. The Marines waited tensely at the rail until the
two ships lurched together. Then, a few at a time, they jumped
to the heaving deck of the *Sabine.* It was a slow and dangerous
job. Finally small boats were put over the side and the Marines
who could swim leaped into the sea to be picked up by the boats.
In the final accounting, all the men of the battalion, except one
corporal and six privates, were saved from the sinking *Governor.*
Reynolds also managed to save most of the battalion's arms and
about half of the ammunition, but as far as the attack on Port
Royal was concerned it had to proceed without the Marines.

It would appear that whatever fate guided the destiny of Reynolds' battalion possessed a grim sense of humor. During the
early part of March, 1862, Reynolds embarked his battalion on
board the transport *McClellan,* under orders from DuPont to
seize and occupy Fernandina, Georgia. The battalion arrived
only to find the town already occupied by Union troops. Less
than a month later they were ordered to St. Augustine, Florida,

for the same purpose. While they were en route to their destination, the Confederate forces evacuated St. Augustine in the face of a landing force of Marines and sailors from the *Mohican* and the *Wabash*. All the troops necessary to garrison the city were furnished by the Army. Once again there was no need for Reynolds to land his battalion.

By this time DuPont had reached the conclusion that there was no longer a need for a Marine battalion in his South Atlantic Blockading Squadron. The battalion returned to Washington, D.C., where it was eventually disbanded and the personnel transferred to various ships' detachments.

One of the most interesting, and potentially most dangerous, incidents of the Civil War was the "Trent Affair." Not a shot was fired by the Marines involved. Yet, by innocently carrying out their orders, they nearly plunged the Union into a war with Great Britain.

From the outset, the British were extremely interested in the war between the North and the South. Most British liberals saw little difference between the Confederacy's struggle for independence and the industrial movements in Europe with which they had long sympathized. As Henry Adams wrote, "The English mind took naturally to rebellion—when foreign."

Normally, English humanitarians would have sided with the North, applauding a war against slavery. But, both Lincoln and Seward repeatedly avowed that slavery was not an issue of the struggle. In the face of such declarations, Englishmen of humanitarian instincts were unable to decide whether their sympathies should lie with the South or the North.

There was no doubt where the commercial classes of England stood. For quite obvious reasons, they favored the South. The Union advocated a high protective policy. The Confederate constitution forbade high tariffs, a fact which was capitalized upon by Southern propagandists. The textile industry of England depended largely upon southern-grown American cotton. British shipping interests were vitally interested in the same commodity,

since cotton represented a large portion of their commerce with
America.

In view of the circumstances, it is hardly surprising that the
North had few vigorous partisans in the England of 1861.

With little industrial capacity, few commercial ships, and the
Northern blockade of its ports growing tighter, the South turned
speculative eyes on England. Early in November two prominent
Confederate diplomatic agents, John Slidell and James M. Mason, set sail for Southampton on board the British mail steamer,
Trent, out of Havana. Slidell enjoyed an outstanding reputation
in the field of diplomatic prowess. It was widely believed that if
Slidell and Mason reached England the breaking of the blockade
would be only a matter of time.

Afraid of upsetting the delicate balance of British neutrality,
the North was powerless to prevent the Confederate agents from
reaching their destination. At least so they thought, until over-
zealous Captain Charles Wilkes sailed his Union sloop *San Jacinto* and her Marines into diplomatic waters.

Learning of the plans of the Southern diplomats, and acting
wholly without orders from Washington, Wilkes positioned his
ship to intercept the *Trent*. On the morning of November 8, the
British ship appeared on the horizon. As she came within range,
the *San Jacinto* sent two shots screaming across her bow. The
Trent hove to.

Wilkes sent Lieutenant Fairfax with a boarding party of Marines and sailors to the *Trent* to remove Slidell and Mason as
prisoners of war. The boarding party was met by the irate British captain who vigorously protested the detention of his neutral
ship as an act of war. Fairfax's request to be allowed to search
the *Trent*, and permission to examine her passenger list, was met
with a curt refusal. Fairfax then told the captain that he had information that Slidell and Mason had taken passage on the *Trent*
at Havana. Further, that he intended to satisfy himself whether
they were aboard before allowing the ship to continue.

By this time a crowd of curious passengers had gathered on
the quarterdeck where the conversation was taking place. Hear-

ing his name mentioned, Slidell stepped forward from among the assembled passengers and identified himself. Fairfax attempted to induce Slidell and Mason to accompany him to the *San Jacinto*. Slidell refused, saying that he intended to remain on the *Trent* and could be persuaded to leave only by force. The Marines in Fairfax's boarding party were only too happy to accommodate Mr. Slidell, who abruptly found himself neatly stowed in one of the *San Jacinto's* small boats alongside. Mason and the two diplomats' secretaries were quickly added to the cargo, and the *Trent* was allowed to proceed.

News of the seizure caused considerable fury in England. The outraged British press screamed of the "ruffianly conduct of an impudent pirate," and made uncomplimentary remarks about the strong-arm methods of the U.S. Marines. From London Henry Adams wrote, "This nation means to make war." Underscoring Adams' words, 11,000 of Britain's best troops embarked for Canada on transports which were serenaded by a volunteer band playing, "I Wish I Were in Dixie." One of the transports provided a rather amusing anticlimax to the British troop movement. Unable to enter Canada's ice-bound St. Lawrence River, the transport put into Portland, Maine. America's Secretary of State, William H. Seward, graciously allowed the British troops to march across Maine to reach Canada.

Three weeks after the seizure of Slidell and Mason, England dispatched an ultimatum to Washington. Finally, after a long and heated debate in Lincoln's Cabinet, the embarrassed President released the Confederate prisoners.

One of the few recorded instances of Union and Confederate Marines meeting face-to-face occurred in 1862. The meeting had some rather unusual aspects. The captain of a Confederate ship requested the U.S. Marines, who were his prisoners, to guard some captured stores from his own men, then attempted to enlist them in the Confederate States Marine Corps.

It all began on December 1 when the mail steamer *Ariel* cleared New York harbor bound for the west coast. Among other passengers on board were two companies of Marines, including six officers. One company was en route to Mare Island, California, for garrison duty; the other to be divided among the various ships' detachments of the Pacific Squadron.

East of Cuba, lookouts aboard the *Ariel* sighted a strange ship astern and closing fast. The stranger was flying the colors of the United States. Within a mile of the *Ariel* she opened fire with her bow gun, struck her colors and ran up the flag of the Confederacy. The first two rounds whistled harmlessly through the *Ariel's* rigging, but the third carried away her foremast.

With over 200 passengers aboard, the captain of the *Ariel* had little choice but to heave to. As a boatload of armed men approached from the other ship, the captain reminded his Marine passengers of the large number of women and children aboard. Thus, the Marines stood docilely by as the Confederate boats pulled alongside. The leader of the boarding party informed the captain of the *Ariel* that he had been captured by the famous Confederate raider *Alabama*.

The Marines were ordered to surrender their arms. A prize crew of Confederate sailors was placed on board, and the captain and his first officer taken to the *Alabama* to discuss ransom terms.

Within a few minutes the senior Marine officer on board the *Ariel*, a Major Garland, was ordered to report to Captain Semmes of the *Alabama*. Semmes informed Major Garland that he was to return to the *Ariel*, rearm as many of his Marines as he thought necessary, and mount a tight guard over the whiskey stores on board. Semmes explained to the astonished major that he didn't place much trust in his rebel crew. Garland carried out the orders of the Confederate captain, and in doing so probably became the only prisoner of war guard commander in history assigned to protect the spoils of war from his own captors.

Having assured himself that the captured liquor supply was properly guarded, Captain Semmes decided to do a little recruiting for his Marine detachment. As a recruiter, he selected the *Alabama's* Marine officer, Lieutenant Beckett K. Howell. Howell, a former U.S. Marine, was the brother-in-law of Jefferson

Davis, President of the Confederate States. He had resigned his commission at the beginning of the war to join the Confederate States Marine Corps. Assembling all the Yankee Marines on the *Ariel* not standing guard over the whiskey, Howell made a recruiting speech. He pointed out that any Marine who joined the *Alabama's* detachment was certain to share in more prize money than he would ever see fighting for the Union. He also cited the fact that the pay of Confederate Marines was exactly double that being paid by the North. He ended his speech by saying that he was sure there were many among them who held Jefferson Davis in much higher esteem than they did Abraham Lincoln. He neglected to mention the family ties between himself and the Confederate States President. But, Howell's efforts were unsuccessful and he returned to the *Alabama* without obtaining any recruits.

After considerable discussion between the two ships' captains, the *Ariel* was ransomed for $261,000. Her officers, crew, and passengers were paroled, and she was permitted to proceed on her way. A careful check of the whiskey stores showed that the Marines had scrupulously carried out the Confederate captain's orders.

By 1864 the number of Marine detachments at sea well exceeded 100, absorbing a large percentage of the enlisted personnel of the Marine Corps. On May 12th of that year death brought Colonel John Harris' tour as Commandant to an end. The selection of his successor proved to be a startling departure from the traditional custom of selecting the next senior Marine officer as Commandant. Shortly after attending Harris' funeral, the Secretary of the Navy, Gideon Welles, remarked that the Commandant's death "gives embarrassment as to a successor." Welles went on to state his conviction that the higher ranking Marine officers, "are not the men who can elevate or give efficiency to the Corps."

Under the authority of a law passed in 1862, and with the approval of the President, Welles retired all the officers in the Marine Corps senior to the major who was his personnel choice for

Commandant. On June 10, 1864, Jacob Zeilin, who had received his permanent promotion to major less than three years previously, was appointed as the seventh Commandant of the Marine Corps.

As the war dragged to a close a tremendous apathy toward active service developed in the Union forces. Desertions had long been a serious problem. Following the Battle of Antietam, the records of the Union Army showed over 30,000 troops on unauthorized absence. During the first year of the war, the Marine Corps lost 298 men by desertion, a figure considerably less than the average for the prewar years. In the last year of the war the number had increased to almost 1,000. The losses from desertions far exceeded those suffered in battle. In the final tally, only 77 Marines had been killed in action, while 257 died from disease and other causes.

On April 9, 1865, General Robert E. Lee, Commander-in-Chief of the Confederate Armies, surrendered to General U. S. Grant at Appomattox Court House. The Yankees and the Rebels were again countrymen.

8

★ ★

★ ★ ★ ★ ★

War, Insurrection and Rebellion

The THREE DECADES following the Civil War witnessed the uneasy transition of the Navy from sail to steam power. This was not, as one might expect from viewing the end result, a simple process. All naval tradition was based on sail, and tradition, particularly in the Navy, dies a slow and lingering death. Steam powered ships continued to carry a full sail rig almost to the turn of the twentieth century. And they used it. Doctrine held that ships should cruise under sail at all times, except when the wind failed altogether. Efficient propellers which would enhance a ship's performance under steam were shunned in favor of less efficient ones which would least impede her performance under sail. As a result, the Navy sailed ships which were capable of only second class performance, under either sail or steam. Captains were under orders to use fuel only when it was absolutely necessary. In fact, a bill was once brought up in Congress to hold the ship's master personally responsible for the cost of any coal burned under circumstances which he could not justify.

The question naturally arose as to what part the Marines would play in this new Navy. Their traditional functions were gradually atrophying. With each passing year, the demand for sea-going Marine detachments grew less and less. What was to be their role?

The answer was not immediately apparent. When it finally did appear, it was the product of naval necessity. From that necessity evolved what has constituted the Marine Corps' primary mission ever since.

The transition from sail to steam power imposed inherent arbitrary limits on a fleet's maneuverability. A fleet was automatically bound to its base of supplies. Coal, and later oil, was what sustained a fleet. Such fuel, in sufficient supply, was obtainable only at well-stocked bases belonging to the United States or an ally. In the closing decade of the 1800s America had few bases of its own, and no allies.

But the bases would have to be obtained, one way or another—and the Navy would have to obtain them. The big question was, what part of the Navy? Today, it appears fairly obvious that the Marine Corps was made to order for this function. But the situation was considerably different at the time.

What the Navy had in mind was a much larger mission than had ever been performed by the Marine Corps. The Corps had enjoyed considerable success in splashing ashore, a few boatloads at a time, to impress the local citizenry with the might of the United States. But, to seize and defend an advanced base against a well organized enemy was a military maneuver for which there were few parallels in history.

The Navy divided itself into two camps on the question. One side held that the Marine Corps should be abolished, and the Navy enlarged to take care of the function. The other side argued that the Marine Corps was already a force in being, with considerable experience in fighting land campaigns. The Corps, they insisted, should be expanded and given the job. The debate was still going on in 1898 when the issue was drawn by an immediate need for such a force—and the Marine Corps had it.

On the evening of February 15, the United States battleship *Maine* lay at anchor in the quiet waters of Havana harbor. Ostensibly, the American man-of-war had arrived in Cuba merely to pay a courtesy call upon the Spanish. But anyone who read the newspapers, especially those owned by William Randolph Hearst, was well aware that Cuba was in the third year of a going revolution. The average American, who knew only what he read in the newspapers, had a pretty hazy conception of just what was going on in Cuba. The headlines screamed of Spanish barbarity in blood-red type, and the editorial pages hinted broadly for American intervention. Outside of a few misplaced citizens and a few cane fields, owned by American firms, the United States had little stake in the Cuban revolution. But things were dull at home and Mr. Hearst had a lot of newspapers to sell. He received considerable assistance from the imaginative pen of Frederic Remington, an artist whom he had sent to Cuba to sketch the war. Remington couldn't find any war to illustrate, so he spent most of his time dreaming up sketches of bestial looking Spanish policemen leering at innocent Cuban maidens. The sketches went rather well with the red headlines.

Finally the *insurrectos* got around to burning some of the American-owned cane fields. A group of young Spanish army officers generated a pretty fair demonstration to protest the replacement of their favorite general, who had been dubbed "The Beast" by American newspapers. And, although the demonstrators did nothing to endanger the lives of Americans, the State Department got a little jittery. So, Captain Charles Sigsbee, United States Navy, having exchanged the usual amenities with the Spanish authorities, sat in his peaceful cabin of the mighty battleship *Maine,* composing a letter to his wife, when suddenly his ship blew up.

Witnesses later testified that the explosion could be heard 11 miles away. Members of the crew heard two distinct blasts. The first was a sharp report, like the crack of a pistol. The second was a tremendous roar that devoured the crew's quarters, twisted steel beams and enveloped the forward third of the ship in a cloud of searing flame. Captain Sigsbee stumbled into the smoke-filled companionway and began to grope his way toward the bridge. He had gone only a short distance when he collided with his orderly, Marine Private William Anthony. The young Marine apologized to his Captain. Then, clicking his heels together in the position of rigid attention, uttered the words that made him a national hero. "Sir," he said calmly as he rendered a snappy salute, "I beg to report that the Captain's ship is sinking."

There were two boards of investigation; one American, the other Spanish. Both collected and weighed their evidence as carefully and honestly as possible—and arrived at contradictory conclusions. The results of the Spanish investigation showed that the *Maine* had been destroyed by an internal explosion. The American investigators concluded that the ammunition in the forward magazine of the ship had detonated as a result of an initial explosion outside the hull.

The United States Naval officers who comprised the board of investigation made no attempt to fix the blame on anyone. It would hardly have been just to do so, since neither theory has ever been disproved. But justice, in the tarnished traditions of yellow journalism, is never allowed to interfere with an opportunity to increase circulation. The American tabloids held trial on the Spanish government and arrived at a unanimous verdict of guilty. The sentence was war. And since a great many readers were voters, Congress also clamored for vengeance for the 232 sailors and 28 Marines who had died on the *Maine*. On April 19, 1898, Congress passed a resolution declaring that Cuba was a free and independent nation. The resolution also authorized President William McKinley to employ American troops to force Spain to relinquish her control over the island. Five days later Spain declared war on the United States.

The Spanish-American War became a shooting reality on May 1 when Commodore George Dewey steamed his American squadron into Manila Bay in the Philippines. In less than eight hours of furious fighting, Dewey destroyed the Spaniards' Philippine flotilla. On the following day the Spanish authorities surrendered the Naval Station at Cavite, and the Governor promised there would be no firing on the American vessels.

Except for Dewey's brilliant victory at Manila, the Spanish-American War was fought along the southern coast of Cuba, in the region of Santiago. It had become apparent to naval tacticians that if a war with Spain ever developed it would be necessary to have an operating base in the Caribbean. The only way to obtain one was to seize it. It was also apparent that the widely scattered U.S. Army was incapable of handling the job.

On April 16, a full week before Spain declared war on the United States, the Marine Corps' Commandant, Colonel Charles Heywood, had received orders to organize a battalion for service in Cuba. Heywood ordered every available Marine within reasonable distance to the Brooklyn Navy Yard. To command the new battalion he selected Lieutenant Colonel Robert W. Huntington, a full-bearded veteran of the Civil War. By April 22, Huntington had organized his 647-man battalion into five infantry companies and one artillery battery, equipped with four three-inch rapid fire cannon. As the Navy Yard's band blared "The Girl I Left Behind Me," the battalion set sail for Key West, Florida, and some intensive training.

While Huntington's battalion fought flies, mosquitoes and a rugged training schedule at Key West, the Marine Corps was expanding to wartime strength. On May 4, legislation was enacted which authorized an increase of 24 officers and 1,640 enlisted men. A typical new recruit was given six weeks' indoctrination at one of the barracks, then was assigned to a ship or shore station. The proudest moment in a recruit's life was the day he was allowed to don his blue dress uniform and swagger out the main gate. In many instances it was also the day he received the rudest shock of his young life. American civilians, unused to military uniforms, often mistook the Marine private for an officer in the Salvation Army.

By the end of May, Rear Admiral W. P. Sampson, the U.S. Atlantic Fleet Commander, was looking for a good harbor to use as a coaling station. His original strategy of steaming into Havana Harbor and blasting the city into ruins had been vetoed by the Secretary of the Navy, and with good reason. At the outbreak of the war, the Spanish fleet had been ordered from Europe to the West Indies. Until the position of the fleet was known, it posed a threat of unknown proportions. Sampson attempted to intercept the Spanish ships, but American reconnaissance was poor and the enemy wasn't located until the latter part of April—safely anchored in Santiago Harbor. Upon this discovery, Sampson established a close blockade of the harbor, and spent a whole month vainly attempting to lure the Spanish ships out of their snug retreat.

On June 6, Sampson formed up his entire fleet and let go an awe-inspiring bombardment against the fortifications which guarded the entrance to the harbor. When the dust and smoke had settled, the massive bastion of Morro Castle still squatted above the harbor's mouth, as sinister as ever. It was at this point in the proceedings that Sampson decided he needed an advanced base to maintain his blockade. As the ideal site, he selected Guantanamo Bay, which lay some forty miles to the east of Santiago.

On June 10, Huntington's Marine battalion waded ashore at Guantanamo to become the first American troops to land on Cuban soil. The landing, made in an area held by an estimated nine thousand Spanish troops, was uneventful. Not a rifle cracked from the dense underbrush as the sweating Marines dragged their equipment across the sweltering beach, toiled up a hill and pitched camp. During the late afternoon of the following day the enemy came to life. Just after sundown the Spaniards attacked one of the outposts, killing two Marines. From then until midnight the enemy made minor probing attacks against the battalion's perimeter. At 1 A.M. the Spaniards launched a determined attack from two sides. According to the novelist, Stephen Crane, who had accompanied the battalion as a war correspondent, it was a night of terror, "a thousand rifles rattling . . . field guns booming in your ears . . . the diabolic Colt automatic clacking, and the Mauser bullets sneering always in the air a few inches over one's head. . . ."

It was typical guerrilla warfare, the attackers cloaked in darkness and firing wildly, the defenders confused but standing fast. Casualties for the night's fighting were surprisingly light;

three killed and five wounded. The second day was a repetition of the first, with an occasional Mauser bullet cracking overhead, but no organized attack until after nightfall. According to Crane, it was another of those "swift nights which strained courage so near the panic point." During the night the Marines lost their sergeant major.

By the end of the third day, Lieutenant Colonel Huntington had his fill of defensive warfare. His active scouting patrols had reported that the only water supply for the Spanish troops in the area was Cuzco Well, six miles southeast of the Marines' position. Huntington decided to destroy the well and force the enemy to withdraw.

On the morning of June 14, Companies "C" and "D" cleared the battalion area and set out for Cuzco Well. The well, defended by a blockhouse and six companies of Spanish regulars and Cuban loyalists, promised to be no easy objective. Captain George F. Elliott, who commanded the force, halted his troops some distance from the objective. He ordered Lieutenant Louis J. Magill to bypass the enemy position with his platoon and cut off any chance of retreat. Elliott then deployed his main body along a semicircular ridge facing the objective, and waited for Magill to get into position.

Before leaving the battalion area, Elliott had been told by Colonel Huntington that the USS *Dolphin* was standing by in the bay to give him naval gunfire support, whenever he signalled the need for it. As Lieutenant Magill's platoon topped the crest of a hill in the rear of the Spanish position, Elliott signalled the *Dolphin* to open fire and launched his attack. The *Dolphin's* barrage was a little high and, although most of it crashed into the objective, an uncomfortable number of shells began falling on Magill's platoon. As Magill frantically looked about for a signalman, Sergeant John H. Quick, clutching an improvised semaphore flag, stood erect in full view of the enemy. As Mauser bullets ripped through the air about him and the *Dolphin's* shells erupted along the hillside, Quick calmly signalled the ship to cease fire. The omnipresent Stephen Crane wrote of the incident, "As he swung his clumsy flag to and fro, an end of it once caught on a cactus pillar, and he looked over his shoulder to see what had it. He gave the flag an impatient jerk. He looked annoyed." It was the only emotion Quick displayed. He was awarded the Medal of Honor for his heroic act. Twenty years later, he won the Distinguished Cross in World War I. He was, General John A. Lejeune once remarked, "a very quiet man."

Thanks to Quick's heroism, the *Dolphin* lifted her fire and the Marines moved in on their objective. The Spanish survivors, with the exception of one officer and 17 privates who were captured, withdrew. The defender's losses, according to the prisoners, amounted to 60 killed and 150 wounded. The retreating Spaniards later reported that they had been attacked by 10,000 Americans. Elliott and his men destroyed the well and returned to camp before nightfall. It had been a good day's work.

With the withdrawal of the Spanish forces from the area, the Marine battalion gained respite from the full-scale night attacks. On June 25, two companies marched into the area west of Guantanamo Bay, but failed to make contact with the enemy. The remainder of their stay in Guantanamo was limited to patrol actions and occasional harassment by snipers and small bands of infiltrators.

While the Marines patrolled the Guantanamo area, the Army's Fifth Corps landed at Daiquiri, 20 miles east of Santiago, and began its drive on the city. A wild-eyed group of amateurs known as the "Rough Riders," led by a big man with a big moustache, Teddy Roosevelt, stormed up the slopes of San Juan Hill to everlasting glory. On the Sunday morning of July 3, Admiral Cervera's Spanish squadron, long bottled up in Santiago Harbor, made a break for the open sea. The light Spanish ships, with leaking boilers, barnacled hulls and defective guns, were hopelessly outclassed. When the shooting was over, every one of Cervera's ships had been destroyed, and 1,782 of his 2,150 crewmen had been captured. Santiago surrendered on July 12.

A month later Colonel Huntington and his Marines, embarked aboard the *Resolute,* lay off the town of Manzanillo prepared to make an assault landing on the following morning. The coming of daylight revealed dozens of white flags fluttering along the shore line. Within a few minutes, a Spanish official arrived at the ship to inform the Americans that a peace protocol had been signed between the two nations.

The Marines returned to the United States where they were given a heroes' welcome. In Washington they paraded down Pennsylvania Avenue to the tune of "There'll Be A Hot Time In The Old Town Tonight," then passed in review before President McKinley. At Portsmouth, New Hampshire, where they were to be stationed, the local citizens held a clambake in their honor, and the Y.M.C.A. presented a Bible to each member of the battalion.

As far as supplying a large armed force was concerned, the Marines had made no great contribution to the victory over Spain. But, they had accomplished something no one else had been able to do—assemble and embark an integrated force at a moment's notice. They had shown the nation a true force in readiness. Huntington's battalion had embarked from Brooklyn within six days after the Commandant had issued orders for its formation. At Guantanamo Bay they had decisively demonstrated the need for Marines as assault troops to be employed with the fleet. An advanced base had been seized and defended by a Marine unit, commanded by a Marine officer.

In a war which had seen many long delays in preparing the nation's military forces for action, the speed with which the Marine Corps had assembled and dispatched their battalion earned them considerable favor with an impatient American public. The calm, military preciseness of Private William Anthony as he reported the sinking of the *Maine* to its captain was the subject of so many newspaper stories that he became a national hero. The quiet, fearless Sergeant Quick, captured for

posterity by the pen of Stephen Crane, became the paragon of
military virtue. To the ordinary citizen, the Marines had come to
symbolize the spirit of aggressive adventure and quiet heroism.
Although it probably wasn't realized at the time, the Marine
Corps had taken a giant stride along the uneven road to its
ultimate destiny.

Accurately weighed on the balance scales of history, the
Spanish-American War amounted to very little. But it was followed, almost at once, by events in the Philippines which
amounted to a great deal more.

There were Marines with Admiral Dewey's squadron during
the capture of Manila Bay, but not enough to avert the drawn-
out tragedy that followed. The Admiral later testified before
Congress that he might have averted the Philippine Insurrection
if a Marine force comparable to Huntington's had been made
available to him. But his only landing force was the ship's detachments of his own small squadron.

When Dewey steamed into Manila Bay, the Filipinos had
been prepared to stage a revolution against the Spanish. When
their new conquerors could make no convincing display of
force, they simply turned their well organized movement against
the Americans.

World War II would prove the Filipinos to be among the
most devoted, loyal and courageous allies any nation ever had.
In 1899 they proved themselves courageous, cunning and some
of the most resourceful guerrilla fighters the world had ever
seen. It took three years of fighting and diplomacy to bring them
around to our point of view. But once that had been achieved,
they never seriously deviated again, even under the brutalizing
influence of Japanese occupation.

Dewey called for a battalion of Marines in March of 1899
when the insurrectionists began to pose a serious threat to his
naval base at Cavite, on the southern shore of Manila Bay. The
battalion, which left the New York Naval Shipyard on April
13, numbered 15 officers and 260 enlisted men. In July another
request for Marines, from the Commander-in-Chief Asiatic

Squadron, added a second battalion to the growing Marine forces in the Philippines. By the end of the year a third battalion had been added and the entire force, boasting 46 officers and 947 enlisted men, was organized into the first Marine regiment in Corps history. Lieutenant Colonel George F. Elliott, the commanding officer, was rapidly rising. As a captain, he had led two of Huntington's companies against Cuzco Well at Guantanamo only two years previously. Three years later he was to become the tenth Commandant of the Marine Corps.

For the next three years the duties of the Marines in the Philippines were many and varied. In October of 1899 a force of 356, led by Lieutenant Colonel Elliott, captured an insurgent stronghold at Novaleta, a few miles south of Cavite. The attack was planned as a diversionary tactic, designed to draw attention from a movement by U.S. Army troops against Cavite Viejo. But a report of the action tends to belie that it was purely diversionary in nature.

Because of the rough terrain, Elliott divided his command into two small battalions; one under the command of Captain Henry C. Haines, and the other under Captain B. H. Fuller. Advancing with the two battalions abreast, the command soon plunged into a dense undergrowth of thorn bushes in a low, marshy area, intersected by tide-water runs. The forward scouts had advanced about a mile when the well-hidden enemy opened up on them with heavy fire. Deploying both units, Elliott slowly advanced against the stubborn enemy. After three hours of hard fighting, the command finally broke through the concealing undergrowth. The objective, a village of nipa huts dominated by a large blockhouse, lay some 1,000 yards to the front, across open rice fields. Approximately 250 yards from the enemy's main entrenchments lay a small dyke and a line of old abandoned rifle pits. Establishing a base of fire along the edge of the jungle, the Marines, sometimes armpit deep in mud and water, advanced across the open rice paddies to the protection of the dyke.

Lieutenant Colonel Elliott reported the final phase of the attack as follows:

"Here the men were gotten fairly well straightened out, but were unable to charge immediately, as they were absolutely 'blown' from the fast pace and heavy ground.

"Four buglers sounded the charge . . . and they finally broke forward in a dogged advance, without cheering, as they were breathless, and the enemy abandoned the entire length of the trenches, but kept up a short fire from nipa huts from the further side of the narrow unfordable river which was directly in front of their works. The men of the right wing were the first in the works, as those on the left were blocked by lagoons and thorn bushes. The blockhouse was burned, as were all nipa huts from which firing was seen, and which were used by the garrison as barracks or shelter. A great deal of personal bravery among men and officers was shown, even up to reckless bravado, of which I highly disapproved, and I believe they will fight as well but with better judgement in the future."

In addition to the incessant jungle fighting, Marines were called upon to perform such duties as port captains, district commanders, customs inspectors, internal revenue collectors and military governors. In many instances it was necessary to completely reorganize entire districts and institute a new form of government. A typical example was reported by Captain H. L. Draper who, with a force of 120 Marines, was ordered to occupy Olongapo, a town north of Subic Bay, and clear the surrounding area of insurgents.

"A patrol system has been inaugurated in and about Olongapo. This insures peace and tranquility to the town. No more robberies by *ladrones* have occurred since this was established, and the population of the town is increasing daily by the ingress of men from the insurgents and families from the mountains.

"To promote the general welfare and secure the regular routing of peaceful life for the Filipinos in Olongapo, I held an election for municipal officers. . . . This election was held with the usual Filipino ceremonies, secret ballot, and resulted in the election of men in whom I have some confidence for president, vice-president, and secretary of Olongapo. . . . The officers were installed by me in their offices with due and appropriate ceremonies."

"After announcing the result of the election, I made a speech to the newly elected officials and electors to the effect that my government guaranteed to every man the fruit of his own toil, the rights of life and liberty and the pursuit of happiness, and the right to worship God as he saw fit, and only demanded in return obedience to the laws.

"I find that the new government works excellently. . . . The municipal government having recommended, I have appointed five native policemen, uniformed in machetes and old full-dress helmets, so that they may be distinguished by the patrols at night.

"Since my arrival here forty families have moved into Olongapo, where no person lived before; government has been organized, the peaceful people are protected; an English school has been started, with Lieutenant Thorpe as teacher; rations have been issued to save from starvation some of the natives; medical attendance and medicines have been supplied when needed, and a constant scouting of the surrounding country maintained."

Of all the locations in which Marines served in the Philippines, there was none which has remained as vividly, or as long, in the memories of Marines as Samar.

By 1901 the areas occupied by Marines had been fairly well cleared of insurrection. But far to the southeast, on the island of Samar, the *insurrectos* still terrorized the countryside. On September 28, the soldiers of Company "C" of the U.S. Army's Ninth Infantry were suddenly attacked without warning as they ate their dinner in their mess hall. In a few, short, bloody minutes the attacking band of Moros had massacred the entire company.

The military district commander called for immediate reinforcements, and a battalion of Marines was withdrawn from Cavite to fill the request. The battalion was commanded by a major answering to the multi-syllable and somewhat redundant name of Littleton Waller Tazewell Waller. He was a rather short man, possessed of a large military moustache and an even larger military ego. One of his caustic fellow officers would later write of him, "He was the only officer I've ever known who was really as good as he said he was." Possibly somewhere behind this observation lies the explanation of the reason he never became Commandant. In most respects he had a better claim to that position than any of his contemporaries.

The battalion arrived at the southern coastal town of Basey at the end of October. For the next two weeks the Marines sent large combat patrols into the surrounding jungle to track down the guerrillas, who usually operated in small bands. As a result of this daily harassment, the rebellious Moros gradually withdrew from the southern coastal area of Samar. By the middle of November they had fallen back to their jungle stronghold, a honeycomb of caves in the face of the towering cliffs above the Sojoton River. The Moros considered their retreat impregnable. To reach the caves, an attacker had to climb the sheer face of the cliffs which rose over two hundred feet above the river. Ascent could only be made by means of bamboo ladders and narrow ledges. At the top of the precipice the Moros had suspended tons of rock in large cages, held in place by vines. A few blows from a machete, and the mass of rock would be sent cascading down the face of the cliff, smashing anyone below.

Determined to rout the insurrectionists from their last stronghold, Waller made plans for an attack on the position. Dividing his force into three groups, he sent two of them overland by different routes. The other he embarked in boats for movement up the river. The plan called for the three groups to join in the vicinity of the objective for a combined attack against the stronghold. However, due to a misunderstanding on the part of Captain David D. Porter, the two land columns met and pushed on without waiting for Waller. The force soon came upon the main trail leading to the enemy's outlying position, across the river from the Sojoton cliffs. Advancing rapidly, the Marines charged into the camp only to find the Moros had fled, leaving behind their still cooking food.

Moving to higher ground, the point of the column discovered two other camps on the opposite side of the river, about 150 yards away. The enemy, busily preparing food, were unaware of the surveillance of the Marines. Captain Porter cautiously deployed his column into a firing line and emplaced a Colt automatic gun. At a signal from Porter, every available weapon in the force opened fire. Taken completely by surprise, the Moros fled, leaving 30 dead sprawled throughout the camp site. Porter then led his men down to the bank of the river where they crossed, using two abandoned dugout canoes and a raft.

Towering above them were the cliffs of the impregnable stronghold the Moros had spent three years in preparing. In two of the fiercest hours of fighting in the Philippine Insurrection, the Marines scaled the cliffs and drove the insurgents from their positions. It was a day long to be remembered. But, thirty days later some of the Marines who had scaled those cliffs were to pass them on a march that would be even longer remembered.

The march was the result of a request by the military district commander, Army Brigadier General Jacob M. Smith. General Smith asked the Marines to determine a route across Samar for a telephone line which would connect the east and west coasts.

To make the march, Major Waller selected 50 Marines and 20 natives to help carry supplies. The detachment moved out of Lanang by boat on the morning of December 28. The plan was to work up the Lanang River as far as possible, then to strike out across country. Due to the many rapids they encountered as they worked upstream, the Marines soon had to leave their boats and continue on foot.

Crossing and recrossing the swollen jungle streams, the Marines doggedly plunged on through the almost impassable jungle. No food was to be found along the route of march, and by the end of the first week their rapidly dwindling supply of rations was becoming a critical problem. Many of the men, their clothing continually wet from fording streams and the incessant tropical rain, were becoming ill. A three day march across rugged volcanic mountains had cut many of the men's shoes to ribbons and left their feet swollen and bleeding.

After holding a conference with his officers, Major Waller decided that the shortest way out of the difficulty was to push on to the west. Selecting Lieutenant Frank Halford and 13 of the men who were in the best condition, Waller started west. The remainder of the group he placed in charge of Captain Porter, with orders to follow slowly along the trail. Waller's intention was to reach the west coast as quickly as possible and send a relief expedition back for Porter's group. Late in the afternoon of the next day, Waller and his men came upon a native shack. Rushing the shack, they captured five natives. One of the natives was persuaded to act as a guide, and the party pushed on, reaching the coast on January 6. The condition of the group when they finally reached the coast is indicated by a portion of Waller's official report of the march.

"Most of them had no shoes. Cut, torn, bruised and dilapidated, they had marched without a murmur for 29 days." The march had covered over 190 miles.

A relief party, which, despite his poor condition, Waller joined the following day, was dispatched immediately to locate Captain Porter's group. The group searched for nine days without success. On the tenth day, Major Waller was stricken with fever and had to be carried out of the jungle to the hospital at Basey.

The first day after Waller pushed on to the west Porter continued to follow his trail, as he had been ordered. By nightfall it was evident to Porter that many of the men were unable to continue, even at the slow pace he had set. Leaving Lieutenant A. S. Williams in charge of the men, Porter selected seven Marines and six natives and started back to Lanang to get help. Fearing that starvation was certain if they remained in camp, Lieutenant Williams and his men slowly followed Captain Porter's trail toward Lanang. One by one the men dropped by the side of the trail. The native carriers became mutinous and four of them attacked Williams with bolos. The lieutenant killed two of them with his pistol, and the other two disappeared into the jungle. On the morning of January 18 a relief party, sent by Captain Porter, reached Williams' small group of survivors and brought them back to Lanang. Despite Williams' superhuman efforts, ten Marines had been left along the trail.

For many years after this tragic episode the officers and men of the Corps paid a traditional tribute to the courage of the survivors of the march by rising in their presence with the following words: "Stand, Gentlemen, he served on Samar!"

Incident to the operations in the Philippines, the comic opera capture of Guam was to play a far greater part in history than could be visualized at the time. As a result of the blissful ignorance of the Spanish governor that his country was at war with America, Guam was painlessly acquired as a coaling station for the U.S. Navy, and garrisoned by Marines. At the end of the war, the United States bought the island from Spain for a nominal sum. But the U.S. had no interest in the rest of the Marianas Islands which Spain, intent on liquidating her deteriorating empire, sold to Germany in 1899. The opportunistic Japanese seized the German-owned island early in World War I.

While the Marines and the U.S. Army were having their troubles in the Philippines, great ferment was taking place in the Far East. In June of 1900 the so-called Boxer Rebellion broke out in China.

The Boxers comprised a loosely knit society of highly nationalistic Chinese who were determined to expel all foreign elements from their country. There were many such elements. Because of the enormous profits to be realized in trade with China, practically every maritime nation of importance had obtained "concessions" in that country. With the increase of unrest in China, each of the interested nations established military guards for their embassies in Peking. When the Boxers rose in force, these guard detachments suddenly found themselves in a state of siege.

Because the guard detachments were small, the various countries concerned hurriedly organized an expedition for their relief. As a result, for the first time in history, Russian, Japanese and American troops marched into combat, shoulder to shoulder in a common cause.

Of the U.S. Marines involved in the rebellion, three names deserve mention. The successful defense of the American Legation was commanded by Captain John T. Myers, one of the ablest officers to ever wear the uniform. Under his command was a young, rather small and extremely hard-bitten private named Dan Daly, who earned the first of his two Medals of Honor during the affair.

The other was a brilliant young lieutenant by the name of Smedley D. Butler, who was to twice win the Medal of Honor— and end his Marine Corps career under house arrest.

But the ultimate destinies of these men lay far in the future as they marched inland from the China coast, brushing aside fantastic numbers of poorly armed, poorly organized and wholly untrained Chinese Boxers.

The *dénouement* of this incident was anticlimactic. The beleaguered legations held out with no particular difficulty. When the relieving force arrived, Smedley Butler scaled the city wall and forced the main gate to admit the column. For that he was breveted to the rank of captain at the age of 20. Twenty-five years, several wars and two Medals of Honor later, he was fired as head of the Philadelphia Police Department.

There will always be argument among Marines as to the substance of the contribution Smedley Butler made to the Marine Corps. But few, if any, would deny the statement that he probably contributed more than any other individual to its colorful reputation. As he led his men in the mopping up operations of China's Imperial City, the day was not far distant when he would begin to establish that reputation.

9

★　　★　　★　　★　　★

The "Banana Wars"

FOR THE FIRST thirty years of the twentieth century, with the interruption of a World War, most of the Marine Corps spent most of its time in Latin America and the Caribbean. The victory over Spain had ushered in an era of "Yankee Imperialism," and the spirit of Manifest Destiny, long dormant, was once more abroad in the land. The phrase that had served as a rationalization for the conquest of Texas and California, now served as an excuse for a "large policy" in the Caribbean.

The intervention of the United States in Panama in 1903 constituted one of the less savory incidents in our history. It also caused our motives to be suspect throughout Latin America for several decades to come.

The United States, President Theodore Roosevelt in particular, was extremely anxious to obtain a concession to land through which to build a canal across the Isthmus of Panama. The area then belonged to the South American Republic of Colombia. Through diplomatic channels, a treaty was drawn up between the two nations. Colombia agreed to lease the land for $10,000,-000, plus an annual rental of $250,000. The U.S. promptly ratified the treaty, but the legislature of Colombia, kept stalling and finally adjourned without passing the necessary legislation.

There followed some plain and fancy finagling on both diplomatic and political levels. For some time an abortive movement had been brewing in Panama to revolt against Colombia, and set up an independent republic. The leader of this movement, Dr. Manuel Amador-Guerrero, visited Washington in the fall of 1903, and is known to have called at the White House. Another visitor was Colonel Philippe Bunau-Varilla, the representative of a French company which had a similar concession and was anxious to liquidate its assets. While it can not be said that President Roosevelt played an active part in fomenting the revolt that ensued, he certainly did nothing to discourage it. Bunau-Varilla contributed $100,000 to the Amador cause with the understanding he would be granted full powers to negotiate a treaty with the United States, should the revolution succeed.

When the revolt broke out early in November, it just so happened that several U.S. warships were within easy steaming distance of the area. It also just so happened that an expeditionary battalion of Marines was standing by in the Caribbean. Thus, when Colombia attempted to send troops to put down the revolt, American forces, under the pretense of protecting American lives and property, would not permit them to land. The United States then promptly recognized the independence of Panama. Shortly thereafter the U.S. concluded a Canal Zone treaty with the government of the new republic, on the same terms originally offered Colombia.

Before it had been in office a year, the Amador government was threatened by revolution which, collaterally, threatened the security of American lives and property. Marines therefore remained in Panama for many years, preserving law and order, patrolling the Canal Zone—and incidentally discouraging any ambition on the part of Colombia to reconquer her lost province.

The aspect of U.S. intervention in Cuban domestic affairs differed essentially from its intervention in the affairs of other Caribbean countries. This island nation which had been turbulent for two centuries under Spanish rule, could hardly be expected to achieve political maturity overnight.

The Treaty of Paris, which formally concluded the Spanish-American War, ceded Cuba to the United States as a territorial possession. Under international law, the island belonged to the U.S. on the same basis as Ceylon belonged to Britain, Madagascar to France, or Java to the Netherlands. When the United States gave Cuba her independence in 1901, this country assumed certain obligations which were specified in what was known as the Platt Amendment. This amendment was subsequently written into the Constitution of the Republic of Cuba. It read: "The Governor of Cuba consents that the United States may exercise the right of intervention for the preservation of Cuban independence, the maintenance of government adequate for the protection of life, property and individual liberty, and for discharging the obligations with respect to Cuba imposed by the Treaty of Paris on the United States, now to be assumed and undertaken by the government of Cuba."

It took a considerable amount of "intervention" for the preservation of Cuban independence. Between 1906 and 1917 Marines were required to step into Cuban domestic affairs on eight different occasions. Notable among these were those with the Army of Cuban Pacification, during the Negro Rebellion and the Sugar Intervention. Depending upon the situation at the time, the strength of Marine Corps units in Cuba varied from a brigade of 3,000 to a company of 25. As a part of the Army of Cuban Pacification in 1906, a brigade under the multi-named Colonel Waller garrisoned no less than 24 stations throughout the island.

During the Negro Rebellion of 1912, a provisional regiment was assigned to troublesome Oriente Province. Their mission consisted primarily of maintaining law and order in the towns throughout the province, and guarding mining property, sugar plantations and railroads against the frequent raids of the insurgents. The Cuban government specifically requested Marine guards for each of their railroad trains in the area. For four months Marines rode on every train that moved. Six months after peace had been restored and the Marines removed from

Cuba, the Navy Department received an itemized bill from the railroad for transportation of the Marine guards. "It amounted," the Navy Comptroller said, "to a hell of a lot of railroad tickets!"

In 1912 the Marines paid one of their many return visits to Nicaragua. This time it was to safeguard the country's only railroad, and to maintain some semblance of stability in an area uncomfortably close to the soon-to-be-completed Panama Canal. Nicaragua was torn by one of its perennial revolutions, with both parties seeking control of the railroad. After a few trains had been destroyed and several stretches of track torn up, the United States became interested.

Ships' detachments proved inadequate for a task of this magnitude, and a Marine expeditionary battalion of 354 men was sent up from Panama. The battalion, which was commanded by the energetic and somewhat flamboyant Major Smedley D. Butler, arrived on August 14. Whether or not it was here that he first earned his nickname of "Old Gimlet Eye" is uncertain. But it is certain that this particular operation marked his emergence as a colorful character in the eyes of the country at large. Newsmen found him to be good copy—so much so that one wrote a series of feature articles about him, describing all sorts of bizarre goings-on. No doubt many of them were true, but whether he actually settled one critical issue by grabbing a recalcitrant native general by the moustache in front of his troops remains a matter of conjecture.

In any event, Butler carried out his assignment quickly and effectively. Upon its completion, the Marines were promptly withdrawn, except for a small guard detachment permanently stationed at the U.S. Legation in Managua. The eventual withdrawal of this detachment in 1925 was to lead to the worst civil war in Nicaragua's history.

It has always been difficult for the people of the United States to understand the frequency of revolutions in Latin American countries. The inclination is to attribute the reasons to unstable temperament and political immaturity. The basic cause, however, has been a concept of government diametrically different from ours.

For many years in Latin American countries, profit was tacitly recognized as being correlative with the power of a high position. This fact was faced realistically. The Chief of State sought that position in order to profit from the national treasury. His followers backed him for whatever gain they might be able to realize in lesser governmental positions.

For the most part, U.S. interventions in Latin America were minor matters of short duration, usually localized. Since the Navy made a practice of keeping warships within easy reach of potential trouble spots, it was usually a simple and expeditious matter to land a ship's detachment of Marines, restore order, then pull out in a matter of a few days. Because foreign interests in these countries were generally limited to the coastal regions, it was seldom necessary to push far inland.

However, when Woodrow Wilson became President, he inaugurated the policy of not recognizing a government unless it came into power through constitutional means. Since many revolutionists paid mere lip service to constitutionality, the picture became considerably complicated. Lack of U.S. recognition was a severe, and often fatal, handicap to any Latin American administration. Many times it resulted in an overthrow by still another revolutionary faction, with no more claim to constitutionality. Thus Marine intervention became more than a simple matter of restoring law and order, then withdrawing to leave the stronger native faction to run its own country. In many instances the U.S. assumed the responsibility for insuring, by one means or another, that the government in power achieved at least the appearance of constitutionality. All too often the United States had to maintain troops on the scene to protect such a government against die-hard opposition.

It was such a situation that caused our intervention in Mexico in 1914.

For many decades our relations with our immediate neighbor to the south had been tranquil. President Porfirio Diaz had made himself an effective dictator, and ruled his country with an iron hand. All disorders, actual or incipient, were sternly suppressed by as much force as appeared necessary. Thus, the average Mexican, while lacking the rights and privileges that the citizens of a democracy take for granted, at least enjoyed a measure of domestic tranquillity for a change. However, advancing age loosened Diaz's firm grip, and he was finally ousted as the result of a revolution in 1911.

The immediate agent in Diaz's overthrow was one Francisco Madero, a capable man of liberal leanings and a friendly disposition toward the United States. Although he won power by revolution, he went through the motions of being constitutionally elected president to satisfy the Wilson administration, and the situation appeared most promising.

Unfortunately, as often happens in the wake of an overthrown dictatorship, other revolutionary factions were abroad in the land. Before Madero had time to accomplish much in the way of reforms, he was murdered by adherents of a general named Victoriano Huerta, who promptly proclaimed himself President, without even a gesture of becoming elected. This did not sit well with the Wilson administration, which refused to recognize him. Huerta did not like this refusal, and liked it less and less as months passed with no weakening in the U.S. position. International ill will was burgeoning while disorders spread throughout Mexico.

It became evident that serious trouble was all but unavoidable. To cope with the situation, the U.S. Navy stationed all available ships off various ports along both coasts of Mexico, with the Marine detachments alerted to land on short notice. Marine expeditionary forces were organized and standing by in both Panama and the southern United States, and one regiment was embarked with the fleet off Vera Cruz.

The U.S. Army had begun massing troops along the Rio Grande in case of border trouble. It had also organized an expeditionary force for possible use elsewhere.

The first overt trouble occurred at Tampico, where the governor seized and jailed the boat crew of a U.S. war vessel which had landed to obtain supplies. The men were shortly released, but Huerta adamantly refused to render the apologies considered appropriate to such an international incident. It appeared for a while that intervention would occur at this point. Before it did, focus of interest shifted to Vera Cruz. A report was received by the Navy that a German freighter was headed for that port, carrying a consignment of arms and ammunition to Huerta.

On April 21, the Marine regiment, which had been standing by with the fleet for over a month, was ordered ashore. Their mission was to seize the customs house and other water-front installations in order to prevent the landing of the cargo from the German ship. The Marines carried out their landing against no initial resistance. They were soon reinforced by the newly arrived contingent from Panama, and the ships' detachments from the fleet. When they started penetrating farther into the city to protect the approaches to their positions, they came under fire of increasing intensity.

It soon became apparent that the whole city would have to be taken under control if the water-front foothold was to be maintained. All the available Marines were rushed to the scene, and the Navy landed a sizeable contingent of sailors to back them up.

Some confused street fighting followed, with much sniping at the troops from windows and roof tops. This entailed the laborious process of searching all the houses along several lines of advance, ferreting out snipers and confiscating all firearms. Inevitable casualties resulted and medals were awarded. By the standards of later wars, the casualties suffered would not be considered as severe. By the same standards, awards of the Medal of Honor, that being the only combat decoration the United States bestowed at the time, might well be considered excessive.

In any event, the job was done in short order. The city had been secured, order restored, and a system of strong points established to guard the inland approaches when the Army contingent reached the scene on April 28 to take over a share of the burden.

The arrival of these troops made possible relief of the sailors, but only part of the Marines were withdrawn. Ships' detachments and other elements attached to the fleet returned to their regular duty stations. The Marine expeditionary force, now organized as a brigade, remained in occupancy along with the Army troops until late November when the Mexican political situation seemed reasonably stabilized.

The basic reason underlying our interventions in Caribbean and Central American countries can be stated quite simply; if we did not intervene somebody else would. The United States was not the only nation with citizens and investments to protect in that turbulent part of the world. For a European power to step in would not only violate the principle laid down by the Monroe Doctrine, but would also jeopardize the approaches to the Panama Canal; hence, it could not be tolerated. Since we would not permit European powers to intervene in the Western Hemisphere, it was up to us to intervene in their behalf. In effect, this was the policy laid down by Theodore Roosevelt during his administration and implemented by Woodrow Wilson when the situation demanded.

It was this so-called "dollar diplomacy" concept that underlay our operations in those two Caribbean nations, Haiti and the Dominican Republic. At the time these two countries were undoubtedly the two worst trouble spots in the Western Hemisphere.

No nation in modern times has experienced anything quite comparable to the chaos that afflicted Haiti during the 110 years of her independence prior to 1915. Indicative of these conditions is the fact that twenty-six individuals—two emperors, one king and twenty-three presidents—had succeeded each other to power. Many of them had died most unpleasantly. It is a matter of record that only one of the 26 voluntarily retired at the end of his term.

The situation that made such a turnover possible was the existence in the northern mountains of a gentry known as Cacos. Commentators of the time have expended thousands of words trying to describe what constituted a Caco, without producing a very definitive answer. In general, they were a hereditary caste of bandit-soldiers that had been on the scene since the beginning of the republic. They were characterized by the fact that they would rather fight than work, and rather loot than fight. Thus, any presidential aspirant with some financial backing had only to make a tactful approach to a few Caco chiefs in order to muster a force which the incumbent usually found impossible to cope with. The Haitian Army consisted of an understrength mob of wretched conscripts who would desert, or go over to the opposition, at the promise of a small bribe.

The United States had particular cause for concern with the Haitian situation. Both France and Germany, as well as the U.S., had extensive investments in the country and were threatening intervention on their own behalf. In 1914 a German cruiser actually put a landing force ashore, only to learn of the outbreak of war in Europe. Upon receiving the news, the ship hurriedly sailed for home. Later France also landed troops, but withdrew them upon assurance that the U.S. would protect their interests. The constant presence of the U.S. Atlantic Squadron in adjacent waters lent considerable weight to such assurance.

Early in 1915, an aspirant by the name of Vibrun Guillaume Sam appeared on the presidential scene. The United States reposed high hopes in Sam. He had the appearance of a strong man, and he proved amenable to certain admonitions imposed upon him by Admiral Caperton, commanding the Atlantic Squadron. Unfortunately, instead of proving his country's salvation, Sam managed to serve only as a symbolic figure for the climax of Haiti's long reign of terror.

When he felt his grip slipping, Sam arbitrarily arrested two hundred members of what he deemed the opposition party and incarcerated them in the city prison at Port au Prince. He then issued orders that they were to be immediately shot, should matters become direly threatening. By July matters had become threatening, and Sam fled to sanctuary in the French Legation. Upon the flight of his chief, the commandant of the prison carried out his orders and murdered 167 of the prisoners in cold blood.

Repercussions were devastating. Once the initial shock had worn off, mob fury rose to a pitch hitherto unknown, even in Haiti. The mob stormed the French Legation, dragged Sam out from behind a dresser where he had hidden himself and literally tore him limb from limb. They also cut out his heart and ate it! They then lashed a rope around his torso and dragged it through the streets of the city.

Admiral Caperton, hurrying down from the north in his flagship, reached Port au Prince just in time to witness this interesting spectacle.

This was obviously the last straw, even apart from the violation of the French Legation's diplomatic sanctity. The Admiral promptly landed all available Marines from his ships' detachments, and hurriedly dispatched a request to the State Department for additional help. By early August a Marine expeditionary brigade had been landed at Port au Prince.

The occupation of Haiti took place with practically no resistance. The Marines were able to maintain order with very little bloodshed until Philippe Sudre Dartiguenave, a member of the Haitian senate, had been elected as the new president. Immediately thereafter, things took a decided turn for the worse.

In the "election" which made him the Chief of State, Dartiguenave had defeated a candidate by the name of Rosalvo Bobo who had been supported by the Cacos. When Bobo failed to gain power, the Cacos realized they could expect no support from the Haitian Government. In addition, it appeared doubtful that a worthwhile revolution could be engineered as long as the Marines occupied the principal towns. The immediate solution to this unacceptable state of affairs appeared to be a Caco rebellion, which immediately got underway.

Colonel L. W. T. Waller, commanding the brigade, took immediate steps to stamp out the rebellion, and established a regimental headquarters at Le Trou in the heart of the Caco district of northern Haiti. His initial step in the campaign was a peaceful attempt to dissuade the Caco leaders from their rebellious resistance to the American occupation. Obtaining funds from the Haitian government, Waller made a standing monetary offer to any Caco chief who would turn in his arms and disband his group. Although Waller's Marines managed to collect something over 1,000 rifles in the period of a month, the campaign was not very successful. Many bands of marauders continued to harass the countryside.

Having made what he considered a reasonable attempt to solve the problem by peaceful means, Waller next issued an edict declaring that all those who refused to disarm would be considered as bandits, and dealt with accordingly. Waller's plan for dealing with the bandits consisted of two techniques which he had successfully employed in the Philippines. One was to use heavily armed patrols to make a thorough reconnaissance of the area and hunt down the enemy. The other was a series of attacks on the known Caco strongholds.

For the next month Marine patrols probed deep into the bandit country, inflicting heavy losses on the Caco bands and keeping them on the move. Typical of the patrol action was a 6-day, 120-mile, reconnaissance led by the redoubtable Major Smedley Butler. The patrol, a mounted detachment consisting of 2 officers and 40 enlisted Marines, left Fort Liberte on the morning of October 22. Just after dark on the evening of the 24th, the patrol was crossing a river in a deep ravine when it was ambushed by approximately 400 Cacos.

The Cacos had selected an ambush site approximately 300 yards from one of their many forts. Concealing themselves in the dense underbrush, they were practically invisible in the darkness. The opening fusillade killed one horse and wounded two Marines. Butler's men, long since veterans of this type of fighting, quickly fought their way forward to a good defensive position. They remained there throughout the night, surrounded by the Cacos who kept up a continuous but poorly aimed fire. At the first light of dawn, the Marines launched a swift attack in three directions out of their defensive position. The Cacos, thoroughly confused by the sudden change in Marine tactics, scattered to all points of the compass, leaving eight dead and ten wounded behind.

Captain William P. Upshur and Lieutenant Edward A. Osterman, advancing from two directions with thirteen enlisted Marines, captured the Caco fort, putting the garrison to flight and killing fourteen more bandits. The Marines then proceeded to burn the fort and all the native houses to be found in the vicinity. In his report of the affray, Major Butler tersely summed up the action by noting, "Swept clear the district within one mile of all Cacos. Patrol proceeded." Total Marine casualties for the incident: three slightly wounded men; one dead horse.

By the end of October the vigorous patrol action of the Marines had driven the bulk of the Cacos into their last retreat—Fort Riviere. This most famous of all Caco retreats was an ancient French stronghold which had been the focal point of many a Haitian revolution. The massive fortress stood atop a four thousand-foot height in the mountain region south of the town of Grand Riviere. Surrounding the stone building were steep masonry walls which were seven feet thick and varied in height from twenty to twenty-five feet. The Cacos had long boasted that, with a garrison of one hundred men, they could stand off any military force in the world. On November 18 they were afforded the opportunity to make good their boast.

For several days Marine patrols had been closing in on the stronghold from different directions, cutting off all retreat. Colonel Waller had high hopes that this would be the final drive to crush Caco resistance. To command the forces that would make the attack on the stronghold, Colonel Waller selected Major Butler.

During the night of November 17, Butler quietly surrounded the fortress with his attack force, cautioning them against giving away their positions. Selecting Sergeant Ross L. Iams and Private Samuel Gross to accompany him, Butler began a stealthy reconnaissance of the enemy position, looking for a weakness in its defenses. As the three men crept through the dense underbrush along the steep fortress walls, it became apparent that it would be virtually impossible to scale them against determined resistance. Butler and his two scouts had almost completed a circuit of the fort when Sergeant Iams discovered a deep ditch leading into the undergrowth from the base of the wall. Quickly contacting Major Butler and Private Gross who were reconnoitering a short distance away, Iams led them to the ditch.

Upon closer examination, they discovered that the ditch led from the mouth of a drain, about three feet in diameter. Motioning Iams and Gross to keep a sharp lookout, Butler crawled into the drain and disappeared. In what seemed to the waiting lookouts to be an awfully long few minutes, the major emerged from the drain and the three Marines faded quietly into the underbrush.

Soon after daylight the next morning, upon Butler's signal, all units opened fire and began to advance toward the fort. Taken completely by surprise, some of the Cacos attempted to escape over the walls, only to be cut down by the accurate fire of the advancing Marines. Under cover of the confusion of the attack, Butler quickly led 27 hand-picked men to the drain opening. As the battle raged above them, Butler and his men crawled, single-file, through the drain which opened into the center courtyard of the fortress. Before the Cacos realized what was happening, the Marines were in their midst. In the epic hand-to-hand battle that followed, the Marines tore into the enemy with rifles, bayonets, machetes, clubs and rocks, until the last Caco had fallen.

The burial detail counted 72 dead Cacos, including seven known bandit chiefs. Miraculously, the attacking Marines suffered only a few minor wounds. Major Butler, Sergeant Iams and Private Gross, the first three men through the opening into the courtyard, received the Medal of Honor for their heroic actions.

Transporting a ton of dynamite to the scene, the Marines proceeded to demolish the fortress, and with it the last vestiges of Caco resistance. With the fall of Fort Riviere, the remaining Caco groups in northern Haiti disbanded, their members retiring into the mountains of the deep interior. For the first time in more than a century, the turbulent affairs of Haiti began to assume an unaccustomed state of peace.

With the threat of revolution allayed, at least for the time being, steps were taken to return the control of the country to native authorities. To provide for the maintenance of law and order, a constabulary called Gendarmerie D'Haiti was organized in November 1915. Since there were no Haitians with sufficient experience in such matters, the task of organizing and training the Gendarmerie fell to the Marines. This shortage of qualified Haitians resulted in an unusual situation. Until Haitians could be trained to fill officer billets in the Gendarmerie, it was necessary for Marines to assume the command functions. Such Marines enjoyed the unique distinction of serving as members of the military forces of the United States and Haiti at the same time. Even more unique was the status of the enlisted men assigned to the Gendarmerie. Initially, Gendarmerie officers of the rank of captain, or above, were Marine Corps officers. Gendarmerie officers of the rank of first or second lieutenant were Marine Corps sergeants. A sergeant in this category found himself in the unparalleled position of being both an enlisted man and an officer at the same time, in addition to serving two countries.

By February of the following year, the newly formed constabulary was sufficiently trained to assume their military and police duties. Gradually the Marines were withdrawn from Haiti, until only six hundred remained by the time the United States entered World War I.

For the next two years the island republic enjoyed a period of relative peace, at least to all outward appearances. But beneath the surface smoldered ever-increasing dissatisfaction with the policies of the Haitian administration. Cause of much of the dissatisfaction was the *corvée,* a system of legally enforced labor which the Haitian peasants found extremely distasteful. The *corvée* was used by the administration as a means of providing free manual labor for an ambitious public highway program. All Haitian men were required to either pay a road tax, or work out the amount of their tax as a laborer on a road gang. From their reactions it was apparent that neither course of action appealed to the Haitians.

The greatest resistance to the *corvée* was found in the east central part of the country where a Caco chief by the imposing name of Charlemagne Peralte was busily engaged in generating a revolt. Charlemagne began by organizing small groups of hill bandits under his leadership. Finding that his organization failed to grow fast enough to suit him, he began recruiting disgruntled peasants. Eager for still further expansion, he began recruiting any peasants who happened to be available, utilizing a method that was both simple and highly successful. The prospective recruit was approached by one of Charlemagne's recruiters and given his choice of two alternatives—either join the group, or be shot. By the late fall of 1918, Charlemagne's followers membered approximately 3,000, and he had succeeded in terrorizing most of northern Haiti, which included one fifth of the population of the entire country. With the peasants abandoning their land for the protection of the towns, a serious shortage of food supplies soon developed and the uprising began to assume the proportions of a full scale revolution.

By the spring of 1919, the revolt had reached a point where the Gendarmerie was no longer able to cope with it alone. A belated request for assistance was made to the Marine Brigade. On March 25, four companies of Marines from the Seventh Regiment at Guantanamo Bay, Cuba, were transferred to Haiti to aid the desperate Gendarmerie.

With the coming of summer, the Marines and the Gendarmerie carried on an intensive campaign against the bandits. During July, August and September, eighty-three encounters took place with the Cacos. Several shooting encounters also took place between the Marines and the Gendarmerie. Because of almost complete lack of coordination at the higher echelons, there were many instances when the Marines were unaware that Gendarmerie patrols were operating in the same area. On a number of occasions patrols failed to recognize each other, and wound up in a casualty producing fire fight, much to the delight of Charle-

magne Peralte. Charlemagne would have had more cause for delight, and enhanced his probability of longevity, had he been
aware of the plans of Marine Sergeant Herman H. Hanneken.

Hanneken, then a captain in the Gendarmerie, had long been
convinced that the revolt could be brought to a speedy conclusion by the capture, or death, of Charlemagne. After considerable thought on the matter, Hanneken conceived a bizarre plot,
more likely to be found among the pages of a dime novel than
the staid chronicles of history.

After considerable undercover work, Hanneken managed to
arrange for a trusted Haitian civilian to organize his own Caco
band. With the connivance of Hanneken, the new bandit leader
soon earned himself a reputation as one of the most successful
"generals" in the area. Several times his mountain retreat was
attacked by Hanneken's *gendarmes* who always managed to
come off second best in the fight. Hanneken once led an attack
himself, then appeared in public for the next two weeks with his
arm in a sling, after circulating the report that he was wounded
during the attack. Soon after Hanneken was "wounded," the new
Caco chief became one of Charlemagne's favorites.

About the time the new bandit leader had appeared on the
scene, one of Hanneken's best *gendarmes,* posing as a renegade
Caco, joined Charlemagne's band. Within a few weeks, the *gendarme* had gained Charlemagne's confidence to the point where
he was acting as the bandit leader's adjutant.

When both his trusted adjutant and favorite "general" suggested there would be greater profit in attacking some of the
larger towns, Charlemagne agreed. He also agreed that the town
of Grand Riviere presented a likely objective, especially since
the Marine garrison had recently been reduced to about one-
fourth of its normal complement. Calling his group leaders together in a council of war, Charlemagne laid out his plan to attack Grand Riviere. The attack was to be a concerted affair,
with about half of the bands under Charlemagne's leadership
taking part. Charlemagne would not take part in the attack him-

self, but would await the results in his mountain command post, not far from Grand Riviere.

Within a few hours after the council meeting, Hanneken received a message indicating the time of attack, and assurance that his plan was proceeding according to schedule. Hanneken then contacted the officer in charge of the Marines who had been withdrawn from Grand Riviere as an enticement to Charlemagne to attack. Plans were made to have the Marines arrive at the town just in time to reinforce the small garrison which had remained there.

On the day of the attack, Hanneken and his Gendarmerie lieutenant, Marine Corporal William R. Button, disguised themselves as Cacos by staining their bodies and donning Haitian clothes. Soon after daybreak, with Button and twenty of his *gendarmes* disguised as Cacos and heavily armed, Hanneken set out for Charlemagne's hideout. After passing many bandits who were on their way to attack Grand Riviere, the group was met at a prearranged spot by the *gendarme* who was Charlemagne's adjutant. Acting as guide, the *gendarme* led the group to a spot approximately a mile from Charlemagne's command post. While Hanneken and his men concealed themselves in the woods, the *gendarme* returned to the camp and informed Charlemagne that a group had arrived from Grand Riviere with news of a great victory. Charlemagne directed that the messengers be brought to him at once.

Returning to Hanneken's group, the *gendarme* gave them the proper countersign for answering the challenges of the five outposts which guarded the trail leading to the command post. With the *gendarme* in the lead, Hanneken and his disguised "Cacos" started up the trail. The first outpost became very excited at the news of the bandit victory and let them pass without bothering to ask them for the password. The second outpost, which was made up of about forty Cacos, challenged the group, but were satisfied with the countersign they received from Hanneken. The third and fourth outposts were also passed without incident. At the final outpost a few casual remarks, passed between the *gen-*

darmes and some of the bandits, aroused the outpost leader's suspicion. Drawing his pistol, he challenged Hanneken who gave the proper countersign, then, feigning exhaustion, staggered past the leader. The leader then grabbed Corporal Button, who was directly behind Hanneken, and demanded to know where Button had obtained the new automatic rifle he was carrying. Button, who fortunately spoke the Haitian dialect without a trace of accent, told him that he had taken it from a Marine he had killed during the attack on Grand Riviere. Apparently satisfied by Button's explanation, the outpost leader allowed the group to pass.

According to the *gendarme,* the area surrounding the command post contained approximately 200 Cacos. As Hanneken's group approached the center of the camp, the *gendarme* pointed out Charlemagne who was standing beside a fire talking to three men. Noticing the group moving toward him, Charlemagne broke off his conversation and watched intently as they approached. When Hanneken and Button were about 15 paces from him, Charlemagne suddenly became suspicious and shouted a warning. The shout had barely cleared Charlemagne's throat when Hanneken sent a pistol shot crashing into his body, killing him instantly. As Hanneken fired, Button opened fire with his automatic rifle, killing the three Cacos who had been talking with Charlemagne. The remainder of Hanneken's group unleashed a hail of fire at any target that presented itself. In less than a minute 10 Cacos had been killed, the remainder bolting for cover in the surrounding brush.

Hanneken quickly organized his group into a defensive perimeter and spent the long night successfully repelling several determined attacks. The following morning the group made their way to Grand Riviere, taking Charlemagne's body with them for positive identification. As Hanneken later told an acquaintance, he had gone to a lot of trouble, and wanted to be absolutely sure that he had killed the right man.

While Hanneken led his group into Charlemagne's stronghold, the reinforced garrison at Grand Riviere had repulsed the attack against the town. Over seventy bandits were killed and many more wounded in what turned out to be the most disastrous raid ever made by the Cacos. Both Hanneken and Button were awarded the Medal of Honor for "Extraordinary heroism and conspicuous gallantry." Not long after Sergeant Hanneken was given a spot promotion to second lieutenant.

With the death of Charlemagne, banditry declined rapidly in the northern area, soon to rise again in eastern Haiti under a new leader. Only by continuous patrolling and constant pressure by the Marines was it eventually wiped out. As conditions continued to improve, the Marine Brigade, which had included 83 officers and 1,261 enlisted men during the height of bandit activity, was gradually reduced. By 1924 the strength had dwindled to about 500 who remained to support the Gendarmerie during emergencies. After a brief flare-up in 1929, the Brigade took no further part in Haitian affairs beyond their mission of training the Gendarmerie. But it was not until August 15, 1934, that the Marines were finally withdrawn from the country.

Coincident with operations in Haiti, the Marine Corps was also involved in the U.S. intervention of the neighboring Dominican Republic which occupies the eastern two thirds of the same island. The causes underlying the intervention and the mission of the Marines bore a marked similarity to those of the Haitian situation. The Marine command, led by Colonel Joseph H. Pendleton, carried the ponderous title, "Provisional Detachment, U.S. Expeditionary Forces, U.S. Naval Forces Operating Ashore in Santo Domingo." With a peak strength of 1,338 Marines, the force's first major task concerned the putting down of a revolution in 1916. Having properly disposed of the revolutionists, the Marines spent the next eight years chasing bandits, training the Guardia Nacional, Santo Domingo's counterpart of the Haitian Gendarmerie, and playing a major role in the governmental administration of the country. American administrators, many of whom were Marines, laid great stress upon improving the public health, education, public works and the financial condition of the Republic. The ultimate success of these endeavors is indicated by the final report of Marine Brigadier General Harry Lee, Military Governor of the Dominican Republic from 1922 to 1924.

"The occupying force assumed control of a state rife with revolution, banditry, ungoverned and mismanaged. We left a state enjoying peace, and with a loyal and well-developed military force, with fine roads, many schools, a fine military hospital, and, in short, with every promise for a future stable government under Dominican rule."

The years of the Banana Wars were extremely important ones as far as the Marine Corps was concerned. In the many occupations of Latin American and Caribbean countries, the Corps had been called upon to provide the major portion of the forces employed. This demand for forces had necessitated maintaining several expeditionary brigades outside the continental limits of the United States. As a result, the Marine Corps, which had never exceeded a strength of 3,000 during the first century of its existence, had grown to 11,000 by 1917.

The advance base concept, which was to one day provide the basis for one of the most revolutionary doctrines of modern warfare, had its origins in the capture of Guantanamo Bay. Both in Cuba and the Philippines the lack of a trained, ready force to undertake amphibious operations in conjunction with the fleet had demonstrated a serious shortcoming in the military forces of the United States. As early as 1902 the Marine Corps had organized an advanced base regiment for training with the fleet. In 1910 the Marine Corps Advanced Base School, the first school in the country devoted purely to the problems of amphibious warfare, was established at New London, Connecticut. Forty years later the product of such training and experimentation was destined to become the deciding factor in the Pacific phase of the greatest war in history.

New weapons, new equipment, and seventeen years of constant duty under field conditions, had provided an unprecedented opportunity to develop new tactics and improve combat efficiency to a point never before attained. According to a remark made during this period by ex-President Theodore Roosevelt, the three most efficient military-constabulary organizations in the world were the United States Marine Corps, the French Foreign Legion and the Canadian Northwest Mounted Police, each supreme in its own particular field. For the Marine Corps, the time was rapidly approaching when this supremacy was to be put to the acid test on the battlefields of France.

★ ★ ★ ★ ★

10

World War I

THE AMERICAN PEOPLE, in general, demonstrated little enthusiasm for their country's continual occupation with the Banana Wars. Only partially convinced of the necessity of such interventions, they were of the opinion that even these minor league wars were bad enough. Americans, particularly, wanted no part of what was coming to be called, and would continue to be called for the next quarter century, "the World War."

In 1916 Woodrow Wilson was re-elected President partly as the result of the slogan, "He kept us out of war." But despite public sentiment and the best of intentions, it became increasingly apparent that no power on earth could keep us out of war, and still allow America to retain a shred of national honor and prestige. Within the military service, awareness of the inevitable was especially acute. Marine officers began to think seriously about what part the Corps might be expected to play in the coming struggle. Would it have an opportunity to distinguish itself by the brilliant performance of a specialized function, as at Guantanamo Bay?

Actually the Marine Corps performed no special function in World War I, yet it emerged from the war with its prestige and popularity immeasurably heightened. The role it was required to play, however, proved to have a serious drawback. The diversion of Marines into other fields of activity greatly retarded the orderly development of the Corps' amphibious function.

The declaration of war by the United States on April 6, 1917, found the Marine Corps' strength at approximately 13,000, hardly enough men to furnish an adequate police force for New York City. A considerable proportion of this number was busily engaged in the West Indies.

With our actual entry into war, the policy makers felt the urgent need of sending at least a token force to France at the earliest possible moment. The object being to bolster the sagging morale of the Allies. But what were we going to use for troops? The Army had a few well trained regiments of regulars, but far too few. The National Guard held promising potentialities, and the draft would supply plenty of men—some time. But some time was not an acceptable answer to a need which was immediate.

The term "well trained" applies only in a broad sense. The troops available were well disciplined and thoroughly grounded in military fundamentals. But there was nothing in our national military experience to prepare them for the conditions and techniques of the sort of war they would be called upon to fight. This was especially true of the Marine Corps. Chasing bandits, and discouraging an occasional Latin-American revolution could hardly be looked upon as cogent preparation for trench warfare in Europe. Additional specialized training was obviously required. Until adequate facilities and experienced instructors could be found in this country, it was decided to provide this training abroad where the Allies already had such facilities.

The Army mobilized its best units for immediate overseas service. The Marine Corps, the nation's "force in readiness," lived up to its slogan by fielding a war-strength regiment. This was accomplished, as in the time of Archibald Henderson, by stripping posts and stations and ships' detachments of every available man. In addition, all men possible were withdrawn from Haiti and the Dominican Republic where the Marine-trained native constabularies were at last showing signs of becoming effective. This regiment was designated the 5th Marines, and was among the first U.S. units to reach France, landing at St. Nazaire on June 27, 1917.

Later, as the Corps' training program slipped into high gear and strength allowances were raised, a second regiment, the 6th Marines, and a machine gun battalion followed. Each of these units was built around a cadre of regulars, filled to strength by comparatively new recruits. In France these units were joined with the 5th Marines to form the 4th Marine Brigade, the largest tactical unit of Marines ever assembled up to that time. Together with the Third Army Brigade, they formed the U.S. 2d Division.

The advent of war raised the ceiling on the Marine Corps' authorized strength. By August 1917, it had risen to 30,000 and eventually reached an unprecedented 75,000, including 269 female reservists. But even such increased quotas proved wholly inadequate to cope with the vast influx of eager young men who, drawn by Marine prestige, clever recruiting methods and the exuberant patriotism of a somewhat naive era, flocked to the recruiting stations. This combination of conditions enabled the Marine Corps to exercise a much higher degree of selectivity than was possible for the other services. This applied not only to the high physical standards which had long been a Corps requirement, but to various other considerations as well. One individual who enlisted during that period wrote to his parents stating that of his group of 220 who had applied, only 16 were selected. Although this was before the days of intelligence and aptitude tests, recruiting sergeants had their own methods of insuring that only those applicants they personally approved met the required standards. One of the 220 who failed to meet the standards was a rugged-looking six-footer who gave every appearance of being a perfect physical specimen. He also gave evidence of not being on very intimate terms with soap and water. In answer to a direct question, he was unable to recall exactly when he had taken his last bath. The recruiting sergeant held a brief conference with the examining physician, who then gave the applicant a test for color blindness. Although the man had passed this same test an hour previously, he failed the reexamination miserably and had to be rejected for failing to pass the physical exam.

Upon acceptance, recruits were sent to one of the two Marine Corps recruit depots. Those from east of the Mississippi went to Parris Island, South Carolina, and those from the west to Mare Island, California. There the recruits entered an unfamiliar, rough and sometimes terrifying new world.

Exactly when and how the famous—or infamous—institution of Marine "boot" training developed can not be determined exactly. Prior to 1915 no standardized system of recruit training existed. The newcomers were assigned to certain duty stations, where they received their basic training in small increments. Under this system, recruits were often exposed to instructors with widely divergent ideas as to what constituted good training. However, in 1915 the installation at Parris Island, which the Navy had used as a disciplinary barracks, was turned over to the Marine Corps. Marine recruit training activities were centered there, and the institution of Boot Camp, in essentially its present form, had evolved by 1917.

The original plan for recruit training envisioned organizing recruits into standard companies, commanded by an officer and staffed by non-commissioned officers. Somewhere between the planning and the execution stage, the small Corps discovered that it could not spare key personnel on such a scale and still carry out its other commitments. For this reason, by mid-1917 the non-coms had taken over. Companies made up entirely of boots were commanded by a sergeant, with one or two corporals, or privates, as assistants. Normally there was one officer to a four-company battalion, and he confined himself primarily to administration.

Such responsibility called for commensurate authority. Thus the "D.I. at P.I."—Corps jargon for a Drill Instructor at Parris Island—evolved into an institution unique in our armed forces; a non-commissioned officer with a greater degree of direct con-

trol and authority over his men than most officers. Marine recruits learned early in their training that all beings, except themselves, are classified according to rank. At Parris Island, the
D.I. was junior only to God.

The training course was deliberately made tough and exacting.
The underlying motive was to effect a man's transition from
civilian to military life as fast and as thoroughly as possible.
Harsh disciplinary methods have sometimes been described as
sadistic by horrified civilians who can claim no personal experience, nor have any real conception of what such training is all
about. It is extremely significant that, with surprisingly few exceptions, men who have been through boot camp training are
extremely proud of their achievement. Normal individuals
emerge with a sense of accomplishment and a common bond
with their fellow Marines, achieved through the consciousness of
having survived a trying experience together. Analysts attempting to establish the reasons which make Marine Corps *esprit de
corps* the extraordinary force that it is, invariably cite boot camp
training methods more than any other factor.

From Parris Island most graduate boots were sent to the
newly acquired base in Quantico, Virginia, for advanced and
specialized training. There they were incorporated into new
regiments if any were forming or, after casualties in France began to mount, into replacement battalions. Some were sent directly from boot camp to the West Indies to relieve veteran
troops for combat service overseas. This arrangement proved to
have some unhappy results. Many of the newcomers were im-
mature in comparison with the experienced men they relieved.
They lacked the maturity and poise necessary to conduct themselves in the required manner. Many of them had enlisted with
the express purpose of fighting in France and were sorely dis-
contented to find themselves chasing bandits in the mountains
of the Dominican Republic and Haiti instead. There was a
rumor current at the time that boys caught enlisting under age
were made field musics—the Marine equivalent of bugler.
Those who failed to qualify on the rifle range were assigned as

cooks. While it is not possible to document the fact that such a system of job classification was used, many a World War I Marine will still testify that the Corps boasted the world's worst cooks and buglers during that era.

Although American troops continued to arrive in France in increasing numbers, it was apparent that the French and British held little confidence in their new allies, most of whom were still undergoing the process of advanced training. General Foch, Commander-in-Chief of the Allied forces, wanted to use the Americans to fill out his own ranks, incorporating U.S. units with understrength French divisions already in existence. Major General John J. Pershing, Commander-in-Chief of the American Expeditionary Forces, however, was adamant that the A.E.F. should operate as an integrated component of the allied command. After some extended controversy on the subject, Foch finally yielded.

Because of this difference of opinion, and possibly for other reasons, the Marine Brigade was not committed to combat until March, 1918, and then in a quiet sector southeast of Verdun. The plan was to break in the newcomers gently, orienting them by degrees to the peculiarities of trench warfare. The Marines soon grew restless. Nothing much happened beyond small-scale raids back and forth across "no man's land." This was not the Marines' idea of fighting a war. Indeed, there was no precedent in the history of warfare that quite paralleled the stalemate that had gradually developed on the Western Front between 1914 and 1918. As the result of bitter experience, both the Allies and the Germans had reached the point where they considered offensive warfare in the open a virtual impossibility.

The newly arrived Americans, their fresh viewpoint unmarred by this bitter experience, accepted this concept with reservations. No war in history had ever been won while the armies involved were lodged in a stalemate. If this war were ever to be won, the fighting must somehow be brought into the open. Across "no man's land" the Germans had finally arrived at the same conclusion. Knowing the Allies to be even more battered than themselves, they mustered all their strength in the Spring of 1918 for an all-out effort to break through.

Thanks to superior numbers, excellent planning and a high degree of tactical surprise, the Germans achieved their break-through in the Somme region. The British Fifth Army, bearing the brunt of the onslaught, was so shattered that it ceased to exist as a tactical force. The French on their flank, likewise battered, fell back, fighting in increasing disorder. By late May the German advance elements, with no organized resistance to their front, were approaching the Marne River, scene of their initial repulse in 1914.

This critical situation called for the Allies to throw in all the reserve they could muster. But General Foch had no such re-serves, except for the Americans in whom he reposed little con-fidence. But Foch had no choice; Pershing detailed the U.S. 2d Division, which included the 4th Marine Brigade, into the gap.

As the 9,444 Marines of the 4th Brigade moved up toward their assigned sector, they began encountering the war first hand. Down the Paris-Metz road streamed a column of pathetic refugees, fleeing the German advance with such household possessions as they could move. Mingled with them were the shattered elements of French combat troops, dirty, battle-shocked and weary. One of the high ranking French officers drew Captain Lloyd W. Williams aside, explained that a general retreat was in progress, and ordered the Marines to withdraw.

The Marine captain eyed the French officer in amazement. "Retreat, hell!" he exploded. "We just got here!"

When the head of the German column came in view, the advanced Marine elements hurriedly deployed along a low ridge, facing the enemy across a wide stretch of open countryside. The Marines opened fire as soon as they got into position. This seemingly premature action the veteran Germans interpreted as a sign of the jitters. In European warfare, small arms fire was not considered effective beyond a range of approximately 200 yards. European armies, since the days of Frederick the Great, had been taught to fire at an aiming point, rather than an individual foe. Many of them still used the system of a company or battalion aiming point, generally the knees of an approaching enemy column. Using this system, known as "the uniform dispersion of fire," the defending units were supposed to be able to establish a zone of protecting fire. The Marines had opened fire at a range of approximately 800 yards. Much to their bewilderment, the Germans soon discovered that they were sustaining casualties.

The Marine Corps' long preoccupation with training in rifle marksmanship was beginning to pay off in something besides mantelpiece trophies. The men lay coolly in their positions, rifle slings adjusted to their arms, estimating range and windage, carefully squeezing off aimed shots.

The Germans deployed, and as additional elements arrived, commenced a determined advance across the open ground. With their casualties mounting at an alarming rate, the Germans concluded that their opponents were armed exclusively with machine guns. Upon this startling conclusion, German officers gave orders to their troops to dig in, deciding to await reinforcements before proceeding with the attack.

The seemingly irresistible German surge had been halted, at least temporarily. With forward momentum lost for the moment, the time for a counterattack had come.

Key objective in the attack sector assigned the Marine Brigade was a patch of woods called the *Bois de Belleau*. All approaches to the objective were across a wide area of open ground, spotted with fields of waist-high wheat. The Germans had prepared trenches and machine gun nests in the wood's edge, and the Marines' first assault, which they made in line formation, was bloodily repulsed. On the next try they adopted a formation of aligned columns. Again casualties were heavy, but several elements over-ran the German forward positions and gained a foothold within the wood. Reinforcements poured in, while the Germans, still fighting desperately, began preparing the rocky, wooded terrain for a defense in depth.

What ensued was to a large degree prophetic of the type of

fighting which would fall to the lot of another generation of Marines in another war, fought half-way around the world. It became a bloody business of close-in slugging through brush-covered terrain, against a dug-in enemy, armed with automatic weapons. It took the Marines twenty days to secure the objective. On June 26, A.E.F. Headquarters received a rather cryptic message, "Woods now U.S. Marine Corps' entirely." When the Brigade emerged on the far side of Belleau Wood, it had written a new, bright chapter in the Corps' history. In appreciation of the achievement, the grateful—and somewhat surprised—French re-named the now battered patch of woodland *Bois de la Brigade de Marine.*

It was during this action that Gunnery Sergeant Dan Daly, the "quiet man" who had won two Medals of Honor, added a new phrase to U.S. military lore. Exhorting his platoon to jump off in the attack, Daly leaped out of the trench, bellowing, "Come on, you sons of bitches! Do you want to live forever?"

The price for Belleau Wood had been high. The Marines had suffered 55 per cent casualties: 1,062 killed and 3,615 wounded. But there was little rest for the weary, battered Brigade. The German advance had been definitely stopped. Now Allied strategy called for seizing the opportunity of throwing it into reverse, while the enemy was still off balance. Fresh replacements poured in to fill the casualty-depleted ranks. In mid-July the 2d Division was on the move again, this time to the sector north of Paris to attack the German salient extending to the Marne.

The action at Soissons was more spectacular than that at Belleau Wood, and in some respects bloodier. There was small consolation in the fact that it did not last as long. It took the form of a sweeping charge across open ground against entrenched positions. The U.S. troops, which included the First and Second Divisions, were assigned the key objectives. The casualties were nothing short of fantastic. The 2d Battalion, 6th Marines, commanded by Major Thomas Holcomb, suffered more than 50 per cent casualties in the 30 minutes required to secure its objective. Other units sustained comparable losses, with the Brigade casualties amounting to over 2,000 during the two days of intensive fighting. The two American divisions were given credit for spearheading the initial attack which started the general retreat of the German Army, that was to continue until the war was over.

On July 28, Brigadier General John A. Lejeune became the commanding general of the 2d Division, achieving the rare distinction of being the only Marine ever to command an Army division.

Under Lejeune, the division next saw action in the St. Mihiel offensive which began on September 12. During the four day battle, the division captured over 3,300 prisoners. At least 40 of these were credited to a German-born Marine, Sergeant Major William Ulrich of the 2d Battalion, 6th Marines. While reconnoitering a patch of woods, Ulrich's patrol surprised a detachment of 40 Germans who had fled when fired upon by the Marines. Much to the amazement of the remainder of the patrol, the Sergeant Major took out after the fleeing enemy, spouting a barrage of German at the top of his voice. In a few minutes he returned, herding the entire detachment before him, with their arms raised high above their heads. "They were willing to listen to reason," Ulrich explained to his commanding officer.

Next came the big offensive in the Meuse River-Argonne Forest area, with the objective of driving the Germans back far enough for the Allies to intercept the principal railway communications converging in the vicinity of Mezieres. The 2d Division, at the urgent request of Marshall Foch, was transferred to the Fourth French Army which had been assigned the sector west of the Argonne Forest.

The attack jumped off on September 26 and went well until the Fourth French came up against Blanc Mont Ridge, keystone of the German defenses in the sector. The 2d Division was assigned the task of taking the ridge and launched their assault on October 3, with the 6th Marines leading the attack. By nightfall the regiment had taken the first objective and Corporal John H. Pruitt and Private James J. Kelley, both members of the 78th Company, 2d Battalion, had earned two of the twelve Medals of Honor awarded to Marines during World War I.

The advance to the second objective was led by the 5th Marines the next day. October 4 proved to be the darkest day of the entire war for Marines. When the objective was finally taken, the 5th Marines had lost over 1,000 men, either killed or wounded in a single day's action. Blanc Mont fell to the 2d Division the following morning. The Marine Brigade, with 494 killed and 1,864 wounded in the week-long assault, received its third citation from the French Army.

For their final action of the war, the 2d Division returned to the Meuse-Argonne sector, this time as a part of the American First Army. Assigned to the center of the First Army sector, the division took part in the drive through the famed Hindenburg Line, which began on November 1 and lasted until the Armistice.

For so small a service, the Marine Corps' commitments during the war were indeed formidable. The terrible casualties suffered by the 4th Brigade necessitated a constant flow of replacements. Altogether 12 replacement battalions, roughly the equivalent of another brigade, were sent overseas. The occupation forces in Haiti and the Dominican Republic had to be maintained. In addition, at least a skeleton expeditionary force, prepared to cope with emergencies, was required in the U.S., in keeping with the Corps' primary mission. Then, in the summer of 1918, came orders to organize a second brigade for service in France.

This unit was designated the 5th Marine Brigade. As ultimately constituted, it consisted of the 11th and 13th Marines and the 5th Machine Gun Battalion. Like its predecessor, it was built around a cadre of veteran regulars beefed up by wartime volunteers, most of them fresh out of boot camp.

To obtain the nucleus of regulars, the Marine Corps again had to scrape the bottom of its manpower barrel. As before, the troops were drawn from far and wide; posts and stations in the U.S., ships' detachments, the Philippines, Guam, Hawaii, Haiti and the Dominican Republic.

The 5th Marine Brigade was organized at Quantico, Virginia, during the summer and early fall of 1918. The 13th Marines sailed for France on the 13th of September in a 13-ship convoy. According to a well-timed news release, the regiment was accompanied by 13 black cats as mascots and the crossing took exactly 13 days. The 13th Marines was commanded by the ubiquitous Colonel Smedley D. Butler who obviously had a fascination for the usually sinister number 13—and a shrewd eye for publicity.

The voyage was marred by two incidents which might have gone far toward weakening Butler's, and the regiment's, faith in the magic numeral. First, the terrible influenza epidemic of 1918 hit the convoy at sea, with the medics wholly unprepared to cope with it. By the time the 13th reached France, it had suffered nearly as many casualties from the disease as the 5th had at Belleau Wood. Second, the USS *Henderson*, carrying the 3d Battalion, was rammed and nearly sunk by another ship in the convoy the first night in the submarine zone. Indicative or not, fate had no happy lot in store for the 13th Marines.

The regiment landed in Brest in the rain. Those still on their feet marched six miles uphill, in the rain, under transport packs. At the end of the march they pitched pup-tents, in the rain, in one of the worst mud holes in France. Veterans who had been around that long swear that they had never encountered the like of Brest until the Bougainville and Cape Gloucester operations in World War II. In the tropics at least the rains were seasonal. At Brest that year, rain fell 358 days.

The 11th Marines followed in October, and the last component, the 5th Machine Gun Battalion, arrived almost simultaneously with the Armistice. With their arrival the Brigade was assembled as a unit—and the war was over.

What employment the high command had in mind for the 5th Marine Brigade has never been clear. The Brigade had been shipped overseas without being designated to assignment with any particular division, an exception to the usual procedure during the war. Certain optimists visualized the possibility of the unit being teamed up with the 4th Brigade to form a Marine division for the first time in history. But this was wishful thinking in its purest form. The A.E.F. could hardly have been enthusiastic about having a Marine division in the field, since the Army would have had to furnish the artillery, engineer and service components of such a division. Still less would it have been inclined to break up and reorganize one of the finest fighting outfits in France, the 2d Division.

The truth is that the 4th Marine Brigade, as part of the 2d Division, shared this sentiment. The Brigade had gained the reputation of being shock troops, fighting alongside two of the best regiments in the U.S. Army, the 9th and 23d Infantry. They had little desire to be brigaded with green troops, even though they were fellow Marines.

So the 5th Brigade remained an orphan, while the war it had come to fight folded up in its face.

There was one high officer in the A.E.F. who was more than willing to adopt the orphan. The Army's Major General James G. Harbord had commanded the 4th Brigade at Belleau Wood and Soissons. As a consequence, he held Marines in very high regard. Subsequently he had been promoted to command of the 2d Division, then kicked upstairs to command the Service of Supply. This was an unrewarding position which at the same time entailed great responsibility. General Harbord sorely needed reliable troops to guard his key depots. When he learned that a Marine brigade was available, he requested that it be assigned to him.

The 5th Brigade spent the long, dreary months between the Armistice and their eventual return Stateside guarding supplies for General Harbord, who rewarded their service with a fine letter of commendation.

From an overall standpoint, the experience which the Marine Corps gained in World War I was to be of little value in the development of their role in amphibious warfare. Perhaps the single exception to this broad generality lay in the genesis of Marine Corps aviation which occurred during the latter part of

the war. From this rather inauspicious beginning would evolve
the concept and doctrine of close-air support which was to play
such a vital part in the world's second global conflict, still some
23 years in the future.

When the United States entered the war, Marine Corps aviation consisted of five officers, thirty enlisted Marines and no
airplanes. During the summer of 1917, this group which had
been in training at the Naval Air Station, Pensacola, Florida,
was transferred to Philadelphia and organized the Marine Corps'
first aviation unit, known as the Marine Aeronautic Company.
By June of 1918, four tactical squadrons and a group headquarters had been formed with a total of 91 officers and 825
enlisted personnel. Since the Marine Corps still had no aircraft
of its own, training was accomplished by using both Army and
Navy facilities and planes.

In late July three squadrons and the group headquarters arrived in France and were designated the Day Wing of the Northern Bombing Group, based at Calais. The Group, which included a Night Wing composed of Navy squadrons, had been
assigned the mission of carrying out bombing operations against
German submarine bases along the English Channel.

The first bombing mission flown by the Marines, which took
place on October 1, had some unusual aspects as bombing missions go. The planes, which were De Havilands borrowed from
the French, carried loaves of French bread and canned goods
in place of their conventional bomb load. Their target, located
near the town of Staden, Belgium, was a French regiment which
had been without food for several days as a result of being cut
off by the Germans. Led by Captain Francis P. Mulcahy, the
flight made four successful "bombing" runs at an altitude of
100 feet in the face of heavy German machine gun and anti-
aircraft fire. The Marines returned for a repeat performance the
following day, again completing the mission without casualties.
As a result of the aerial food delivery, the beleaguered French
regiment was able to hold out until ground forces came to their
rescue.

By October 13 sufficient planes had been received for the Marines to make their first and, as it turned out, only raid against the German submarine bases. The day following the raid the Germans began their general withdrawal and abandoned their submarine bases as one of the first steps. Thus, after only one raid the Northern Bombing Group found itself without a mission, and was subsequently assigned in support of the British Army with which it operated until the end of hostilities. During this relatively short interval, the Marine Wing conducted numerous attacks against rear area targets and succeeded in shooting down four enemy planes.

By the time the Armistice was signed, Marine Corps aviation had grown from the original 35 to approximately 2,500 personnel and boasted 340 airplanes. As far as the air war was concerned, the score wound up a tie, with the Marines losing four pilots against four enemy shot down. Of far greater import was the fact that the aviation component, which had demonstrated the potentiality of becoming a major factor in warfare, had become a permanent part of the Marine Corps.

At 11 a.m. on the 11th of November 1918, the war fought "to make the world safe for democracy" was officially terminated. In the final accounting, the Marine Corps ledger showed a balance of 2,455 dead; 8,894 wounded; 2,468 assorted medals and the everlasting nickname of "Devil Dogs"—bestowed by a respectful enemy at Belleau Wood. The accounts also showed some unfinished business in the jungles of Latin America.

★ ★ ★ ★ ★

11

Evolution of a Mission

THE PERIOD BETWEEN World Wars was destined to become the most fruitful in Marine Corps history, not only for the Corps itself, but for the contribution it was to make to the defense of the nation and to the art of war. But this bright future was by no means evident during the aftermath of World War I, nor for a number of years to come.

By the Spring of 1920 the Marine Corps had pretty much returned to a peacetime status. The dust, generated by the sloughing off of strictly wartime elements, had settled sufficiently for the Corps to examine its position in the national defense picture. What it saw was not too discouraging. As after every war in the country's history, Congress proceeded to drastically reduce the armed forces as quickly as possible. This affected the Marine Corps by reducing its total strength from an all-time high of 75,000 to 15,000, still the largest peacetime establishment the Corps had ever enjoyed.

The Marine Corps of 1920 was an unbalanced unit in several respects. Gone from the ranks were the "high-hearted" mass of wartime volunteers and the regulars, somewhat to their surprise, missed them. This was especially true among the officers. Regulars who had held commissions before the war had risen in rank very rapidly. The vacuum thus created in the lower ranks had been filled by "90-day-wonders" who had signed on for the duration. Even though the Corps had been greatly reduced, the post-war departure of these officers left an abundance of field grade officers and an insufficient number of company grade officers to fill the required billets.

However, as with every service in every war, there emerged from the ranks of the wartime warriors certain individuals who liked the military service and found themselves adapted to it. The answer to the junior officer problem was largely solved by integrating the best of these into the regular Marine Corps. This gave rise to some troublesome problems regarding the relative seniority of wartime regulars and those newly integrated from reserve status. A typical example is the case of two officers, both of whom were to serve as the Commandant of the Marine Corps. Throughout the war, Lemuel C. Shepherd, a regular, outranked Clifton B. Cates, a reserve. When Cates was promoted to captain and integrated into the regular Corps, the order was abruptly reversed, apparently owing to the relative dates of their original commissions.

Matters finally reached such a state of confusion and disgruntlement that headquarters hit upon an extraordinary expedient. The last group of reserve lieutenants to be integrated took rank arbitrarily in alphabetical order, without regard to previous relative seniority. To the clamor of protest that this naturally aroused, the harassed headquarters retorted curtly that all concerned could either take it or leave it. Thirty-five years later one of these unfortunates, whose name occurred close to the bottom of the alphabet, still spoke bitterly of the incident. The gross injustice visited upon him in his youth still rankled, although by this time he wore three stars on his shoulders.

As they looked around them at the newly evolving peacetime national defense structure, forward-looking Marine officers began asking each other, "Where do we go from here?"

Only a comparative minority sought the answer to this question. As with all branches of the armed forces, the Marine Corps contained a sizeable element who simply did not give the matter any thought at all. There were those who regarded the service as a sinecure and enjoyed the easy-going, and generally dull, routine of garrison life. There were those who heartily subscribed to the thesis that if you kept your nose clean, routine promotion came eventually on a seniority basis. The Marine system of limited tours of duty kept such a life from becoming too monotonous. About the time a man got fed up with his current duty assignment, he was transferred to another spot, or to sea, and the whole scene changed, superficially if not basically. Indeed it was a good life for those who liked that sort of thing, and many did to the extent of not bothering to look beyond it. At a later date, a caustic general was to scornfully characterize such officers as "navy yard Marines."

The leavening effect of the war produced antipodal reactions. While many sank gratefully back into the safe monotony of routine, there emerged a few in whom the experience had engendered a heightened understanding of the profession of arms, and a keen intellectual curiosity regarding the art of war. When General Lejeune was appointed Commandant in 1920, the thoughts of this small group were assured a hearing. In addition, their activities were assured of such support as lay within the Corps' power to furnish. Lamentably, such support was more often moral than material.

However, even the seriously progressive element was split sharply into two factions during the early years following the war. One faction pointed to the inescapable fact that Marines had gained their greatest distinction in the Corps' history while fighting side-by-side with the Army in an extended land campaign. They held that the 4th Brigade had proved itself at least equal to the very best units the Army would field. Thus, it did not appear illogical to visualize the Corps' future in terms of extended land warfare along Army lines.

The other faction held that to duplicate the Army's functions, however well the Marines did so, would mean merging the Corps' identity with that of the Army. This, they maintained, would eventually lead to merging the units physically, and the Corps would eventually lose its separate identity. This faction clung to the concept which had evolved so slowly following the Spanish-American War. This was the concept of the Marine Corps as the Navy's land arm, whose primary function would be the seizure and defense of advanced bases, in order to extend the operating radius of the fleet.

The old Advanced Base Force had been redesignated the Expeditionary Force, but its basic mission and organization—what there was of it—had changed little. It was still, as it had been all along, pretty much of a hit or miss proposition, a sort of catch-all for Marines not at the moment engaged in more active duties. Thus, personnel were in a constant state of flux, and the maintenance of anything resembling a permanent staff was next to impossible. Although the stated mission was to "seize and defend," training was concentrated on the "defense" aspect to the virtual exclusion of "seizure." "Seize," as the term was understood in those days, meant simply occupying an undefended island or area by landing troops. There were many such areas in the Caribbean where the Navy was principally preoccupied with the possible need for enforcing the Monroe Doctrine and the defense of the Panama Canal approaches.

The main objective under this concept was to install the strongest possible defense in the shortest possible time. This was to be accomplished by mounting coast defense and antiaircraft guns, digging defensive works, and setting up beach obstructions. If the preparations could be completed before the enemy had time to react in force, the mission was a success. For wasn't it a military axiom that the power of modern defensive weapons rendered impossible any seaborne attack against a defended position?

Or was it?

Students of the problem began to ask themselves, and each other, some embarrassing questions. Suppose, just for the sake of argument, that the hypothetical enemy were to beat us to the advance base site of our choice. How were we to go about wrest-ing it from them? All hands had to admit reluctantly that they did not have the slightest idea. All attempts at offensive thinking ran head-on into the gloomy spectacle of the British debacle at Gallipoli, the crowning example that proved the axiom about the power of modern defensive weapons.

Or did it?

When the League of Nations awarded Japan mandates over former German island groups in the Pacific, following World War I, a new element entered U.S. naval strategy. At long last there came, faintly audible, a voice that had been crying in the wilderness for seven years.

Earl Hancock Ellis, familiarly known as "Pete," was a brilliant young Marine staff officer with a gift of military prophecy that bordered on omniscience. As early as 1913, he had delivered a series of lectures at the Naval War College in which he predicted that eventually the United States would have to fight Japan, if it were to realize its manifest destiny. He pointed out that the techniques of amphibious warfare would be indispensable toward that end, and strongly urged that a program of development be undertaken at once. The Navy, and the country at large, preoccupied with the threatening conflagration that would soon engulf Europe, paid little attention to the earnest young Marine.

The awarding of the mandates to Japan in 1920 meant little to a nation just emerged from the "war to end all wars," and quite eager to forget the whole unpleasant business. Nor did the U.S. strategists grasp at once the full significance of the potential threat to our trans-Pacific lines of communication and our outlying bases. The peril to Guam was too obvious for anyone to miss, once the Japanese possessed the remainder of the Marianas to the north and the Carolines to the south and southeast. But Guam served merely as a fueling station, a place of no great importance. That the Philippines might also be imperiled was a thought too far-fetched to be worthy of debate. So the Navy contented itself with recommending the strengthening of Guam defenses to a point where the island would be able to hold out long enough for the Pacific Fleet to come to its relief. And that was that.

Ellis pointed out, in vain, that any advance across the Central Pacific would carry the Fleet far from its Pearl Harbor base. Such movement must be made through waters flanked, for a large part of the distance, by mandated islands which the Japanese could readily convert into air bases, should they feel so inclined. To emphasize his point, Ellis drew up a detailed plan of trans-Pacific operations to be used in the war he predicted was bound to come. It was known as Operation Plan 712 H, "Advanced Base Operations in Micronesia." In essence the plan was based on a series of limited objective operations, designed to seize successive, strategically placed islands for the U.S. to use as advanced bases. The accuracy of his foresight, and the soundness of his strategic concepts appears uncanny in retrospect. On July 23, 1921, Commandant Lejeune officially approved Ellis' plan. From that day until the U.S. advance across the Central Pacific began in World War II, it stood as the Marine Corps' basic doctrine for the war in the Pacific. When the advance did begin, it followed Operation Plan 712 H in many details and most essentials.

It is one of the ironies of fate that this far-seeing officer was never afforded the satisfaction of seeing his amazingly accurate prophecies come true. Nor did he play a further part in developing the doctrines which he was mainly instrumental in originating. Destiny had decreed a strange fate for Pete Ellis—a fate which remains one of history's insoluble mysteries.

Ellis was a high-strung man in whose mind the potential war against Japan had become such an obsession that he was tottering on the edge of a nervous breakdown. Whether he had always been a heavy drinker is not apparent. But in the early 1920s he was beginning to show all the earmarks of dipsomania, possibly as the result of attempting to assuage the tensions growing out of his obsession. But restlessness continued to drive him. Shortly after completion of his plan, he determined to study first hand the region about which he had so prophetically written. To his mind Japan's announced policy of excluding foreign visitors from the mandated islands indicated only one thing; they were fortifying some of these islands. Pete Ellis wanted to see this for himself.

Whether General Lejeune really knew what Ellis intended to do, or not, remains a moot question. Regardless, the Commandant granted Lieutenant Colonel Pete Ellis a year's leave of absence and authorized him unlimited foreign travel, no questions asked.

In August of 1922 Ellis turned up in Tokyo in the guise of a representative of a U.S. trading company, seeking to explore the possibilities of new export markets in the South Seas. He made his identity and true mission known to a few selected higher-ups in the Navy and diplomatic circles. A truly sick man by now, suffering from nephritis, he spent over a month in the U.S. Naval hospital in Yokohama. The commanding officer of the hospital knew the real reason for Ellis' presence in Japan. As a doctor, he also knew the seriousness of Ellis' illness, and regretfully made the decision to send Ellis home for further treatment. On the night of October 6, Lieutenant Colonel Ellis disappeared from his hospital bed and official sight.

It is known that he somehow wangled passage on a Japanese ship bound for the islands out of the port of Kobe, 280 miles south of Tokyo. Where Ellis went and what he found there will probably never be known. If he was looking for fortification activities, he must have been disappointed. American forces discovered the hard way two decades later that the Japanese made no effort to fortify the mandated islands until after the outbreak of World War II, the single exception being Truk, in the Carolines, which they developed into an advanced naval base. Ellis is believed to have visited Truk, and to have explored its extensive lagoon by small boat when the Japanese refused him permission to go ashore. However that may be, the first definite word of his whereabouts reached Tokyo in the form of a terse dispatch from Japanese authorities in the Palau Islands announcing he was dead.

Ellis' last days can be reconstructed only through hearsay, much of it derived years after the event. It is not a very elevating story. An extremely sick man, he was befriended by a half-caste trader and took up residence among the natives on the island of Koror, the Japanese administrative capital for all of the mandated island territories. He lived in a thatched hut furnished by the local native chief, until he tore it apart one night in the belief that there was more liquor concealed within its grass walls.

Koror being a sensitive spot, the Japanese naturally kept him under surveillance. In his rare lucid moments, Ellis realized this and had a number of run-ins with Japanese civil policemen and soldiers. Of his last day of life it is recorded simply, "By nine o'clock he was roaring drunk and by three o'clock he was dead." The Japanese immediately cremated his remains and sent a dispatch to Tokyo regarding his demise.

Did he drink himself to death? Or did the Japanese accelerate the process by spiking his liquor with some lethal agent, as they could have easily done? The seeming haste with which the Japanese destroyed any possibility for a post mortem provides a strong inclination to suspect the latter. It is, however, a fact that speedy cremation has long been an established Japanese custom. It is extremely doubtful that anyone will ever know, for the man who might have provided the solution to the mystery of Pete Ellis was prevented from doing so by an odd quirk of fate.

Upon receiving word of Ellis' death, U.S. naval authorities dispatched a chief pharmacist by the name of L. Zembsch from the naval hospital in Yokohama to bring back his ashes. What happened to the pharmacist in the Palaus is something else that will never be known. He returned to Yokohama with his mission accomplished, but in a state of semi-shock and unable to speak coherently. Horrified doctors rushed him to the hospital. Upon examination, it was discovered that he had been drugged, while other evidence indicated that he had been badly mistreated. After two weeks of hospitalization, Zembsch's condition had improved to the point where the doctors felt that he ultimately would be able to tell them what had happened to him. But before

they could nurse him back to rationality the great Japan earth-
quake of 1923 destroyed the hospital, claiming Zembsch as one
of its victims. Thus vanished from the face of the earth the last
clue that might have shed some light upon the mystery of Pete
Ellis—a prophet without honor in his own time.

Although Ellis might have been called the pioneer advocate
of offensive amphibious doctrine, he was by no means the only
Marine officer thinking along those lines in the early 1920s.
Colonel Robert H. Dunlap, who was coming to be regarded as
one of the soundest and most progressive thinkers in the Corps,
had seen eye-to-eye with Ellis for some time. Upon several occasions he had brought his higher rank and prestige to bear in
support of the younger man.

Impatiently seeing his constructive efforts repeatedly thwarted
by the bugaboo of Gallipoli, Dunlap undertook an exhaustive
analytical study of that operation. His findings satisfied him
that the Allied debacle had resulted from faulty planning, poor
organization and wretched execution, rather than unsound basic
doctrine. He published his findings, and a number of men who
had been groping in their own minds for an answer began thinking along Dunlap's lines.

It can not be said that the Marine Corps rushed in wholeheartedly to support this school of thought, nor that the Navy
immediately saw the light and furnished all necessary assistance.
At Quantico, home base of the Expeditionary Force, advocates of
extended land operations were having a field day in the form of
a program of ground maneuvers, utilizing the Expeditionary
Force and any other troops that happened to be readily available. To give point and interest, these maneuvers simulated various campaigns of the Civil War, and many were conducted on
the actual sites.

These activities were by no means the ridiculous waste of time
they might appear. Basic tactical concepts of Civil War times
were by no means as obsolete as the events of World War I appeared to indicate. Many sound military scholars in both the
Army and the Marine Corps recognized this, and a subsequent

war would prove it. Furthermore, the simulated battles provided interesting spectacles. The command at Quantico went to some lengths to see that important political figures and press representatives from nearby Washington were invited. This served to keep the Marines before the public eye as an active military organization, publicity of which the Corps, always at the narrow end of the appropriations pipeline, stood in constant need.

Just how such activities served to prepare the Expeditionary Force for its basic mission of acting in cooperation with the Fleet was something else again. However, the advocates of amphibious warfare were able to get in a few licks of their own. Some of their mounting enthusiasm was beginning to rub off on important people in the Navy. As a result, it became possible to obtain sufficient cooperation in the form of warships and small boats to stage a series of small landing exercises. Two were conducted during the winter of 1922, one at Guantanamo Bay and one on the island of Culebra, just off Puerto Rico. In the spring of the following year, there was a landing exercise at Panama, and another during the summer on Cape Cod, Massachusetts. Two landing exercises which involved reinforced regiments were held at Culebra and Panama in 1924, and one which simulated a force of 42,000 Marines in the Hawaiian Islands the following year.

Unrealistic though these were, they engendered an appalling state of confusion which clearly indicated how much both the Marine Corps and the Navy had to learn in order to master this exceedingly complex business. Far from being discouraged, the Marines set about solving their many unexpected problems. They were making substantial progress when the sudden pressure of outside events created a demand for the entire strength of the Expeditionary Force, and more. This state of affairs brought the amphibious training program to a dead halt.

First came the intervention in Nicaragua in 1927. This followed the pattern of previous involvement in Caribbean countries before World War I. The Latin-American political shenanigans involved had a strangely familiar ring to the few Marines who bothered to concern themselves with such matters. It was not for the Marine Corps to weigh the rights and wrongs of the case. The decision to intervene came from a higher governmental level, and the Marines once more assumed the role of active implements of U.S. foreign policy.

As usual, the first Marines to land were the detachments of ships which had been hovering nearby. These were followed by elements of the Expeditionary Force until a provisional brigade was formed. It was not surprising, in the face of this display of force, that the contending political factions quickly saw the light. The leader of the rebellion agreed to lay down his arms and disband his "army," and apparently made a sincere effort to do so. But his control left much to be desired. One of his lieutenants, Augusto Sandino, slipped away with a small following and made his way to the jungle-covered mountains of northern Nicaragua. Sandino had avowed intentions of carrying on guerrilla warfare, and rousing the spirit of revolt once more to drive out the hated "Yanqui" interlopers.

It is difficult to appraise fairly the character and the motives of a man like Sandino. His capacity for leadership was demonstrated by his ability to add to his original following, and to keep a force in the field over a protracted period. His limitations in this respect were evidenced by his inability to make his force really formidable. His ability to elude capture for four years, first by the Marines, then by the Marine-trained Guardia Nacional de Nicaragua, attested to his capacity for jungle operations. He expressed sentiments of the most sublime patriotism in his public utterances, and with considerable eloquence. His declarations that his only motive was to oust the foreign intruders failed notably to arouse the national spirit. The government in power hated and feared him, and placed him beyond the pale of the law. Even the former rebels with whom he had sided distrusted him, and failed to rally to his standard.

In short, Sandino was without official status in his own country, an outlaw with a price on his head. Among his followers there may have been a scattering of true patriots who desired to oust the foreigners. Perhaps there were partisan die-hards who were against the government as a matter of principle. But one can not ignore the logical conclusion that most were simply idle men of the time-honored Caribbean stamp who took to banditry as an accepted means of livelihood. It is ironic that Sandino gained far greater, and more idealistic, support from the bleeding hearts and the do-gooders in the United States than he ever did from the people of his own country.

The mission of the Marines boiled down to a matter of containing Sandino in the sparsely settled highlands where he constituted only a local nuisance, and preventing his movement into more prosperous regions to the south. This was accomplished by setting up small garrisons at strategic points, and covering the intervening ground by a system of patrols. The Marines had every hope of quickly running Sandino to earth and bringing the whole business to a speedy conclusion. Under the circumstances, this proved to be a virtual impossibility. Sandino and his men knew the terrain far better than the Marines could ever hope to. Many local inhabitants, whether through fear or more noble motives, provided the bandits with an intelligence network that kept Sandino appraised of every Marine movement that threatened him.

Strangely enough, Sandino was doing the Marines a favor, though he certainly did not realize it, nor could anything have been further from his intention. It was not until many years later, when they were fighting in other jungles on the other side of the world, that Marines would fully appreciate the value of what they had learned in Nicaragua.

The first experience lay in the field of jungle patrolling. Marines had operated in tropical jungle in both Haiti and the Dominican Republic. But this had been a haphazard business compared to the more extended and systematic procedure employed against Sandino. Patrols were in the field constantly. On many occasions they ran into skillfully contrived ambushes and sustained casualties in short, sharp flurries of fighting. These they learned to cope with. Not above borrowing a page from the book of a skilled enemy, the Marines learned how to set up similar ambushes themselves.

One of the most significant operations conducted was known as the Cocos Patrol, the name being derived from the river along which it operated. This patrol, of approximately company strength, was commanded by Captain Merrit A. ("Red Mike") Edson.

The Cocos Patrol was unique in that it started from the lowlands along the east coast and moved west and north to effect a junction with the main body of Marines deployed in Sandino's backyard. Its purpose was to protect the comparatively rich mining developments in the area which Sandino's men had begun to raid.

Edson has often been called the infantryman's infantryman. A man with sound tactical concepts, he was anxious to try out his textbook knowledge under field conditions. He knew everything "the book" had to say about scouting and patrolling, but it bothered him that the authors had never seen the jungles of Nicaragua. He determined to use his patrolling mission as a practical laboratory for testing accepted jungle tactics.

The situation could hardly have been better suited to his purposes. His force was operating under wartime conditions in the face of an armed enemy. The danger which lurked constantly in the dense undergrowth and tall trees kept his men alert. Occasional skirmishes inured them to being under fire. There was just enough action to impress all hands that this was more than a routine drill. Yet there was not so much as to imperil the expedition seriously, nor to hamper Edson's experimentation in learning techniques by trial and error.

Edson's primary object was to find the means by which patrols could be pushed along jungle trails at the greatest possible speed, compatible with tactical security. To arrive at the best method, he experimented with many types of formations, some conventional, others not. In the course of this experimentation, he evolved what many students of the subject consider the origin of that uniquely Marine development, the "fire team." This tactical group was to be refined in another war on a vastly greater scale than bandit chasing in Nicaragua.

The basic concept was simple enough. The fire team consisted of a small group of Marines, specially trained to work together. Once an enemy ambush, or strong point, had been discovered, the central element of the fire team had the mission of building up a base of fire to hold the enemy in position. The other elements moved out to the right and left in an effort to flank the enemy position. It was a maneuver which required swift reaction by all members of the team, and extremely close coordination. Edson was quick to appreciate the value of the Browning Automatic Rifle, the good old work horse of World War I. It proved to be an excellent weapon to quickly develop and sustain the desired base of fire. Regardless of the size of the fire team Edson experimented with, the BAR always occupied the key spot.

Edson's mission, of course, involved a great deal more than field training. It required much back-breaking labor to get boats and supplies upstream on a swift river. Before he had gone very far, maintaining his supply line to the east coast proved so difficult that the expedition had to depend upon air drop for rations, supplies and ammunition.

This brings up the second major technique developed by the Marines during the campaign against Sandino—employment of aviation in support of ground troops.

The Marine air component which had accompanied the Expeditionary Force to Nicaragua consisted originally of nine obsolescent De Havilands of World War I vintage. These were based in a cow pasture on the edge of Nicaragua's capital city, Managua. At the outset, the planes were confined to flying reconnaissance missions over the mountainous area where Marine ground patrols and outposts were operating. It was on such a mission on a midsummer's morning that two Marine pilots suddenly found themselves flying over a vigorous combat action raging through the village of Ocotal.

Sandino was making a decisive effort to strike the blow which might well determine the success or failure of his cause on a national scale. His following had reached the peak strength he could expect in local operations. But he was politician enough to realize that a decisive stroke inflicted upon the Marines might bring many dissident elements all over the country flocking to his cause. He was military man enough to sense that the time to strike was ripe.

Ocotal seemed a logical place. The Marine garrison numbered only 62, reinforced by 48 members of the new, only partially trained, Guardia Nacional. Ocotal also lay far beyond ready supporting distance. At 1 a.m. on the morning of July 16, Sandino hurled an estimated six hundred men against this small outpost. Although it was launched under the cover of darkness, the assault achieved only partial surprise, thanks to an alert Marine sentry. The Marines and Guardia detachment were quartered in two fairly substantial buildings, and by dint of some furious fighting were successful in beating off repeated assaults.

With the coming of daylight, Sandino withdrew his forces beyond the edge of the village, and regrouped for a new form of attack. If his troops had been even partially trained, he might well have overpowered the garrison by sheer weight of numbers. But when his night attack failed, Sandino realized that even less could be accomplished during daylight. He wisely shifted to the tactic of attrition. He knew that the Marines could not retreat, and that they lacked the strength to stage a successful sortie against such odds. It would take at least a week for supplies and reinforcements to reach them. Thus, if Sandino could entice them into expending their ammunition quickly, the garrison would soon be at his mercy.

What the two reconnaissance planes saw when they flew over Ocotal was a vigorous fire fight in progress. The pilots promptly dove to their ground compatriots' support, expended their machine gun ammunition in strafing attacks against the bandits, then roared off for home to rearm and obtain reinforcements. Five planes, led by Major Ross E. Rowell, commander of the air unit in Nicaragua, returned to Ocotal loaded with light bombs, in addition to their machine guns. They found the fire fight still in progress. Few of the Nicaraguans had ever seen a plane, and none had any conception of its combat potential. Instead of dispersing, they gathered in curious groups to observe the antics of these strange machines.

It was the last time many of them made this mistake. The planes peeled off and roared down in power dives, straight at the astonished besiegers of Ocotal, and released their bombs. Survivors of the resulting carnage ran screaming for cover, pursued by strafing machine guns.

This incident, coupled with others which had taken place in Haiti and the Dominican Republic, has led partisan scholars to claim that the Marine Corps invented dive bombing. This would be difficult to substantiate. Both British and U.S. Army aviators had been experimenting with the idea of aiming bombs by aiming the plane. But the Marines have considerable justification for their claim to being the first to use this technique in combat.

At the National Air Races in Los Angeles, in 1933, Marine aviators staged an exhibition of dive bombing to the considerable edification of at least one of the spectators; Major Ernst Udet, the great German ace of World War I. At the time no one considered it unusual that one of the world's most famous flyers should be so interested that he took copious notes during the exhibition. Nor was it unusual that he later sought out the pilots and engaged them in long technical discussions of the technique they employed. It was far more than mere coincidence that the outbreak of World War II in Europe found the Allies completely unprepared to cope with the dreaded Stuka dive bomber which Udet is credited with developing.

Air support of ground troops had effectively raised the siege of Ocotal. In January 1928, Lieutenant Christian F. Schilt added another chapter to the Marines' book of air support. Two Marine columns operating in the vicinity of Quilali were ambushed by seven hundred bandits. While planes covered the relief expedition, an emergency airstrip was prepared by burning and leveling a part of the town. Using a two-seater Corsair, Schilt made

10 trips into Quilali, landing on a small rutted road, loading his plane with wounded Marines and taking off in the face of heavy hostile fire.

So successful were these techniques that they were adapted on a wider scale to apply to all Marine activities in northern Nicaragua. Patrols, by the nature of their missions, often moved far afield from their bases of supply. It was a distinct handicap to have to transport the supplies to keep them in the field for the required length of time. With resupply by air systematized, the patrols gained much greater freedom of action. It was seldom possible for the planes to land, but a system of air drops of supplies was worked out whereby the ground troops could indicate by means of signal panels what they needed and where they wanted it dropped.

The planes also supported the patrols by reconnoitering their routes in advance. In the dense jungle it was seldom possible to detect enemy activities from the air. But once a patrol had made contact, dive bombing and strafing in close air support proved of great value in dispersing the bandit ambushes and strong points.

Viewed in retrospect, these activities might appear crude and small scale. But the original concept of the Marine air arm, and the justification which made it possible, was its potential value in supporting the operations of ground troops. Such techniques had remained in the realm of theory throughout World War I where the minor activities carried out by Marine aviation had no tactical relation to Marine infantry operations. Some experimentation with the theory had taken place in Haiti and the Dominican Republic, but this had been largely hit-or-miss in nature. However, after the techniques and mutual understanding worked out in Nicaragua, the foundations of the Marine air-ground team had been so firmly established that further refinements became primarily matters of adaptation.

Although considerable Marine Corps energy had been devoted to extensive operations in Latin America and the Caribbean during the post-war period, it had also been required to maintain a force of varying size in China. The beginning of the Chinese Nationalist movement in 1923 had generated another attempt to rid China's economy of foreign domination. The resulting outbreaks, reminiscent of the Boxer Rebellion of 1900, had repeatedly required the landing of Marines from the Asiatic Fleet during the early 1920s.

By 1925, China was seething with intermittent civil war, as the Nationalists continued to extend their control over the country. As the result of the Nationalist retaliatory measures against members of the opposing faction, the situation became critical in Shanghai in 1927. With the Americans of Shanghai's great International Settlement seriously threatened, the 4th Marines were dispatched from San Diego, arriving in late February. The following month several Americans were killed when Nationalist forces captured Nanking.

With the situation rapidly growing more serious, additional protection was ordered for Americans residing in various Chinese cities. The 6th Marines were hurriedly reorganized in Philadelphia for duty in China. By early summer over 4,500 Marines in China had been organized into the Third Reinforced Brigade and placed under the command of Brigadier General Smedley Butler. The Brigade spent the next two years "trouble shooting" all manner of emergencies, most of which were quickly and peacefully resolved when the Marines appeared on the scene. With general political conditions relatively stabilized by 1929, the bulk of the Brigade was returned to the United States, leaving the 4th Marines in garrison at Shanghai.

The year 1933 marked the most crucial turning point in Marine Corps history. Withdrawals from Nicaragua and China made the Expeditionary Force once more available for resumption of the amphibious program which had been interrupted in the middle twenties. But if actual amphibious training had been dormant these several years, thought along doctrinal lines had matured considerably. Thus, when the Marines again took part in fleet exercises, the basic faults of the Expeditionary Force concept became clear.

For one thing, the Expeditionary Force lacked the personnel stability it so badly needed. Members were continually being transferred before their training had advanced beyond the basic stages. As a result, few of its personnel ever attained the degree of specialized training necessary to expertly perform the complex job of amphibious warfare.

Conditions could not be remedied under the existing organization, since this impermanence reached to the highest levels. Because of this, no continuity of effort or cumulative constructive learning from experience was possible. Staff members who had taken part in one year's exercises were likely to be on the opposite side of the country when the next annual maneuver got under way.

Obviously these drawbacks could not be remedied under the existing system. A complete re-evaluation of the functions of the Expeditionary Force was called for. More important, its basic position as a component of the Naval service required reassessment. Such a re-evaluation was undertaken by establishing a staff at Quantico to work out plans for organizing a striking force which could be rapidly mobilized.

At this time Major General Ben H. Fuller was Commandant of the Marine Corps. His right hand man in the post of Assistant Commandant was Brigadier General John H. Russell, recently returned from a distinguished tour of duty as the American High Commissioner to Haiti. With Fuller's approval, Russell undertook to give substance and form to the new concept.

Essentially, the concept provided for the Expeditionary Force to be set up on a permanent basis under the command of a general officer with a permanent staff. Within the Naval Service itself, this force was to be incorporated as an integral component of the U.S. Fleet, under operational command of Commander-in-Chief, U.S. Fleet. Since the designation "Expeditionary Force" seemed in many respects a misnomer, it was suggested that its title be changed to either the "Fleet Base Defense Force," or "Fleet Marine Force."

By this time many important and influential naval officers had become interested in the budding Marine Corps concept of amphibious and advanced base operations. How keen this interest had become was soon testified to by the prompt approval and acceptance of General Russell's proposal. The title "Fleet Marine Force" was selected and it became officially designated a type force component of the U.S. Fleet on December 8, 1933.

Unfortunately, the only major amphibious operation in modern warfare had proved a failure. Consequently the laborers in the vineyard of Quantico had to begin with a negative approach. It was their task to determine what ought to be done on the basis of careful study of what ought not to be done. That reliable old whipping boy, the Gallipoli fiasco, was trotted out and belabored lustily. Every move of the British and their allies was subjected to minute scrutiny and the reasons for its failure analyzed in detail. In addition, the existing doctrine which had evolved through the years as a result of maneuvers and training exercises held by the Expeditionary Force was carefully scrutinized. The resulting study gave planners a firm basis on which to sketch constructive methods whereby the apparent failures of the past could be obviated in the future.

The results of this large scale, collaborative effort were published in 1934 under the modest title, "Tentative Manual for Landing Operations." Since the manual was admittedly tentative, tests under field conditions brought about a few minor revisions. In 1938 the Navy took over the whole project and reissued the revised manual under the title, "FTP—167" (Fleet Training Publication). Two revised versions had been issued by 1941 when the Army belatedly awoke to the probable nature of operations in the coming war and "borrowed" FTP—167. They put its contents practically verbatim between Army covers, and issued it as Field Manual 31-5, "Landing Operations On Hostile Shores."

Thus did the pioneering effort of the Marine Corps produce the basic doctrine which was followed throughout World War II by all branches of the U.S. forces and our allies as well. Viewing the results in retrospect, the authors of *The U.S. Marines and*

Amphibious War have this to say regarding the extraordinary document: "If later publications by all the services during and before World War II can be considered the Holy Writ of modern amphibious warfare, then the *Tentative Manual for Landing Operations . . .* deserves to be thought of as a sort of combination Pentateuch and the Four Gospels."

The basic doctrine involved in putting assault troops ashore in the face of opposition and sustaining them there had been laid down. The techniques and tactics employed to implement these doctrines were something else again. Some of those prescribed in the Tentative Manual and FTP—167 proved to be more concerned with wishful thinking than the harsh realities of war. Every effort was made to test them under simulated combat conditions during the series of amphibious exercises between 1934 and 1941. But the limitations in such simulation did not become fully apparent until the troops involved faced the actual reality of combat.

The development of specialized amphibious equipment went hand-in-hand with the evolution of amphibious tactics. It was an equally hard problem, though in different ways.

When the landing exercises began, the only craft available for landing purposes were the Navy's standard ships' boats. These demonstrated their inadequacy from the outset. They were too slow for tactical assault purposes. They were also extremely difficult to handle in even moderate surf, a function for which they had never been designed. Finally, they were incapable of handling heavy or bulky equipment. Although some ingenious experimenting was done to adapt the standard 50-foot motor launch for the handling of light tanks and medium artillery pieces, it soon became obvious that no adaptation would ever prove satisfactory. The only practicable course was to start from scratch and develop special craft.

The story of the Marine Corps' struggle to obtain adequate landing craft is a long drawn-out one, fraught with discouragement and heartbreak. It was pursued with the inadequate funds characteristic of the period and in the face of such obstructive bureaucratic procedures as to call down a Congressional investigation on the hapless neck of the Bureau of Ships.

The Marines stuck grimly to their guns and eventually obtained a powerful ally whose contribution to ultimate success would be difficult to overrate. This individual was Andrew J. Higgins of New Orleans, a civilian boat builder. Higgins was not above using his influence to go over as many heads as necessary to put his own and the Marine Corps' ideas across. Thanks to this collaboration, Higgins not only developed prototype models, but had the accepted craft in production when World War II arrived. After much experimentation, these boiled down to the LCVP (Landing Craft Vehicle and Personnel), a 36-foot craft capable of carrying 36 fully equipped Marines, or a light vehicle; and the LCM (Landing Craft Mechanized), a 50-footer which could transport a light tank, or 100 personnel. Both were equipped with a bow landing ramp by which men, cargo and vehicles could be discharged expeditiously directly on the beach.

Another civilian who contributed significantly to the development of landing equipment was Donald Roebling. Son of a wealthy manufacturer, young Roebling had been sent to Florida for his health. There he set up a well equipped hobby shop in order to indulge his mechanical bent. Among the first fruit of his experimentation emerged a curious contraption which he called the "Alligator." This machine, a true amphibian, he had designed for rescue work in the Florida Everglades. Track propelled on land, it derived its propulsion afloat from flanges set in the track to serve as a series of small paddles. Thus, it could make the transition from one element to the other with hardly a noticeable pause.

The story of how the Alligator became a major item of Marine equipment sounds like a sea story. It is, however, a well documented fact.

World War II made the armed services and the general public extremely familiar with the appearance of the LVT (Landing Vehicle, Tracked) or Amtrack, as it became known. But back in

1937 when *Life* magazine published a photograph and a short article of Roebling's first model, it appeared almost fantastic. Rear Admiral E. C. Kalbfus commanding the Battleship Force, U.S. Fleet, chanced to see this article. Probably more or less in a spirit of jest, he clipped the page and mailed it to his friend the Commandant of the Marine Corps. The Admiral enclosed the clipping with a note to the effect that if this contraption were capable of the performance claimed for it, it might be a useful addition to the fleet of weird craft the Marines were in the process of developing.

The Commandant, not at all sure that he wasn't being kidded, wrote a dead-pan acknowledgment and bucked the clipping to the Marine Corps Equipment Board at Quantico. The strange contraption was no jest to the Equipment Board. Instead, Roebling's brain child set their collective imaginations afire. If this odd-shaped monstrosity could be adapted to military use, they could visualize it as the answer to the Board's prayers of more than a decade. At the first opportunity, they sent an officer to Florida to consult with Roebling and see the Alligator demonstrated.

The rest is history. The original model proved readily adaptable, the principal change necessary being the substitution of steel hull construction for the original aluminum. Roebling and other engineers concentrated on working out refinements and improved models, several of which were on the drawing boards by the time war came.

The decades of the twenties and thirties were years of fruitful development for the Marine Corps. They were also decades which embraced the development of the most titanic conflict in history.

The seeds had been sown when the Treaty of Versailles emerged as a dictated, rather than a negotiated, peace. The Allied treaty makers had met at Paris in an atmosphere of hatred and greed; hatred for the enemy and greed for colonies and reparations.

Germany, stripped of her colonial possessions and resentful

of defeat, chafed under the restrictions of the Treaty. Nurtured by fourteen years of confusion and the guiding hand of a fanatical Austrian named Adolph Hitler, the National Socialist Party seized control of the government.

Italy, long discontent with what she considered a disproportionate share of the spoils, turned to Fascism and Benito Mussolini, who hungered for glory.

Japan, with the door to further expansion securely closed by the League of Nations, looked with increasing resentment on the power of the United States and Great Britain in the Orient. The country had been dealt a severe blow by the world depression of 1929. Seeking a short cut to prosperity, she turned to the mainland of Asia for the basic resources to supply her industrial requirements. With the threat of forceful deterrence lessened by the cutdown of military expenditures in Western nations, she seized Manchuria in 1931. Six years later came the invasion of China, and the world recoiled at Japanese atrocities chronicled by the "rape of Nanking." In the early fall of 1940, the growing Empire of the Rising Sun began its encroachment on Indo-China.

At Pearl Harbor, on the Sunday morning of December 7, 1941, the prophecy of Lieutenant Colonel Pete Ellis became a stark reality, echoing in the crashing thunder of falling bombs.

★ **12** ★

★ ★ ★ ★ ★

The War Against Japan

WHEN THE CALL CAME, the Marine Corps made good its boast of being the nation's force in readiness. It did so, however, with immediate results that had not been entirely anticipated. It is paradoxical that this immediate availability materially impaired the Marines' state of readiness to perform their highly specialized function of amphibious warfare.

The first call came in the Spring of 1941, with the United States involved in World War II on the side of Britain, in a status euphemistically described as "short-of-war." This entailed two major considerations. One concerned maintaining the security of the Western Hemisphere by preventing the Nazis from taking over the Caribbean possessions of conquered France and the Netherlands. The other involved safeguarding the trans-Atlantic supply routes upon which Great Britain was wholly dependent for the materials necessary to continue her war effort, and for domestic subsistence.

The most sensitive spot within the Monroe Doctrine area was the French island of Martinique, in the Caribbean. The fall of the homeland had caught a small French naval squadron there, which included an aircraft carrier loaded with 106 U.S. planes, originally destined for France. Rear Admiral Georges Robert, commanding, promptly declared for the Vichy government and displayed a marked indifference towards pointed suggestions that the U.S. would be glad to provide the island with "protection." For a period of several months during late 1940 and early 1941, the project of seizing Martinique by force preoccupied the U.S. strategic command. The 1st Marine Division, based at Quantico, Virginia, was held on the alert for swift action, while Admiral Robert's backing and filling held the situation in suspense.

A seemingly potent threat to the southern supply route to Britain lay in the Spanish and Portuguese islands lying off the northeast coast of Africa. During the Spring of 1941, reliable intelligence sources indicated the possibility of Hitler striking south from newly conquered France into the Iberian Peninsula with the consent of Franco Spain, a move which Portugal would be powerless to resist. To forestall the Nazis gaining possession of the offshore islands belonging to these powers, Great Britain and the U.S. drew up plans for seizing them. The British were to take over the Cape Verde Islands and the Canaries. The U.S. would occupy the Azores—with, of course the specific consent of Portugal.

Like many plans, this one looked good on paper until the question arose as to where the troops to accomplish all this were to be found. The U.S. Army had about 1,500,000 men. But most of them were either newly acquired draftees or recently called up National Guardsmen. According to existing legislation, none of these could be sent outside of the Western Hemisphere unless they volunteered for such service. The relatively small hard core of Army regulars had long since been split up to form cadres for new units. Clearly the Army could not provide the necessary troops.

The only likely candidate left was the 1st Marine Division, already tentatively earmarked for an attack on Martinique. To bring the division up to the strength necessary to carry out either operation, Marine Corps Headquarters ordered attachment of a reinforced regiment from the 2d Marine Division on the West Coast. The regiment selected was the 6th Marines. But to provide this regiment and its reinforcing elements with the necessary personnel meant stripping the woefully understrength 2d Division, leaving it a "division" in name only.

The 6th Marines assimilated its reinforcements, combat loaded three transports and four destroyers, and sailed from San Diego within six days of receiving its orders. While the regiment was en route, several developments took place which radically altered its intended mission.

To begin with, Portugal objected strenuously to the U.S. occupying the Azores. Next, France declined to permit its near-ally, Germany, to move into Spain. Then, British intelligence received information that Hitler was planning to strike to the north, instead of south, attacking his erstwhile ally, Russia. In the face of such an event, the importance of the Azores became negligible and Britain faced peril from another direction. About this time, Admiral Robert drifted into one of his conciliatory moods, which eliminated Martinique as an immediate target.

The reinforced regiment from the West Coast put in at Charleston, South Carolina, to find its original orders to join the 1st Marine Division canceled. In their place were orders redesignating the unit as the 1st Marine Provisional Brigade. The troops were more surprised than pleased to receive an issue of winter clothing.

It was thus that a highly trained amphibious unit was diverted to the last place on earth where amphibious training was needed —the bleak, treeless waste of Iceland.

The Brigade's orders stand as a classic example of brevity and clarity: "Defend Iceland against hostile attack." The good citizens of Iceland were not particularly happy at the advent of U.S. Occupation, nor were the Marines overly enthusiastic about their assignment. News of the attack on Pearl Harbor only confirmed their conviction that they were wasting their time in the middle of the wrong ocean.

It is, of course, in the Pacific where the main story of the Marines really begins.

The deployment of Marines in small detachments scattered about the Pacific made it inevitable that some of them would be among the first U.S. troops to fall into enemy hands when the Japanese struck.

In view of the deepening peril, the 4th Marines, the "old China Regiment," had been permitted to fall far below strength. Individuals were rotated Stateside without any replacements being furnished. The regiment's strength had been reduced to 804 when it was evacuated to the Philippines during the last week in November, on the last two transports to get safely out of China. But war had come by the time one of these ships returned to China, and it was captured by the Japanese before it could retrieve the 4th's small rear echelon and the Marine Legation guard detachments at Peiping and Tientsin. These were left with no alternative save surrender.

Last minute efforts were made to reinforce the outposts on the islands of Wake and Midway. Twelve Marine fighter planes of Squadron VMF-211 reached Wake four days before the Japanese struck. Seven of the planes were destroyed by the first Japanese air strike of thirty-six twin-engined bombers.

The surviving planes and the Marine ground defense garrison of 15 officers and 373 enlisted men held out for 16 days against incessant air attack and one attempted amphibious landing, which was handily repulsed. During the course of these events, the Marines exacted a heavy toll from the enemy: 21 planes shot down, 11 planes damaged, 3 destroyers sunk and over 500 enemy personnel killed.

The odds, however, were so great that it could only be a matter of time before the island fell. The Japanese received substantial air reinforcements from carriers returning from Pearl Harbor. Under the cover of darkness during the early morning of December 23, they achieved a landing by the expedient of beaching two of their transports. One detachment of this landing force was wiped out to the last man. Hard fighting continued into the daylight hours. When the Island Commander learned definitely that the relief force which had been dispatched from

Pearl Harbor had turned back, he saw nothing to be gained by holding out any longer. Consequently, he ordered the surrender of Wake and its 1,000 unarmed civilian construction workers.

Guam, neither reinforced nor fortified when the opportunity afforded, fell easy prey to the Japanese from the neighboring Marianas and Carolines. The Marine garrison of 153 had only the standard equipment for a small infantry unit in peacetime. In fact, the only available weapon larger than a .30 caliber machine gun was a 3-inch antiaircraft gun mounted on the minesweeper *USS Penguin,* which was sunk in Agana Harbor by an early Japanese air attack. After continued softening-up by air, the enemy effected two seaborne landings with approximately 7,000 men on December 10. With the enemy inflicting severe life and property losses on the hapless native population, the Navy governor surrendered the island.

The island of Midway received sporadic shelling by two Japanese destroyers, dropped off by the enemy's main attack force headed for Pearl Harbor. The shore bombardment killed 4, wounded 29 and did relatively light material damage. The ships withdrew, however, without attempting a landing. According to inconclusive evidence, one ship was apparently set afire while withdrawing, but Japanese records indicate that neither was lost. Indeed, one of them, the *Ushio,* achieved the dubious distinction of being the only Japanese vessel participating in the December 7 attacks still afloat when the war ended.

Similarly, and on an even smaller and less effective scale, wandering Japanese submarines paid visits at various times during the ensuing months to Johnson and Palmyra Islands. True, MacArthur's people still held out in the Philippines and would continue to do so for several months to come. But this area had already fallen into the backwash of war, and their gallant and protracted resistance had no effect on the Japanese timetable of conquest. For all practical purposes, the strategic picture in the Pacific had jelled firmly by the time Spring of 1942 rolled around.

From an overall viewpoint, the Japanese conquests had

reached alarming proportions. Besides crippling the U.S. Pacific Fleet, they had mopped up a combined U.S., British, Dutch and Australian naval force operating in the Far East, while in the process of seizing the Netherlands East Indies. In addition to that area and the Philippines, the Greater East Asia Co-Prosperity Sphere embraced Indo-China, Thailand, Malaya, and a good portion of Burma on the Asia mainland. Across the Pacific their conquests included the island groups of the Marianas, Carolines, Marshalls, Gilberts and Palaus. They had also gained firm footholds on the Bismarks, the northern Solomons and eastern New Guinea where they literally camped on Australia's northern doorstep.

It was at this stage of the proceedings that greed welled up to confound the most successful Asiatic conquerors since the hordes of Genghis Khan. The Japanese had accomplished all they had originally planned. But their initial objectives had been attained with such unexpected ease that they did not want to stop once these had been realized. The efforts of the Japanese jingoists to push their conquests beyond reasonable bounds led to two actions which proved to be disastrous.

That the timing of the Japanese was conspicuously bad is a lot more apparent with the benefit of hindsight than it was at the time. Based on the old maxim about striking while the iron is hot, their decision to quickly follow up their advantage can be soundly rationalized. Their failure arose from the fact that they overestimated both the heat of the iron and their own striking power.

The first step in the extended grand strategy entailed encircling the Coral Sea with Japanese bases, leaving the end of the Allied supply line to Australia dangling at the Solomons. This design was to be initiated by an amphibious assault on Port Moresby in southeastern New Guinea, a move which had already been diagnosed by U.S. intelligence. A carrier task force met Vice Admiral Takeo Takagi's strike force in the Battle of the Coral Sea on May 7, 1942. A careful totaling of the losses on both sides appears to favor a Japanese tactical victory. Yet a strategic victory must be voted to the U.S. since the Japanese losses were sufficient to abort the landing at Port Moresby. For the first time, the enemy had been met head-on and stopped in his tracks. The second time was fast approaching.

Blithely ignoring their failure in the Coral Sea, the Japanese proceeded with the next phase in their new plan—the capture of Midway. With Wake Island already providing an outpost in the Central Pacific, the addition of Midway would extend even farther the perimeter of Japan's defenses. The only people surprised by the Midway operation were the Japanese. Having broken their naval code, the U.S. Pacific Fleet knew of the planned attack, the approximate time and the strength of the attacking force. By June 4, the day of the attack, Midway boasted an air complement of 107 planes, ranging from Army B-17s to Marine F4F fighters. Two hundred miles north of the island the carriers *Yorktown, Enterprise* and *Hornet* waited for the word to launch their planes.

The battle lasted two days. The Japanese lost 4 aircraft carriers, 322 planes, 3 cruisers and other assorted ships. With the carriers had gone the cream of Japan's experienced naval pilots. According to the Japanese authors of *Midway: The Battle That Doomed Japan,* "The catastrophe of Midway definitely marked the turning of the tide in the Pacific War. . . ."

The naval victory at Midway had set the stage for a quick follow-up offensive. The activities of the Japanese themselves provided the cue to where it could be launched with the best prospects of decisive success. The archipelago known as the Solomon Islands runs from a point about five degrees below the Equator, adjacent to New Britain, for several hundred miles in a southeasterly direction. The several large islands and innumerable smaller ones lie in two parallel chains, separated by a wide channel.

Throughout the spring, British and Australian Coastwatchers lurking in the hills had reported steady Japanese penetration southward along both of the twin chains. Their need for the Solomons was self-evident. Defensively, these islands covered the approaches to Japan's powerful advance base at Rabaul in New Britain. Offensively, they thrust far forward to threaten the vital American supply line to Australia, now screened by the New Hebrides and the Fijis.

In June the U.S. high command arrived at two momentous decisions. The first offensive against the Japanese would be launched at Guadalcanal, next to the last island in the southern chain of the Solomons. The assault troops would be the 1st Marine Division, a portion of which was already busily engaged establishing a training base in New Zealand.

It was not without reason that the participants labelled the Guadalcanal attack "Operation Shoestring." Everything was in short supply, from troops and ships to rations and equipment. Intelligence information regarding the target area was as scarce as the time in which to obtain it.

The advance echelon of the 1st Division reached New Zealand June 14, travelling by transport from the East Coast of the United States, via the Panama Canal. It consisted of the 5th Marines (Reinforced) and Division Headquarters. The division was under the command of Major General A. A. Vandegrift. Since sufficient shipping was lacking to lift the division as a unit, the 1st Marine Regiment was ordered to proceed overland to the West Coast and await the necessary sea transportation. The understrength condition of the division had not seemed especially important at the time. General Vandegrift had left the States with the understanding that the division would not be committed until around the first of the coming year, and would complete field training in New Zealand.

The advance echelon had barely completed unloading and moved into camp when the bombshell fell on June 25. With his second echelon still somewhere at sea, General Vandegrift received orders to prepare immediately for assault operations in the southern Solomons—not about the first of the year, but the 1st of August.

The efforts that followed may best be described as frantic. The 5th Marines combat loaded their transports and cleared the

Wellington docks barely in time to make room for the incoming 1st Marines. This unfortunate outfit had to complete unloading and combat reloading in a single operation under the most unfavorable conditions imaginable. Considerable equipment and supplies had to be left behind, some deliberately, some inadvertently because of lack of time for thorough planning. General Vandegrift succeeded in having the target date deferred until August 7, but that was the best he could do. The convoy cleared Wellington on July 22.

The division was one-third understrength, owing to the previous detachment of the 7th Marines to Samoa. To make up the deficit, such available units as the 1st Raider Battalion and the 1st Parachute Battalion, minus their parachutes, were attached to the division. At the last minute the 2d Marines of the 2d Division was combat loaded out of San Diego, California, to serve as floating reserve for the operation.

Such intelligence as could be obtained was quite fragmentary. This was based upon the general recollection of such individuals as plantation owners, traders and labor contractors who had been in the region at one time or another and thought they knew something about the terrain. As it turned out they knew surprisingly little about it. As for the Japanese strength, dispositions and capabilities, one man's guess was as good as another's. The enemy was known to occupy the island of Tulagi, some 18 miles away across Sealark Channel. The Japanese also occupied, in unknown numbers, the big island of Guadalcanal where they had nearly completed an airstrip. Details were wholly lacking.

The combined convoy rendezvoused off Koro, in an isolated area of the Fiji Islands on July 28. There a landing rehearsal was attempted. But landing craft were in such short supply and poor repair that none could be risked actually going ashore. According to General Vandegrift, the rehearsal was "a complete bust!" So the 1st Marine Division departed for the first Pacific offensive as unpracticed as any troops ever employed in a major operation.

The attack came off on schedule shortly after dawn on

August 7, with simultaneous landings on Tulagi and Guadalcanal. By great good fortune complete tactical surprise was
achieved, and the troops waded ashore on both sides of Sealark
Channel without opposition. Tulagi and the outlying islands
protecting its fine harbor were secured after two days of hard
fighting. On Guadalcanal it was a different story. The Marines
secured their foothold and captured the airfield with no more
opposition than a little random sniping. But the worst was yet
to come. Marine amphibious doctrine predicated a successful
assault on complete control of sea and air. At Guadalcanal this
control was obtained only temporarily. The Japanese at Rabaul
reacted by the afternoon of D-Day with the first of a series of
air strikes. These were directed mainly against shipping, instead
of the supplies piled on the congested beaches, and proved
singularly ineffective. But this demonstration of the enemy's
capabilities so alarmed the commander of the supporting aircraft carriers that he announced he was withdrawing from the
area.

The following night a strong Japanese cruiser-destroyer
squadron got through the naval screening force, because of a
combination of poor communications and worse judgment.
Catching the naval defenders flatfooted, the enemy sank four
heavy cruisers, three U.S. and one Australian. With his air support and now a large portion of his surface strength gone, the
U.S. task force commander decided he could stay no longer. So
the transports scurried away with a large part of the already
short supplies, and the floating reserve still not embarked. The
Marines ashore were left very much on their own, with the
Japanese in undisputed control of both sea and air. "Operation
Shoestring" was already beginning to fray.

The Marines tightened their belts and went on short rations,
supplemented with supplies captured from the enemy.

During those first weeks the Japanese were able to pour in
troops and supplies almost at will. In short order they made
landings on both flanks of the Marine perimeter. The objective
of the repeated assaults they staged was the recapture of the air

strip, now named Henderson Field after the Marine squadron commander killed at Midway. Thus developed the essential pattern of the first three months of fighting on Guadalcanal— the Japanese attacking the airfield, the Marines defending it along a wide flung perimeter stretched painfully thin in places.

While the planes operating from Henderson Field were predominantly Marine, Navy and Army planes also shared a good portion of the work. The effectiveness of these planes did much to slow down Japanese reinforcing activities. Such activities were further curtailed as U.S. Navy forces became more active in adjacent waters. The naval battles were extremely bitter and hard fought, with the Japanese Navy giving as good as it received. But the Japanese could not afford the losses they were taking. Finally, in a series of almost continuous naval actions during November, they lost 12 troop-laden transports. This ended their attempts at large-scale reinforcement and resupply, which were abandoned in favor of piecemeal operations by destroyers and landing craft, staged down through the islands.

Meanwhile, the Marines were learning a number of useful things. They learned the technique of jungle fighting and patroling under such Nicaragua veterans as Colonel Merritt A. ("Red Mike") Edson and Colonel W. J. ("Wild Bill") Whaling. They learned much about the enemy as a fighting man. They learned that he relied more on treachery and some mystic divine guidance than upon sound military doctrine. They also made the interesting discovery that because a man is a brave and stubborn fighter does not necessarily mean that he is an especially skillful one. Once and for all, the legend of Japanese invincibility, engendered by their earlier successes against negligible opposition, was blasted. A Marine sergeant, being questioned by an Army intelligence officer, put this feeling in a nutshell.

"Hell!" he snorted. "They aren't supermen; they're just tricky little bastards!"

As the Japanese capability for sustaining action diminished, the American capability grew. The supply problem ceased to be serious after mid-September. Reinforcements came in despite enemy interference. The 2d Marines, the original floating reserve, landed on September 14, followed by the 7th Marines from Samoa, who arrived on the 18th. Army troops were also becoming available at long last. The 164th Infantry Regiment arrived in mid-October to be followed by the remainder of the Americal Division, and two other Army divisions.

By early December it became possible to relieve the 1st Marine Division. These men had borne the brunt of America's first Pacific counter offensive for four long months. They were exhausted physically and mentally, and riddled by malaria and other tropical diseases. They were shipped to Australia for a protracted period of rest, rehabilitation and re-equipping. It was a pleasant period that many would remember long after the horrors of Guadalcanal had become only a bad dream.

Command on Guadalcanal officially passed to the Army on December 9 when Major General A. M. Patch relieved General Vandegrift. Elements of the 2d Marine Division had been arriving and remained to help General Patch in the final drive that pushed the Japanese off the island altogether.

Operations during the remainder of 1943 and the early months of 1944 continued to be directed toward the reduction of Rabaul. The conviction had been growing that actual capture of the base would be unnecessary, provided it could be effectively isolated, and its air potential destroyed. Coordinated drives toward this end were instituted in the South Pacific and the Southwest Pacific Theaters.

In the South Pacific the drive moved up the Solomons chain from Guadalcanal, now developed into a powerful base. The first step took place during the summer of 1943, aimed at the island group centering around New Georgia. Its primary objective was the newly developed Japanese airfield at Munda Point on New Georgia.

This was mainly an Army show, supported by the 1st and 4th Marine Raider Battalions and the 4th and 9th Marine Defense Battalions. The fighting generally resembled that which had taken place on Guadalcanal. On several occasions the attack bogged down badly, demonstrating even more emphatically the futility of attempting a war of maneuver in dense tropical jungle. The operation dragged on much longer than had been originally expected. But the outcome was inevitable, and by October 9 the New Georgia group, including the islands of Kolombangara and Vella Lavella which lay to the north, had been secured. With these steps, bases for the air arm advanced that much closer to Rabaul.

The next advance in this theater occurred on November 1. The new 3d Marine Division, reinforced by Raider and Parachute troops, landed on Bougainville, largest and northernmost of the major Solomon Islands. There was no intention of seizing all, or even an appreciable portion, of this large, strongly held island. The landing area selected lay in the Empress Augusta Bay region on Bougainville's west coast. It had been picked for two reasons. Intelligence indicated that it was weakly held and was not susceptible to prompt reinforcement, owing to its distance from the main Japanese troop concentrations. The objective was strictly limited to establishing a beachhead and pushing far enough inland to set up a defensive perimeter around terrain suitable for the construction of airfields. Establishment of these airfields would bring Rabaul within easy fighter range.

The small Japanese defensive force, estimated at only company strength, was incapable of defending the entire landing area. But it had some well integrated emplacements near the right flank of the beach which managed to inflict numerous casualties among the assault waves. This deterrent was overcome in short order, as was a hurried and badly planned counter landing the following day by Japanese troops from Rabaul.

Thereafter the operation became a matter of steadily pushing inland across some of the worst terrain in the world—and under some of the world's worst weather conditions. Several random skirmishes punctuated the advance against what remained of the original defense force and some reinforcements which the Japanese managed to feed piecemeal into the area. This resistance was centered along the southern flank of the advance. Engineers and Seabees performed prodigies of labor in preparing the way for troops across extensive swamps lying immediately behind the landing area, and constructing airfields, once sites had been secured. The Army's 37th Infantry Division came in to reinforce the Marines and take over defense of the left half of the perimeter. By December 10 the air strips were operational, Japanese resistance had been crushed, and the Americal Division arrived to take over the rest of the perimeter. By December 28 the Marines had been relieved for further assault operations.

A bloody footnote remained to be written on Bougainville. By great effort, the Japanese finally succeeded in concentrating an estimated force of two divisions in the area. Early in March they launched a powerful and violent attack against that portion of the perimeter held by the 37th Division. Fighting reached such a crescendo of intensity that every plane on the island was assigned a standby pilot for immediate evacuation. But the 37th proved fully capable of handling the situation. In 17 days of intensive fighting they destroyed all further Japanese capabilities for offensive action on Bougainville.

In the Southwest Pacific Theater, General MacArthur's forces carried out their part of the isolation of Rabaul by pushing westward along the northern coast of New Guinea. In September they captured Lae and Salamaua. In late October they seized Finschhafen and strategically important Huon Peninsula facing Cape Gloucester, on the western end of New Britain Island. Rabaul occupied the northeastern corner, 260 miles away across Vitiaz Straight. MacArthur did not consider it safe to press his advance any farther to the west, as long as the enemy held a strong point which included a two-strip airfield squarely on his flank, across some sixty miles of open water. Therefore, he decided that the Cape Gloucester area must be seized. To perform this assault mission he designated the 1st Marine Division. This unit had been sent to Australia from Guadalcanal for rehabilitation on the proviso that it perform at least two assault missions for Southwest Pacific forces.

Planning for the Cape Gloucester operation involved considerable argument which served to underline the difference between Army and Marine tactical thinking. The Army favored multiple landings at two or more separated points, with the troops converging on a common objective. The Marines favored concentration of maximum force against a single point, and developing the situation from there. Possibly this mode of thought stemmed from the fact that the Marines had never had enough men to be able to afford dispersing them all over the map. In addition, the 1st Marine Division knew only too well from experience the great difficulties in effecting convergence in tropical jungles. They were also well aware of the danger of friendly forces firing into each other when they met.

The tactical argument was finally settled by General MacArthur in favor of the Marine concept. The General decided against the plans submitted by the staff of his own Sixth Army which exercised tactical command of the operation. However, one minor concession was made to Army thinking. While the main force struck east of the Gloucester airfield, one detached battalion was to land around the cape to the southwest. Thus the Army could— and did—point with pride to two arrows on the operation map. As a matter of fact, the detached battalion played no part in the action until several days after the main issue had been decided, when it became involved in a minor action with retreating Japanese.

The Cape Gloucester assault was preceded by a landing on December 15, made by the 112th Cavalry Regiment of the Army's First Cavalry Division. The landing was made at Arawe on the southern coast of New Britain. Exactly what tactical purpose this operation was designed to serve has never been very clear, least of all to the luckless troops who carried it out. These unfortunates were destined to spend the next three months pinned down on an isolated neck of land by a greatly inferior Japanese force, simply because once they had landed they had no orders to do anything else. The avowed purpose of the landing was to obtain a suitable location for a PT boat base, which the Navy kept insisting it did not want and had no intention of developing.

The diversionary effects of the landing, however, were considerable. It succeeded in drawing off a Japanese battalion which otherwise might subsequently have been employed against the Marines at Cape Gloucester. And, like a stick driven into a hornets' nest, it stirred Rabaul into a frenzy of air activity which ultimately diverted a major air strike which might have hit the Gloucester landing before the amphibious shipping had been completely unloaded.

The Japanese defenders of western New Britain numbered somewhere between 7,000 and 10,000 troops. The exact number could not be computed by the Japanese themselves, let alone U.S. Intelligence. Comprised of elements of no less than 68 tactical components, the Japanese force embraced every conceivable branch of the service. Overall command rested in the hands of Major General Twao Matsuda whose principal claim to military competence lay in the field of ocean barge transportation, for which Cape Gloucester had become an important center.

His principal components were two infantry regiments. The 141st Regiment was widely deployed to defend the west and south coasts, and would require at least a week to concentrate in the area of the Marines' attack. All that Matsuda had immediately available to oppose the landing were two battalions of the 53d Regiment, one at the airfield, the other in the Brogen Bay area seven miles to the east.

The Marines attacked on the early morning of December 26, 1943, according to the calendar west of the International Date Line. Back home it was Christmas Day. Partly by luck and partly by shrewd interpretation of inadequate intelligence, they landed unopposed midway between the two widely separated areas of prepared Japanese defense positions. It was really a shore-to-shore operation, rather than a true amphibious assault. The largest vessels employed were LSTs which loaded their troops and equipment in New Guinea and discharged them directly on the Gloucester beaches. While one regiment drove inland to set up a perimeter around the landing beaches, another plunged westward toward the airfield. Hampered more by swampy jungle terrain, monsoon rains and electric storms of indescribable violence than the spotty resistance offered by the Japanese, they secured the airfield on December 30.

This allowed neat timing for Major General W. H. Rupertus, the division commander, to get off a flowery dispatch to his immediate superior, General Krueger of Sixth Army, presenting the airfield as a New Year's present. Krueger, in turn, presented it to MacArthur who radioed back congratulations to each in turn, and all hands in general. For a while the air waves were so crowded with mutual congratulations that little space remained for such mundane matters as rations, medical supplies and ammunition.

Capture of the airfield signalled accomplishment of the 1st Marine Division's primary mission. But the battle for Cape Gloucester was far from over. To secure the airfield against the possibility of counterattack, the main Japanese force had to be destroyed, or driven off. With this end in view, the Marines regrouped and attacked eastward toward the Brogen Bay area.

By this time General Matsuda had managed to bring up his scattered detachments from the south, notably the 141st Infantry. The Japanese had also had time to prepare defensive positions commanding the Brogen Bay approaches. The route of advance lay across extremely difficult terrain. A maze of high, jungle-covered ridges and ravines lay across the axis of attack. The advance was characterized by jungle fighting of the most stubborn and vicious sort, under terrible weather conditions. It finally came to an end on January 13 with the capture of Hill 660, the last dominating height held by the enemy.

With the loss of Hill 660 the Japanese did something unique in the experience of the troops who had fought against them. They broke off contact and, as far as the Marines were concerned, simply vanished. Actually they were conducting a well planned and well executed withdrawal eastward toward Rabaul and intermediate strong points still held along New Britain's northern coast. With their superior knowledge of the terrain, they got away to a long head start before the Marines realized what they were up to and succeeded in locating their escape route.

A series of amphibious leapfrogging operations followed along the north coast, as the Marines sought to intercept the withdrawal and destroy its main components. This maneuver led to the second main attack of the New Britain campaign— the Talasea operation. Talasea is located on the eastern shore of the Willaumez Peninsula, a spatulate finger of land about midway along New Britain's northern coast. A strongly held position there would dominate the main escape routes of Japanese garrisons evacuating in the general direction of Rabaul.

This operation was unique in several respects. It entailed crossing some sixty miles of open sea without naval convoy or air cover, then assaulting a hostile shore without support. It was performed entirely by landing craft, the largest of which were a few LCTs. Air support promised from Army fields in New Guinea failed to materialize when the fields were weathered in. At the last minute, a small Piper Cub observation plane showed up and enlivened proceedings by dropping hand grenades and fused mortar shells on suspected enemy positions. Under this support the Marines made their landing against relatively light resistance, on March 6.

At the end of three days of steady slugging, they had advanced five miles. The Japanese defenders made a desperate last-ditch stand at the edge of a non-operational airfield which occupied the center of the twenty-five-mile-long peninsula. Once this obstacle had been overcome, the Japanese power and will to resist had been definitely broken on Willaumez Peninsula. Mopping up the remainder of the peninsula proved to be routine patrol work for the most part.

The nature of the New Britain campaign makes it very difficult to select a date, or place, where the operation definitely ended. Actually the Army's 40th Infantry Division, which relieved the Marines on April 25th, had begun killing Japanese before the last of their predecessors had left the island. For all practical operational purposes the campaign had ended with the seizure of the Willaumez Peninsula, and the withdrawal of the Japanese forces to the vicinity of Rabaul. There some 40,000 of the enemy, harassed by "milk run" bombing and the guerrilla activities of the natives, sat out the remainder of the war powerless to influence the issue being decided many miles away.

The summer of 1943 saw a considerable increase of Marine strength in the Pacific. Following the Guadalcanal operation, the 1st Marine Division had been transferred to Australia and the 2d Division to New Zealand. Four Raider Battalions, organized into a regiment, were based on New Caledonia. The newly organized 3d Marine Division had displaced to the Pacific in increments, first to New Zealand, then to Guadalcanal. The 4th Marine Division had been activated early in the year. By fall, organization had been completed and the division was undergoing concentrated advanced training at Camp Pendleton, California, preparatory to shipment "beyond the seas."

Such increased strength called for establishing command and administrative echelons higher than division level. The first such command was activated in Noumea, New Caledonia, in the fall of 1942 to exercise over-all command of the troops fighting on Guadalcanal. This originally was designated "I Marine Amphibious Corps," the title later being changed to "III Amphibious Corps." Top command remained in the hands of the Marine Corps, though the staff comprised many representatives of other services. The first commanding general was Major General Clayton B. Vogel, who was succeeded by C. D. Barrett, A. A. Vandegrift, who became Commandant in 1944, and finally Lieutenant General Roy S. Geiger who retained the post until the end of the war. Corps Headquarters displaced from Noumea to Guadalcanal during the late summer of 1943 where it remained until after the Okinawa operation. Its components included all tactical troops operating in the South Pacific Area, in conjunction with Admiral William F. Halsey's Third Fleet. It exercised command over ground and air operations in the New Georgia and Bougainville campaigns during the drive up the Solomons chain against the Japanese stronghold at Rabaul.

The V Amphibious Corps was activated at Pearl Harbor during the late summer of 1943 to command the more recently conceived drive across the Central Pacific. Again top command was held by the Marines, though in this case not without strong opposition by the Army. The commanding general of the Army forces in the Hawaiian area emphasized the point that the Marine Corps was without experience in command at corps level. He strongly urged that the Army take over all details of this function. However, the Commander-in-Chief of the United States Fleet, Admiral Ernest J. King firmly blocked this move within the Joint Chiefs of Staff. He pointed out that the Central Pacific drive would be primarily a naval undertaking under a Navy theater commander, with the Marines spearheading the landing operations. The command went to Marine Major General Holland M. Smith.

The drive across the Central Pacific opened while the campaign against Rabaul was still continuing full blast. Behind its inception lay a long and heated controversy at the top strategic level where the basic concepts of the Navy were opposed to those of the Army.

The drive, aimed straight at Japan by what appeared to be the shortest route, passed through the enemy held islands and the island groups intervening. The more important of these were to be seized for the dual purpose of serving as advanced bases for further operations, and to neutralize certain other islands which were to be by-passed. The basic idea was to bring U.S. striking power within distance of the enemy homeland in a much shorter time than MacArthur's campaign along the northern New Guinea coast and upward through the Philippines seemed possible of achieving.

The campaign opened with an epic battle in the Gilbert Islands on November 20, 1943. More specifically, it started on an island named Betio in an atoll called Tarawa, from which the action took its name.

Betio was typical of the mass of coral atoll islands which dotted the Central Pacific. It consisted of a low-lying coral formation, surrounded by coral reefs up to 1,000 yards in width. Its airfield had been neutralized well in advance of the actual attack. But Japanese labor and ingenuity had converted the island, approximately the size of Central Park in New York City, into a veritable fortress. It was so strongly fortified and garrisoned that its commander had boasted that a million troops could not take it by assault in a hundred years.

But the 2d Marine Division, unaware of the commander's boast, secured the island in three days. The cost in casualties shocked a nation lulled to complacency by previous less bloody conquests, though it would have to accept materially higher casualty lists in subsequent operations. Major General Holland M. Smith who commanded the entire Gilberts operation believed at the time, and maintained afterward, that Tarawa was a mistake. He was convinced that the whole Gilberts group should have been by-passed and the assault staged in the Marshalls, farther west. But the fact is that a Tarawa, by whatever name, had to be fought sometime, somewhere, and the lesson that it taught learned the hard way.

Tarawa served as a testing laboratory for Marine Corps amphibious doctrine; not the basic doctrines themselves, but the means of executing them. The test revealed certain glaring flaws which, had they not been recognized and corrected, might well have rendered impossible the conquest of such places as Saipan, Guam, Peleliu and Iwo Jima.

The first lesson learned at Tarawa concerned the employment of naval gunfire and air support for a landing operation against a thoroughly entrenched and prepared enemy.

The naval gunfire support group, which included three battleships, five cruisers and nine destroyers, was the largest ever assembled in the Pacific up to that time. The carrier support group included five aircraft carriers. During a pre-landing briefing,

Rear Admiral Howard F. Kingman, commanding the Gunfire Support Group of the Task Force, had proudly assured the assembled naval and Marine officers, "We do not intend to neutralize this island. We do not intend to destroy it. Gentlemen, we will obliterate it."

For a while it looked as though this was precisely what was happening. Within a short time after the bombardment commenced, the island appeared a flaming, exploding mass of destruction. The gunfire slacked off in order to give the planes a chance to plaster the target; then the devastating bombardment resumed. But when the transports moved in to the debarkation area, Japanese shore batteries of big 8-inch guns captured at Singapore promptly opened up on them. These huge weapons were necessarily emplaced in the open and should have been the first targets destroyed; yet here they were very much operative, to the great embarrassment of Navy gunnery officers, and more especially to Admiral Kingman.

The enemy guns scored no direct hits, but their near misses caused numerous casualties. The vulnerable transports hurriedly withdrew out of range. H-Hour was postponed half an hour, later another half hour, to give the support group and air further time to work on this unexpected obstacle. Now that the naval guns had begun to concentrate fire on individual targets, rather than bombarding a general area, the big guns were soon put out of action. But when the landing waves finally began their run on the beach, they were assailed by a fury of machine gun and high-velocity weapons, fire that awesomely exceeded anything previously encountered in the Pacific.

What had gone wrong? The naval gunfire bombardment had been executed according to plan. The fault lay not in the execution of the gunfire plan, but in its basic concept. At Tarawa, as it always had before, the preparatory phase called for neutralizing fire, designed to blanket an entire area without regard to specific targets. This seemed to have worked well enough at Guadalcanal, Tulagi, the Central Solomons and Bougainville. But these places all had a common characteristic that appears to have escaped the notice of the naval gunfire planners. At all of these landing sites the Japanese had not been prepared to offer strong initial resistance from well fortified positions. One of the great lessons learned at Tarawa was that the existing doctrine of naval gunfire support was based on a false premise. Area neutralization was of little value against heavily constructed fortifications. They required absolute destruction.

The second lesson learned at Tarawa dealt with the methods of assault across extensive coral reefs. Here Amtracks (LVTs) were employed for the first time as troop carriers. The Amtrack had not been designed as an assault vehicle. No one had thought of using it in that capacity until shortly before this operation. The decision to use them was made when uncertainty regarding the tidal conditions led to serious doubt as to the conventional landing crafts' ability to get to the beach.

When the decision was made to attempt this experiment, there were only enough Amtracks available to boat the first three assault waves. The plan called for the Amtracks to go straight in, unload, then return to pick up the troops carried in those landing craft unable to negotiate the reef—which proved to be all of them. But the Amtrack is at best a slow, clumsy and vulnerable vehicle. They were sitting ducks for the Japanese gunners. Drivers inexperienced in this sort of employment contributed operational casualties, with the result that very few Amtracks remained for ferrying operations. Many of the stranded troops were able to reach the beach only by swimming and wading across the open reef. The beachhead that night was a most tenuous thing. Probably the only factor that kept the Marines from being shoved back into the sea was that naval gunfire, for all its other ineffectiveness, had destroyed the enemy's communication system, preventing them from mounting a concerted counterattack.

The troops occupying the beachhead were a badly jumbled lot. Inevitably, in the face of such heavy opposition, some units had landed out of place and become intermingled with other units. Even those which remained intact were sadly depleted.

Many key leaders had become casualties, and organization, in the conventional sense, had broken down to a serious degree.

But the Marines went on to capture the island in 72 hours at the staggering cost of 947 killed and 2,186 wounded. The Japanese garrison suffered almost complete annihilation: 4,690 killed; 146 prisoners of war, of whom 129 were Korean laborers. According to the December 6, 1943 issue of *Time* magazine, "Last week some 2,000 or 3,000 United States Marines, most of them now dead or wounded, gave the nation a name to stand beside those of Concord Bridge, the Bon Homme Richard, the Alamo, Little Big Horn, and Belleau Wood. The name was Tarawa."

The imprint of the nearly disastrous assault on Tarawa was plainly to be seen in all further operations in the Central Pacific. The situation following Tarawa somewhat resembled that prevailing at Quantico in the early 'thirties when a dedicated group laboriously evolved successful doctrine from a study of one of the most conspicuous failures in modern warfare. Like much belabored Gallipoli, Tarawa's contribution was the results of its failures.

Never after Tarawa would naval gunfire support content itself with area saturation bombardment at extreme range. Henceforth enemy strong points, either previously located by aerial photography or by the actual firing of the pieces, would be pinpointed by point blank fire. This practice was contrary to existing naval tactical concepts. Many officers of the old school didn't like it a bit, and it required much persuasion before they would accept it. A certain admiral, by his reiterated order to his reluctant skippers to "Close in! Close in!" won the lifetime nickname of "Close in Conolly."

Much the same principle applied to air support. Pre-invasion aerial reconnaissance and photography were emphasized in an effort to pinpoint major enemy installations for the attacking planes. With the Japanese proclivity for digging in and their knack for camouflage, only the obvious installations were detectable. But once the action was joined, many others inevitably disclosed their positions. Ground-to-air and shore-to-ship communication systems were worked out by which the troops ashore could bring down call fire on positions which were holding them up.

Tarawa had also made it unmistakably clear that there was to be little resemblance between the tactics employed in the Central Pacific and those which had been used on the big islands of the South and Southwest. The Marines, like the Japanese, had learned jungle lore and jungle fighting by combat. On the atolls of Micronesia, both antagonists were to find the techniques on which they had lavished so much thought, sweat and blood as obsolete as the close-order formations of the Civil War.

No future assault plans envisioned putting assault troops ashore in landing craft across fringing coral reefs. This became the function of Amtracks, now appearing in the Pacific in ever increasing numbers. These would embark the leading assault elements, waddle from ship to shore, land their troops and return to the reef's edge. There they would rendezvous with conventional landing craft, standing by with supporting troops elements which would be ferried across the coral in turn. But, like any other new technique, there was much to be learned before this method of troop transportation reached an acceptable degree of efficiency. Some of these lessons, as well as others, were learned during the campaign in the Marshalls which followed a little over two months after Tarawa.

But transcending in importance the tactical innovations developed in the Marshalls was the concept which caused the attack to be made in the first place.

Lying to the north and east of the Carolines, the Marshalls formed a bastion covering the front and northern flank of the great Japanese base at Truk. Since they lay squarely across the Central Pacific, in enemy hands they denied direct access to the strong points of the inner Japanese defense ring, and flanked the approach to Japan itself. The Japanese had strongly fortified six atolls in the Marshalls group: Jaliut, Mille, Maloelap, Wotje, Kwajalein and Eniwetok, each containing at least one airfield.

To reach Kwajalein, approximately in the center of the archipelago, it was necessary to by-pass the other four strongholds which lay to the east and southeast. The concept was to rely on naval gunfire and aerial bombardment to keep these neutralized and isolated from seaborne support until they "withered on the vine," as a phrase included in the plan so aptly described the process. This was the first major by-passing operation of the war, and it could hardly have been more successful. Four strong enemy defensive bases were eliminated as thoroughly and permanently as though they had been atom-bombed—and without the necessity for costly assault.

Kwajalein, the largest coral atoll in the world, measures 65 miles in length, with a maximum width of 18 miles. The Japanese were known to be established in force on its three main islands. Kwajalein, from which the atoll takes its name, lies at the southeastern tip. Roi and Namur, which for all practical purposes comprise a single island, occupy the northern point of the irregular, triangle-shaped group. Simultaneous attacks were made on Kwajalein and Roi-Namur by the Army's 7th Infantry Division and the 4th Marine Division, respectively. D-Day was January 31, 1944.

The assault on Roi-Namur marked the first action for the 4th Marine Division, which had staged out of San Diego for a combat operation some 4,300 miles away. For most of the troops it was an unusual experience. The first "romantic tropical island" they ever laid eyes on was one which they were called upon to wrest from the enemy to the accompaniment of blasting gunfire and the dull "whump" of bursting bombs. It was, however, a situation that rapidly became familiar to a division which was destined to storm ashore four times in the coming year.

The new division brought with it a tactical inovation in the use of artillery. Setting up artillery on a shallow beachhead is a hazardous operation at best. Furthermore, artillery so employed can seldom realize its full potential effectiveness as a support weapon, even if it can be brought ashore soon enough to be of much use during the early phases. At Roi-Namur, outlying islands within artillery range were seized as a preliminary step and the weapons emplaced to support the main assault. Such tactics produced a situation unique in the Pacific war—the artillery landing on D-Day, while the main body of infantry did not hit the beach until the following day.

The costly naval gunfire lesson learned at bloody Tarawa paid rich dividends in the Marshalls. For two solid days before the landing a mighty task force shelled the objectives until there was virtually nothing left standing above ground. The new technique of pre-assault emplacement of artillery proved highly successful, and the leading assault waves hit the beach under a close-in preparation from their own support weapons. By the time the third wave was ashore it looked like a text book operation. One hour later the Marines were rewriting the book on the basis of another lesson learned the hard way.

The landing technique of using Amtracks was being employed on a large scale for the first time. When the Navy had been informed that LVTs were to be substituted for conventional landing craft as the primary assault vehicle, naval officers, not unnaturally, assumed they should be handled in the same manner. Unfortunately, there were distinct differences in the characteristics of the two types of craft.

By accepted convention, transports launched their landing craft in an assault operation at a minimum of 12,000 yards offshore. This distance was beyond the range of any but the largest Japanese guns, which presumably had been knocked out by naval gunfire. This worked out fine in the case of conventional landing craft, as had been proved by repeated tests. But when an attempt was made to adapt the same technique to the Amtrack, the fundamental weakness of this vehicle became painfully evident. The Amtrack consumes fuel in quantities disproportionate to anything ever experienced with small craft. A half hour following the assault landing, Kwajalein lagoon was strewn with wallowing Amtracks which had run out of gas while trying to get back to the convoy to refuel.

This serious miscalculation pointed up a further limitation of the Amtrack. Underway, it is reasonably seaworthy in not too violent waters. Stalled, it pitches helplessly, shipping water over the sides in even a comparatively calm sea. Before anyone realized what was happening, Amtracks were swamping all over the lagoon.

However, by then, with the beaches secured, it was practical to bring in the supporting elements by landing craft. This meant that many of the troops had to wade ashore across the coral reefs, but at least they could do so without coming under fire. Tanks proved capable of coming in from the reef's edge under their own power, though a few were lost in the process.

Even with the frustrating experience of the Amtracks, it was all over with a suddenness that startled all hands. The key island of Roi, which consisted mainly of an airfield, was secured by early afternoon of the first day. Its Siamese twin, Namur, which was covered with dense jungle, fell during the early afternoon of the following day. On the island of Kwajalein forty miles to the south, the Army's 7th Division, attacking down the long axis of a much larger island, completed the job in three days.

The seizure of Kwajalein gave the United States effective control of the Marshalls. There was one requirement still to be satisfied—a staging base farther to westward. The logical choice was Eniwetok, westernmost atoll of the island group.

The capture of Eniwetok had been included in the overall plan of the Marshalls campaign. Originally, the plan called for a target date some two months following the seizure of Kwajalein, using an entire division in the assault.

The comparative ease with which Kwajalein had been taken caused reassessment of the whole atoll situation. As a result, the decision was made to assault Eniwetok at once, using the floating reserve for the Kwajalein operation. This reserve was composed of two reinforced regiments; the 22d Marines and the Army's 106th Infantry Regiment.

The hurriedly revised attack plan called for the 22d Marines to seize the main island of Engebi which contained an airstrip. The 106th was to attack Eniwetok Island on the southern face of the atoll, which intelligence estimates indicated was held by a comparatively small force of Japanese. The Marines took Engebi on February 17 in a brisk fight that lasted until mid-afternoon. Pausing to look around after they had secured their objective, it appeared to the Marines that nothing else had happened.

Early the next morning, Brigadier General T. E. Watson, commanding the Tactical Group, detached one battalion of the 22d Marines to move down to Eniwetok and find out what was going on. The Marines found the 106th pinned down just inland of the beach by the heavy fire of the defenders. Throwing their weight into the fight, the Marine battalion drove straight across the island, cutting it in two. Once the attack got rolling, the remainder of the island was secured without undue difficulty.

With the fall of the Marshalls, the way at last lay open to the inner ring of Japan's defensive bases. The war in the Pacific was moving rapidly westward toward the Rising Sun.

★ **13** ★

★ ★ ★ ★ ★

Pacific Victory

THE FIRST BLOW at Japan's intermediate defensive ring was aimed at the Marianas Islands. Tactically, it involved considerable risk. Strategically, it constituted an impressive display of the U.S. capability for long-range operations, and a serious threat to Japan's inner defense line.

The Marianas form the final link in an almost unbroken chain of islands extending some 1,400 miles southward from the mainland of Japan. Like giant unsinkable aircraft carriers, the larger islands provided a series of mutually supporting airfields and bases protecting the lines of sea and air communications from Japan to her southern empire. Control of the Marianas would not only sever the enemy lines of communication, but would also provide easy access to the enemy-dominated seas of the western Pacific. Perhaps most important of all, it would provide land bases within bomber range of the home islands of Japan.

Of the fifteen islands which compose the Marianas, only the southern islands of Saipan, Tinian, Rota and Guam were worthwhile military targets. Saipan, keystone of the Marianas defense, served as the Japanese supply base and communications center for the Central Pacific. Among other headquarters, it housed those of Vice Admiral Chuichi Nagumo, commander of the Central Pacific Fleet and Lieutenant General Hideyoshi Obata, administrative commander of the Marianas, Bonin, Marshall and Caroline Islands.

The campaign for the Marianas proved to be the toughest which the U.S. troops had yet been called upon to face in the Pacific. Saipan alone was a sort of multiplied Tarawa. While the latter was taken in a matter of hours by a single Marine division, Saipan required twenty-five days and the undivided attention of two reinforced Marine divisions and one Army division.

The overall operation plan called for the Marine Corps to field an organization much larger and more complicated than it had ever operated before. Roughly, it required the equivalent of two corps; three Marine divisions and a provisional brigade, plus two Army divisions. The command situation caused considerable concern in Army circles, and serious attempts were made in Honolulu to superimpose more experienced Army staffs at the higher levels. This action did not elicit the enthusiastic approval of Major General Holland M. ("Howlin' Mad") Smith, the Marine officer designated for top command.

The Marine Corps had no rank designation for an echelon as high as that now occupied by General Smith. Marine Corps Headquarters handed him the awkward title of "Commanding General Northern Troops and Landing Force."

As the senior Marine officer, General Smith exercised command of the expeditionary troops. More directly, he commanded those forces whose immediate object was to secure the northern Marianas, notably Saipan and Tinian. His troops for this purpose consisted of the veteran 2d and 4th Marine Divisions, and the Army's largely untried 27th Infantry Division.

Seizure of the southern Marianas—in a word, Guam—was assigned to what later became known as the Third Amphibious Corps, commanded by Major General Roy S. Geiger. This Corps included the 3d Marine Division, 1st Marine Provisional Brigade and one of the Army's finest units, the 77th Infantry Division.

The opening wedge was driven in the northern Marianas on the western shore of southern Saipan on June 15, 1944. The 2d and 4th Marine Divisions hit the beach, side-by-side, at 8:43 a.m., to begin one of the bloodiest battles of the Pacific war. The lesson of the Amtracks had been well learned in the Marshalls. In the first 20 minutes of the assault, over 8,000 men were deposited on the shore by 722 clanking Amtracks.

Since the senior Japanese officer, General Obata, was at Palau on an inspection tour at the time, the defense of Saipan devolved upon Lieutenant General Yoshitsugu Saito, commanding general of the Northern Marianas Army Group. To meet the invasion, Saito had two main units; the 43d Infantry Division and the 47th Independent Mixed Brigade. In addition, there was Admiral Nagumo's Navy contingent which included the 55th Naval Guard Force and the 1st Yokosuka Special Landing Force of the so-called Imperial Marines. All told, the defenders of Saipan numbered 29,662, and they knew their business.

It was hard going from the beginning. By night fall of D-Day the beachhead was 1,500 yards deep. At the end of the second day American casualties had mounted to over 3,500, with the other end of Saipan still twelve miles away.

Psychological warfare was nothing new for the Japanese. Veteran American troops had long since come to expect it, and were generally prepared for it. At Saipan, however, the Sons of Nippon came up with a new wrinkle that really had the Marines worried for the first two or three days. Position after position was overrun which contained only one or two enemy dead. Past experience indicated that with such concentrated shelling and intensive fighting, heavy casualties on the defending side were inevitable. Many a BAR man and machine gunner swore up and down that he had seen at least a half dozen of the enemy drop in his sights after a well aimed burst. Yet when the position was taken no bodies were to be found. The mystifying situation was beginning to have a telling effect on the troops when a platoon of the 23d Marines finally solved the mystery. Moving across a ridge, the platoon came upon a deep crevasse literally crammed with enemy dead. The retreating Japanese had been carrying off their dead in an attempt to prevent the attackers from learning the extent of their casualties. It was a tactic which was to become very familiar in subsequent operations.

On June 18 the attack carried across the island to the eastern shore. With the 4th Marine Division on the right flank and the 2d on the left, the advance swung northward. To cover the expanding front, the 27th Infantry Division, commanded by Major General Ralph Smith, was assigned to the center of the lines—a move which precipitated one of the most unfortunate incidents of the Pacific War. For reasons still subject to debate, the Army unit failed to keep pace with the Marine divisions on its flanks. After two days with no improvement in the situation, Marine General "Howlin' Mad" Smith relieved Army General Smith of his command. Due largely to a west coast newspaper's sensationalism, the incident ballooned into a public controversy which succeeded only in creating an inter-Service rancor that lasted for years.

The relentless advance of the Americans ground on, with the Japanese-held portion of the island growing smaller each day. At the end of the third week the main core of resistance was concentrated along the western shore, about seven thousand yards from the northern end. After twenty-two days of steady retreat, the initiative passed briefly to the Japanese on the night of July 6.

General Saito had realized the inevitable for some time. As the repeated and extravagant promises from Japan for air and naval relief failed to materalize, the reality of ultimate defeat grew increasingly apparent to the aging commander. But Saito had been raised under the Japanese warrior code of Bushido, and for the Bushido there is no defeat. Sitting alone in the cave that was his command post, the General carefully laid his plans for the attack. At 8 a.m. on the morning of July 6, General Saito issued his last order—a prelude to the largest mass suicide ever staged in the Pacific.

The order read in part, "The barbarous attack of the enemy is being continued . . . we are dying without avail under violent shelling and bombing. Whether we attack, or whether we stay where we are, there is only death. However, in death there is life. We must realize this opportunity to exalt true Japanese manhood. I will advance with those who remain to deliver still another blow to the American devils, and leave my bones on Saipan as a bulwark of the Pacific."

The blow fell in the Army's 27th Division sector at 4:45 the following morning. A seething, screaming tide of humanity smashed into the division's forward elements and rolled on without pause. There was no stopping the fanatical attackers whose only thought was to kill or be killed. Throughout the division's zone of action savage fighting swirled around a dozen isolated pockets of resistance.

With the coming of dawn, observers in the hills saw a strange phenomenon. Behind the Japanese assault moved a weird procession of bandage-swathed men, amputees and crutch-supported cripples helping each other move slowly toward the front. Some carried rifles or a few grenades. Others carried only a bayonet lashed to a stick. Many bore no weapons of any sort. The sick and the wounded had come forth to die.

The attack was finally contained after a penetration of about 1,500 yards. Artillery, firing point blank at the onrushing horde, killed them by the hundreds. Machine gunners piled up so many dead in front of their positions that they were forced to move their weapons to obtain a clear field of fire. By nightfall the greatest *banzai* of all was over. Based on the number of bodies subsequently buried in the area, over 3,000 of the enemy had fallen in one of the most devastating single battles of the war.

Two days after the great *banzai* the campaign came to a close. The neatly ruled columns of the statisticians told a grim story—3,372 Americans killed in action; 10,952 wounded. The price had been high. News of Saipan's fall hit Tokyo with such stunning force that it brought down the Tojo Cabinet with a crash that shook the entire Greater East Asia Co-Prosperity Sphere.

During the campaign still another devastating blow had been struck to the defense of the Empire.

The Marianas operation had been planned as an overall campaign, calling for the simultaneous seizure of the northern and southern islands. The landings on Guam were scheduled for a few days after those on Saipan. Two factors combined to throw this plan awry—the stiffness of enemy resistance on Saipan, and the sortie of the Japanese fleet in an attempt to break up the landings. The first caused considerable concern, but little alarm. The second necessitated the removal of many key naval units originally assigned to support the landings.

Actually the fleet was fully prepared to meet the threat. In fact, high Navy brass had long been looking forward to an opportunity to meet such of the Japanese fleet as had survived the Battle of Midway, and the attrition of the drawn-out Solomons campaign. But the fact that a threat did exist had diverted much of the naval strength earmarked for support of the southern landings. The result was an indefinite postponement of the Guam operation. The unfortunate troops already en route spent the next 50 days on the crowded transports, while their ships circled aimlessly in waters safely beyond possible Japanese interception. It was extremely rough on morale.

The ensuing naval engagement became known officially as the Battle of the Philippine Sea. Unofficially it was labelled "The Marianas Turkey Shoot." The battle was a plane-vs-ship affair, with the surface forces never sighting each other. Moreover, it brought out in dramatic fashion the fatal flaw in Japanese aviation policy.

This policy stressed quality in favor of quantity. Where U.S. aviation turned out thousands of trained pilots, good, bad and indifferent, Japanese aviation concentrated on the thorough training of a comparatively small number of carefully selected men. The Japanese pilots who fought at Midway and other early actions were probably the equal of any who flew in World War II. But the Midway contingent was wiped out en masse with the destruction of their carriers, while the inevitable attrition of hard fighting soon pared down the rest. With the cream of the crop gone, the Japanese had very little left, and limited facilities and personnel for training replacements.

Training facilities were expanded and training speeded up to the point where it became slipshod. As a result, the inept pilots who flew off the Japanese carriers in the Philippine Sea against the U.S. Navy's best were hopelessly and pathetically outclassed. After three days of most unequal fighting, the Japanese surface forces were hightailing for home waters, with the Americans hotly pursuing but never quite catching up. Comparative losses show over 400 Japanese planes destroyed against a U.S. loss of 26. The damage inflicted on Japanese ships was comparable; three aircraft carriers and two tankers sunk; four carriers, a battleship and a cruiser badly damaged. The death blow had been dealt to Japanese carrier-based air power.

The long-delayed Guam operation got underway on July 21. The time lapse gave Rear Admiral R. L. Conolly, commanding the Southern Attack Force, fourteen days to bombard the island. This he did slowly and systematically. Without doubt, it was the best pre-landing bombardment ever experienced by Marines in the Pacific. But even this was not sufficient to permit an unopposed landing, nor to knock out many of the Japanese strongpoints inland.

Two landings were made simultaneously against the western beaches of the 29-mile-long island, a maneuver which defied the long established military principle of never dividing one's forces in the face of the enemy. The fighting developed much along the lines of that on Saipan, over generally more difficult terrain, but against weaker resistance. After the initial phases, the enemy concentrated their strength on the northern half of the island. The campaign for the first reconquest of American territory in the Central Pacific resolved itself into three weeks of hard, unspectacular fighting. The island was declared officially secured on August 10, but desultory fighting continued in the rugged hills for some time. The natives continued to ferret out Japanese holdouts until the end of the war.

In addition to the satisfaction of retaking former U.S. territory, the capture of Guam provided a much needed advance naval anchorage. Within a relatively short time, Apra Harbor had been developed into a base capable of supporting one third of the Pacific Fleet.

The assault on Tinian was staged from Saipan three days after the III Amphibious Corps made its landing on Guam. Since only three miles separated the two islands, artillery emplaced on southern Saipan was able to deliver preparatory and covering fire over most of Tinian. This gave the attackers a decided advantage. For the second time in the war the assault troops were able to make their landing under cover of their own organic support weapons. In addition, the Marines had the unaccustomed advantage of knowing the terrain thoroughly. Saipan-based planes had been reconnoitering and photographing the neighboring island for weeks.

The Japanese had a few advantages on their side. The drawn-out fighting on Saipan had given the garrison warning of what to expect, as well as some knowledge of Marine tactics. It had also given them ample time to prepare their defenses. The few beaches which appeared suitable for landing purposes had been strongly fortified. The enemy defensive force was positioned to be able to move quickly to any threatened point. Such movement was entirely feasible since Tinian, in contrast to the rugged terrain of Saipan and Guam, was nearly flat.

Tinian has been described as the most perfect operation in the Pacific—the ultimate demonstration of amphibious doctrine and technique. It has also been described as sending a man to do a boy's work. Against a single Japanese infantry regiment with its normal supporting elements, General Smith hurled two reinforced Marine divisions. Thus, the normal odds of three to one, considered essential to amphibious assault against strongly fortified positions, was increased to something on the order of twelve to one. How much this fantastic numerical superiority had to do with the "perfection" of the operation is purely academic.

The fact remains that at Tinian all plans were executed without flaw, and error and confusion was kept to the barest minimum. Warships and landing craft staged a highly convincing feint off Tinian Town, the most strongly fortified Japanese position. The fire support ships bombarded, while the landing craft circled about in the customary manner, preceding their formation into assault waves. This demonstration continued long enough to enable the Japanese to concentrate all their mobile troops for the defense of the threatened area. Then the landing craft abruptly scuttled off southward to land on two undefended beaches, so narrow and shallow that it never occurred to the Japanese that anyone would be foolish enough to attempt a landing there. And for some time they refused to believe it.

By the time the Japanese commander was able to move his force to the scene, it was the dark hours of the next morning. A large portion of the 4th Division was already ashore and well dug in on a fairly extensive perimeter. As they generally did, the Japanese attacked at once, throwing their full strength at a small sector of the strung-out perimeter. There was ferocious close-in fighting, punctuated by an abortive *banzai* charge. The net result, too, was the same as before. The coming of daylight found the backbone of the well-integrated perimeter unbroken.

From that point on, the operation became a parade. The remainder of the 4th Division came ashore, and the 2d Division behind it. Together they deployed across the entire width of the island and swept northward, mopping up everything they came across. Eight days after the landing, the 4th Division overran Tinian Town. The surviving Japanese concentrated on a rugged ridge at the northern extremity of the island. There they dug in, prepared to fight to the death.

The fight for the ridge was as fierce as any that took place during the war, though on a small scale. Twenty-four hours later the last remnants of organized resistance on Tinian crumbled, and the island was declared officially secured. The date was August 1, 1944.

Capture of the Marianas gained a firm foothold in the intermediate line of defense which the Japanese command depended upon to keep the war away from the Empire. To secure the remaining strongpoint in this line required the seizure of the Palau Islands, the key member of which was Peleliu. To **many** at the time, and to many more later, the operation appeared unnecessary. However, Peleliu contained a sizeable airfield and lay squarely on the flank of General MacArthur's imminent advance into the Philippines. So the high command ordered its capture. The task was assigned to the 1st Marine Division, then staging in the Solomons, as a part of the III Amphibious Corps, still engaged on Guam.

Peleliu looked easy—at first. It was only six miles long and two miles wide. It contained an airfield, plain to be seen, an estimated 10,000 Japanese troops, and a number of other disagreeable features which became painfully apparent only after the battle started. All in all, the place appeared so insignificant at first glance that one Marine on an offshore transport was heard to remark, "How the hell could the Japs crowd 10,000 men on that little hunk of real estate?"

The Marines learned the answer to that question early in the operation. The Japanese weren't on it; they were in it.

In some superficial aspects Peleliu resembled the islands of the Marianas. But in most essentials it resembled no other place on earth, at least none the Marines had ever seen. Peleliu proved to be full of surprises, all of them unpleasant. Basically the island was a solid piece of coral and limestone thrust above the ocean's surface by some past volcanic action. On it had settled a meager top soil capable of supporting low, scraggly vegetation, sufficient only to cloak the natural terrain contours against aerial observation. Once naval gunfire and bombing had blasted loose this fragile cover, the high ground north of the airfield stood revealed as a veritable nightmare of terrain. The area was an intricate complex of precipitous coral ridges oriented generally north and south, criss-crossed at all angles by intersecting ridges. These, it was subsequently learned, were honeycombed with natural caves which the Japanese occupied in force. Where the natural caves did not occur in suitable positions, the Japanese had created artificial ones.

The creation of such positions, or any sort of positions in that adamant coral, required elaborate blasting. The Japanese defenders had ample time to do this, but the troops in the assault were preoccupied with other matters. Many a hard-won position had to be relinquished simply because of the Marines' inability to dig in for adequate defense.

The heat was incredible. All day the tropical sun baked the bare corral which exuded its stored heat throughout the night. The occasional rains that fell evaporated instantly, without providing any relief. During the first few days heat prostration cases even exceeded the heavy battle casualties. The whole situation was extremely well summarizd by a *Time* correspondent who opened his dispatch with the statement, "Peleliu is a horrible place. . . ."

The Japanese themselves provided at least one major surprise. Through long experience U.S. commanders looked forward to the enemy breaking his own back by one or more of those fanatical *banzai* charges. But on Peleliu the Marines waited in vain. Not a single *banzai* occurred, nor in any subsequent Pacific operation. Somewhere along the line the Japanese had learned the tactical futility of seeking death for its own sake.

The naval gunfire preparation at Peleliu was singularly ineffective. Three full days of bombardment had been scheduled. On the morning of the third day the admiral commanding the gunfire support group announced, to the consternation of the Marines, that he proposed to cease fire for lack of profitable targets. In justice to the admiral, it must be said that you can't hit what you can't see, or can't locate on aerial photo maps. As far as could be seen, the support ships had destroyed everything worth destroying. Many of the positions which later became so troublesome were located in the maze of ridges and could not have been hit anyway, since they were in defilade.

Nevertheless, when the first waves started across the reef on that memorable morning of September 15, they were assailed by a fury of fire from artillery, machine guns, mortars and high-velocity anti-tank guns. The Marines had a healthy respect for the enemy's 47 millimeter anti-tank gun. It was the one Japanese weapon which exceeded in efficiency anything the U.S. had of comparable caliber. Casualties mounted alarmingly. At one point an aerial observer reported 35 Amtracks burning on the reef or beach. Casualties for D-Day were 210 dead and 910 wounded.

Once ashore, the Marines went about their prescribed missions. In the center the 5th Marines cut the island in half the first day, and secured the airfield on the second. The 7th Marines wiped out resistance in the area south of the airfield two days later. But on the left the 1st Marines almost immediately ran up against that frustrating jumble of terrain, soon to be known as "Bloody Nose Ridge."

Experience indicated that if you hit a Japanese position hard enough and long enough, something was bound to give. Day after day the commanding officer expected a decisive breakthrough. His Marines made some gains frontally and some fairly deep penetrations over to the east. But, owing to the impossibility of digging in, they were unable to hold what they had gained. And the Japanese stubbornly refused to break. The 1st Marines were up against a defense in depth hitherto unprecedented in their experience. After a week of this, the regiment had sustained casualties of 60 per cent, the survivors were completely exhausted, and what remained of the regiment had to be withdrawn.

Frontal assault having proved impractical, the obvious alternative was to attempt flanking the position. This was attempted on both flanks. On the east it proved impossible because of swampy terrain and deep indentations of the sea. On the west, however, a road of sorts traversed the narrow flat between the ridge and the sea. Moving swiftly along this road, the 5th Marines reached the northern end of the island, taking some galling flanking fire from the ridges on their right and the offlying island of Ngesebus on their left. They seized Ngesebus by a miniature amphibious assault with one battalion, and secured all of northern Peleliu.

To replace the 1st Marines the Corps commander brought in the 321st Infantry Regiment, a component of the Army's 81st

Infantry Division. This unit had been engaged in the seizure of the nearby island of Angaur as part of the overall Palaus operation. Although Angaur had fallen without too much difficulty, the 321st knew that it had been in a fight and had won a victory.

The 321st moved across the island, isolating Japanese resistance in the southern end of the ridge system. Since the map labeled the high ground on Peleliu by the improbable title "Umurbrogol Mountain," the isolated Japanese position became known henceforth as the "Umurbrogol Pocket."

For the next month Marines and soldiers hammered at the Umurbrogol Pocket from all directions. From the south, where the first attacks were made, little progress could be achieved. But from the north, east and west they gradually constricted the pocket. It was slow and bloody work.

Peleliu was another of those campaigns which never really had a definable end. It just sort of eventually petered out. For the 1st Marine Division it was over on October 15, when the last of its units were relieved by elements of the 81st Infantry Division.

During the early winter of 1944-1945 an uneasy quiet settled over the Marines in the Pacific. No major actions took place between the withdrawal of the remnants of the 1st Division from Peleliu in October and the assault on Iwo Jima the following February. Hard training continued; no one deceiving themselves for a moment that the war was anywhere over. Re-equipping continued, replacement of material and many new weapons and devices which were at last in production. Fresh troops poured in, replacements for the casualties of the divisions which had fought seven major actions during 1944, and for the weary veterans who had earned their six-months respite back in the States.

The bitter fighting of 1944 had brought out one very clear fact to the U.S. forces. The closer they approached Japan, the better fortified they found their objectives, and the tougher the fighting became. The Marianas had indicated this and Peleliu had underlined it. It remained only for Iwo Jima, the inevitable island, to furnish the final proof.

If the terrain of Peleliu appeared peculiar, that of Iwo was equally strange, though in a different way. Peleliu was, in effect, one solid chunk of jagged coral in which even the simplest field positions had to be blasted out with high explosives. Iwo was composed of loose volcanic ash, somewhat coarser than sand, and rocks so soft that they could be carved with a bayonet or combat knife. Into this the Japanese had burrowed like moles until no defensive installations showed above the surface, although the island was probably the most heavily fortified area on the face of the earth.

The reasons for seizing Iwo were basically different from those which motivated previous operations in the Central Pacific. Although it lay close enough to Japan to be administratively included in the Prefecture of Tokyo, its strategic position on the sea approaches was of small importance. Its seven and a half square miles of area was too small, and its terrain too inhospitable to serve as a staging area or advance base. But its strategic position in relation to air approach was of vast importance.

One of the main reasons for the Marianas campaign had been to capture airfields within bombing range of the Japanese home islands, Tokyo in particular. To the Marines fighting in the Marianas this concept meant very little. None of them had ever seen a B-29, and very few of them had any inkling that such a monster was in the process of development.

When the B-29s appeared in the Pacific and began bombing Japan, they quickly discovered Iwo Jima in their path, a most formidable obstacle for all its insignificant size. Fighter planes swarmed up from its two airfields to intercept the bombers, and its radios flashed alarm of the impending strike to Tokyo. As a result, by the time the big planes reached their target, every Japanese defensive plane was in the air, while alert ground anti-aircraft crews manned their weapons. The B-29s began to suffer an unacceptable casualty rate. Comparatively few were shot down over Japan proper, but many were so badly damaged that they were unable to make it back to their bases in the Marianas. The round-trip to Japan represented their maximum range capabilities. Because of the distance involved, fighter cover was out of the question.

The B-29 was an enormously costly piece of equipment, by far the most costly aircraft of its day. As the losses continued to mount, it became obvious that Iwo Jima had to be eliminated. In Japanese hands it constituted a deadly menace. In U.S. hands, not only would the menace be removed, but it could be converted into a haven for B-29s and a base for accompanying fighters.

The task of eliminating Iwo Jima was assigned to the V Amphibious Corps, with the 4th Marine Division and the new 5th Division making the assault, and the 3d Marine Division in floating reserve. D-Day was designated as February 19.

The Japanese used a new defensive tactic at Iwo. It came as a surprise. The Marines had made a thorough study of Japanese tactics, methods and psychology, and seldom made the same mistake twice. Staff thinkers had often wondered why the enemy seemed to learn nothing by experience, and kept repeating the same mistakes. Actually there were two good reasons, both fairly obvious. One was the inflexibility of the Japanese military mind. The other was the fact that in previous operations no officers had survived to convey in person the lessons learned.

But wisdom gradually filtered through. At Peleliu they had discarded the futile and wasteful *banzai* charge. At Iwo they demonstrated at last they had learned to cope with aerial bombing and naval gunfire. For seventy-two consecutive days preceding the assault, the tiny island had received a blasting from U.S. bombs. Although yard for yard it was the most strongly fortified island in the Pacific, the enemy made no move when the actual landings began under cover of the customary furious naval barrage. The Japanese allowed the advance waves to land practically unscathed, deploy and press inland.

This necessitated the lifting of the naval gunfire barrage to avoid hitting the assault troops. When the barrage ceased, the

Japanese popped up all over the island and blasted the succeeding waves with the most devastating hail of defensive fire imaginable. Casualties among the Amtracks and landing craft were so heavy that for a considerable period the troops ashore were cut off from all support, and meeting the heaviest kind of resistance. For a time the situation was gravely in doubt.

The assault elements needed help desperately, so the supporting troops clinched their teeth and went in, taking murderous losses along the way. Tanks were obviously and badly needed. These got ashore early. Iwo, unlike most of the islands immediately before it, had no fringing coral reef. Landing craft of all types were able to come all the way in and discharge their loads on the beach. Within hours the beach had become so littered with wreckage that it became difficult to find a place to land.

Once ashore, the tanks found themselves bogged down almost immediately in the deep volcanic ash, unable to move over the sharply rising ground just inland of the beaches. The preceeding infantry managed it only with the greatest difficulty, leaving behind footprints that resembled elephant tracks. To provide sufficient traction for the tanks, it was necessary to bring ashore quantities of steel matting designed for reinforcing airfield runways.

From an overall standpoint, the operation was simple enough, though in detail it became bloody and complicated. In spite of all obstacles, on the first day the 5th Division cut across the narrow neck of the island and the 4th Division gained a grip on the main airfield.

The 5th then wheeled to the south and attacked Mount Suribachi, an extinct volcano which dominated the entire island. The mountain itself proved less formidable than its fortified approaches and lower slopes which contained over one thousand separate defensive installations. These were overcome in four days, and on the fifth a patrol of the 28th Marines groped its way to the top and raised a small American flag someone happened to have along. The story goes that Secretary of the Navy, James Forrestal, along as an observer, glimpsed this through

binoculars and suggested that it be replaced by a flag large
enough to be seen all over the island. Accordingly, a ship's flag
was carried up from one of the LSTs on the beach. Hearing of
this, Joe Rosenthal, veteran AP photographer, trudged along
with his camera—and produced what is perhaps the most dramatic and symbolic photograph to come out of any war.

Because this was the second flag-raising, rather than the
original one, some critics have tended to dismiss it as a posed
picture. It was far from that. Japanese resistance on Suribachi
was anything but stamped out. If the men involved were not
actually under fire at the moment, heavy fighting was going on
all around them. In fact, of the six men appearing in the famous
photograph, three were killed on Iwo and a fourth badly
wounded.

Once the airfield had been taken, the 4th Division deployed
across the island, facing north, where they immediately encountered a fantastic complex of prepared positions, organized in
great depth. All hands had expected Iwo to be tough, but nothing in their experience had fully prepared them for anything
quite like this. In welcome contrast to Peleliu's solid coral, Iwo's
volcanic ash permitted the Marines to dig in with little difficulty.
The trouble was that in many areas a foxhole two feet in depth
would uncover a bed of molten sulphur. In other areas under-
ground vents shot up sulphurous steam, often so hot that the
men could cook coffee over it. This was the first operation
against the Japanese to be fought outside the tropics for the
Marines, and many of the men were ill-conditioned for such an
abrupt change in climate.

After Mount Suribachi had been secured, the 5th Division
also turned northward and took position on the left of the advance. But it had already become apparent that, despite the
small size of the island, the two divisions ashore would be inadequate to seize it expeditiously in the face of the formidable
Japanese fortifications. Elements of the floating reserve began to
come ashore on February 21 and take position in the center,
between the 4th and 5th Divisions. Before it was over, two re-

inforced infantry regiments and most of the supporting elements
of the 3d Division were engaged.

There was a considerable sameness about the various operations to the north, all concerned with brutal losses to both sides.
At long last, the remaining Japanese were driven into a deep
ravine and cave system and there effectively sealed off from the
rest of the island. At this point an element of novelty entered
the picture in the several attempts by the Marines to pursuade
Lieutenant General Tadamichi Kuribayashi, the enemy commander, to surrender. It came as a surprise to no one that all
such efforts failed completely, and the work of extermination
continued to the bitter end which came thirty-six days after the
landing.

The three divisions lost 5,931 killed and 17,272 wounded,
by far the largest total casualties suffered by the Marines in any
Pacific operation. In the words of Fleet Admiral Nimitz, "Among
the Americans who served on Iwo Island uncommon valor was
a common virtue." The Japanese defensive force of 21,000
was wiped out save for a handful of prisoners, most of whom were
taken only after being badly wounded.

But there was a brighter side to the picture. Capture of Iwo
greatly accelerated the bombing of the Japanese home islands
and, at the same time, drastically reduced losses of American
lives and equipment. Fighter planes rose from Iwo's airfields to
provide cover for the B-29s over their targets. The island also
provided a haven of safety for those bombers too crippled to
make it all the way home. Three months after Iwo had been
taken, the Army Air Force reported that 850 B-29s, carrying
over 8,000 crew members, made safe landings on Iwo which
otherwise would certainly have been lost at sea. Perhaps the
cost of Iwo Jima was not quite as exhorbitant as it first appeared.

The Iwo Jima operation witnessed the appearance in the field
of a new Marine division, the 5th. It was "new" only in the
sense of being a division, being built up from a strong nucleus
of veteran combat troops who had served in earlier Pacific
operations. After six months of Stateside duty, they had become

eligible for transfer back to the divisions. Others had been crowded out of existing units in the Pacific under the new tables of organization which became effective during the spring and early summer of 1944.

The new organization aimed at streamlining the Marine division and making it more flexible. This was accomplished by transferring supporting troop units to higher echelons where they would be available to reinforce the divisions for special missions. Such units became Amphibious Corps and Fleet Marine Force troops. In the earlier phases of the war, when the Marine Corps had no higher echelons, the divisions had to be entirely self-sufficient and had grown to unwieldy proportions. The reorganization cut division strength from approximately 21,000 to about 17,000.

There was also another "new" division being formed at this time. The 6th Marine Division was quite unlike any the Marine Corps ever put in the field. It was formed by adding a new reinforced infantry regiment and supporting troops to the 1st Provisional Marine Brigade. The Brigade itself had an unusual background. Its major components had fought together on Guam for the first time, both had fought separately before that. The 4th Marines, namesake of the regiment lost in the Philippines, had been created by consolidation of the early raider battalions. These had fought as separate units in the Solomons, and had operated first as a regiment in the unopposed seizure of Morotai during the campaign to isolate Rabaul.

The 22d Marines had long since been an unattached regiment and, as such, had fought at Eniwetok in the Marshalls. The 1st Battalion of the new regiment, the 29th Marines, had been formed in the field from surplus personnel reshuffled under the new tables of organization, and had been thrown into combat at Saipan. The other two battalions had been organized in the U.S. and, like the new 5th Division, contained a backbone of veteran combat troops. Brigadier General Lemuel C. Shepherd, the Brigade Commander, was advanced to two-star rank and assigned command of the 6th Division, staging on Guadalcanal.

All this represented the culmination of a remarkable expansion for a military service which at the outset of war had boasted only two divisions, actually little more than slightly expanded brigades. In numerical strength, the Marine Corps grew from 65,000 men to almost the half million mark in little more than three years.

Inevitably an expansion of this proportion had a tremendous impact on such a small and compact military organization. Some drastic changes had been necessary. There was no room for the non-essentials in a war that was taxing the nation to the utmost. Among the first to go had been dress blues, long a hallmark of the Marine Corps. But blues were useless in combat, and the money they cost could better be spent for weapons and ammunition.

Also quickly into the discard had gone the officer's traditional Mamaluke sword. Career officers had not exactly beaten their swords into plowshares, but had packed them away carefully against the day when peace would come and the "Old Marine Corps" might conceivably return.

But one thing the Marine Corps was determined never to give up, and that was the exacting standards of conduct and discipline traditionally expected of every Marine. They managed to adhere to this policy to an amazing degree. The iron regime of boot camp was never relaxed, despite occasional protests from tearful mothers, irate fathers and others with less sympathetic axes to grind. Oddly enough, there were few protests from the boots themselves, apart from a few misguided and frequently misunderstood letters home. This was true even after voluntary enlistment was arbitrarily stopped and the Marine Corps was dragged, kicking and screaming, under Selective Service.

Actually the impact of Selective Service was not at all as disastrous as Marine Corps imaginations feared it might be. Its most apparent effect was to raise slightly the average age of Marine enlisted personnel. At least during the early stages, draftees were permitted to pick the branch of the service in which they preferred to serve, and the Marine Corps received more quasi-volunteers than it could use. By maintaining its high standards of physical and mental eligibility, the Corps was able to skim the cream of this crop and reject most of the undesirables.

To lessen further any possible stigma attaching to a drafted man in a predominantly volunteer outfit, an ingenious gimmick of dubious legality was devised. A draftee selecting the Marine Corps and measuring up to its standards was promptly discharged and permitted to enlist in the normal manner. However, the time soon arrived when the Corps was no longer predominantly volunteers, and elaborate face-saving became unnecessary.

In all probability, many of these draftees would have enlisted long before had they not been held back by obligations of various sorts. Once in they took hold wholeheartedly. They took the rigors of boot camp in their stride, caught the contagious high *esprit de corps,* and by the time they reached the field were indistinguishable from the volunteers who had preceded them.

The same applied to the officers. By the middle of 1944 the Marine Corps was officered predominantly by reservists who also became indistinguishable from the career men.

The final act in the long, bloody drama of the Pacific took place on Okinawa. No one knew at the time, nor for many weeks afterward, that it was to be the last beachhead of World War II. But there was no doubt in the mind of anyone concerned that it was going to be one of the biggest and the toughest of all. The fact that its five hundred square miles of mountainous terrain lay less than four hundred miles from the Imperial homeland provided a solid foundation for such a conclusion.

The task force for the operation was the greatest armada ever assembled in the Pacific Ocean. Not including the fast carrier and submarine forces which supported the operation, 1,213 ships took part in the landing. The Landing Force was the newly activated Tenth Army, totaling over half a million men, commanded by General Simon B. Buckner. The Marines' III Amphibious Corps, which included the 1st and 6th Marine

Divisions, was designated as the northern landing force. The southern landing force was the XXIV U.S. Army Corps, consisting of the 7th, 9th and 77th Infantry Divisions. In addition to the assault troops, the Tenth Army included the 2d Marine Division as a demonstration force and the Army's 27th Infantry Division as floating reserve.

The 100,000 defenders of the island bastion were commanded by Lieutenant General Mitsuru Ushijima, one of the Empire's most able soldiers. Ushijima's concept of the defense of Okinawa was laid down in "Battle Instruction Number 8," which he issued to his subordinate commanders some three weeks before the attack. It read in part, "The time of opening fire will naturally vary somewhat according to the type of weapons, strength of positions, duties, etc. However, generally speaking, we must make it our basic principle to allow the enemy to land in full. Until he penetrates our positions and loses his freedom of movement inside our most effective system of firepower and until he can be lured into a position where he cannot receive cover and support from naval gunfire and aerial bombardment, we must patiently and prudently hold our fire. Then, leaping into action, we shall open fire and wipe out the enemy. . . ."

Ushijima was a skillful commander who had learned his lessons well. He realized the validity of the ageless military principle that terrain favors the defender, and he capitalized upon it. For the first time in the Pacific the invaders were to be forced to fight the kind of a war most advantageous to the defender—a war of attrition.

On April Fool's Day, 1945, the initial assault wave churned their Amtracks through the drifting smoke of the conventional naval gunfire bombardment to hit the beach at 8:30 a.m. Ten minutes later all the assault waves were ashore. Even this early in the game there was an uneasy feeling among the old veterans that something was awfully wrong. There had been only scattered fire against the assault waves on the way in, but this was small consolation for those who remembered Iwo Jima. Safely ashore and moving rapidly toward their assigned objectives, they still met no organized resistance. The feeling of uneasiness grew.

By noon the 6th Marine Division had taken Yontan airfield, an objective for which they had expected to fight viciously. What was more surprising was the fact that the airfield had been captured virtually intact, with many operational aircraft sitting on the aprons of the field. Something was certainly amiss when the Japanese handed over an operational airfield with no apparent protest. It was a puzzled and apprehensive assault force that dug in for the night along the perimeter of the 6,000-yard beachhead that extended 5,000 yards inland.

The two corps, the Marines' III on the left and the Army's XXIV on the right, had landed abreast on the western coast of narrow Ishikana Isthmus, approximately one-third of the way up the island's 70-mile-long axis. The operation plan was divided into two phases. Phase I called for the seizure of all the island to the south of the isthmus by the XXIV Army Corps; Phase II all of the island to the north by the III Amphibious Corps. The two phases were to operate simultaneously, and were to be mutually supporting whenever the need arose.

As usual the Japanese came up with several surprises, one of which turned out to be the most fantastic weapon of the war. It was pretty well agreed among U.S. tacticians that the *banzai* attack had finally been discarded from the Japanese repetoire of battle. Shortly after dawn of D-Day, Marines of the 2d Division, standing by to make a diversionary feint against the southern coast, learned to their utter amazement that the *banzai* had grown wings and changed its name to *kamikaze*.

The new weapon, whose name translates into "Divine Wind," was a suicide aircraft whose mission was to crash into American vessels. The Marines' rude acquaintance with this latest inovation occurred when two suicide planes crashed into a transport and tank landing ship in their convoy, putting both completely out of action.

The underlying philosophy of the *kamikaze* was identical to that which motivated the *banzai* suicide attacks, a philosophy

largely incomprehensible to the western mind. Captain Rikibei
Inoguchi, Chief of Staff of Japan's First Air Fleet during the
war, attempted to explain it to an American officer in these
words: "We Japanese base our lives on obedience to Emperor
and Country. On the other hand, we wish for the best place in
death, according to Bushido. *Kamikaze* originates from these
feelings. . . . By this means we can accomplish peace. In view
of this—from this standpoint, the *kamikaze* deserved the consideration of the whole world."

The *kamikaze* received a tremendous amount of "consideration" from the U.S. Navy before the Okinawa campaign ended.
From April 6 to June 22, the Japanese launched over 1,900
suicide sorties, employing a total of 1,465 planes. These attacks
resulted in the unprecedented sinking of 26 American vessels
and the damaging of 164 others. The *Kamikaze* was an air-
borne example of the resistance that would be met on land.

By the end of the fourth day the island had been cleanly
severed by the 1st and 6th Marine Divisions. The 6th then
began a swift advance northward against negligible resistance,
backed up by patrols of the 1st Division which had been assigned the task of mopping up behind them. It wasn't until the
12th of April that the Marines hit the resistance they had been
expecting since D-Day. The main enemy position in the northern
sector of the island was located in the center of rugged Motobu
Peninsula, amidst a jumble of precipitous hills, ridges and gorges.

Using the 4th and 29th Marines in a pincers movement, General Shepherd attacked simultaneously from the east and west.
In the face of a well dug-in enemy and formidable terrain, the
action turned into a slow, deadly slugging match. The evacuation
of the wounded and the bringing up of supplies and ammunition
proved to be a major problem. As one observer noted, the
entire island possessed "an excellent network of very poor roads."

After three days of extremely grim work with hand grenades
and flame throwers, the 4th Marines overran the core of the
enemy position. The mopping up of isolated nests of die-hards
required three additional days, and the peninsula was declared

secured on April 20. Much to the Marines' surprise, the fight for Motobu marked the end of organized resistance in their sector of Okinawa. The next ten days, spent in systematic combing of the remainder of the northern two-thirds of the island, failed to reveal any enemy, other than stragglers and local conscripts who had no particular desire to fight with anybody. Phase II was obviously over. On April 30 Major General Pedro A. del Valle, commanding the 1st Marine Division, received orders detaching his division from the III Amphibious Corps and placing it under operational control of the XXIV Corps. It was a pretty good indication that things hadn't been going as well with Phase I down in the Army sector.

For three days following their landing the XXIV Corps' experience paralleled that of the Marines to the north. On the fourth day they reported "resistance stiffening." By April 8 they were advancing slowly against "greatly increased resistance." Three days later they were being mercilessly pounded by the best coordinated concentration of Japanese artillery fire ever seen in the Pacific war. There was no longer any doubt as to where General Ushijima had decided to make his primary defensive effort. The real battle for Okinawa was to be fought in the south—and it had just begun.

The enemy had established three successive defensive lines of great depth. These formed a well conceived belt of mutually supporting fortifications which extended completely across the island. From the capital city of Naha on the west, through ancient Shuri which occupied the key terrain of the system, to the coastal village of Yonabaru on the east, 75,000 defenders waited patiently for the invaders.

By May 11 the entire III Amphibious Corps had joined the Army's XXIV, and the two corps were fighting abreast across the width of the island. It was a slow and bloody struggle. By the third week in May the unceasing drive of the attackers was beginning to have a telling effect on the Japanese. As the days passed, the pall of battle smoke that marked the front lines edged slowly southward. In the center, Dakeshi Ridge, then Wanna

Draw fell to the 1st Marine Division. On the right the 6th Division added Sugar Loaf Hill to the ever growing list of objectives torn from the grasp of the enemy. On the extreme left the relentless attack of the 7th Infantry Division ground on through the mud and rain to smash Yonabaru and move on to the south.

On the morning of May 23 the 4th Marines, infiltrating under the cover of darkness, crossed the Asato Gawa River to establish a bridgehead and launch the 6th Division's assault against Naha. The great Castle of Shuri which dominated the key position of the Japanese defensive was captured by the 1st Marine Division. Two days later the 6th Division overran Naha. With the collapse of the Naha-Shuri-Yonabaru line, organized resistance crumbled throughout the central and eastern sectors of the Tenth Army front. After two months of some of the hardest fighting in World War II, the critical phase of the Okinawa campaign was finally passed.

It took the Tenth Army another month and a lot more bitter combat before the final curtain was rung down on June 30. The final battle report showed the Japanese losses as 107,539 dead and 10,755 prisoners of war. But the cold, impersonal wording indicated merely that, "A large and important contribution to the destruction of the Japanese armed forces was made when this bastion in the Japanese home waters was snuffed out."

The greatest contribution of all had been made by the 7,374 Americans who had given their lives for Okinawa—the last island.

14

Peace and Korea

Returning from one of their never-ending field maneuvers, a column of bedraggled, mud-spattered Marines halted for a short break in front of the Headquarters Building of the sprawling base at Camp Lejeune, North Carolina. Suddenly a door burst open and a highly excited woman Marine ran out, ignoring the steadily pouring rain.

"Hey, you guys!" she cried. "Have you heard the news that just came in? The war's over!"

Stony, dripping silence greeted her. Finally a weary voice rose from the ranks.

"Yeah?" it asked. "Who won?"

Such cynicism was more or less typical of the time. The war, which had begun as high adventure for the early volunteers, had long since become a way of life—a life compounded of rain, mud, grinding monotony, crashing gunfire and fear. A couple of years in the Pacific, then, if a man were lucky, six months stateside duty. After a brief leave, they would send him some place like Lejeune, where there was still rain and mud, to train some more to return to the rain and mud of the Pacific. To many, any other way of life had become a dim, unreal memory.

The suddenness with which the end came left them too numb to appreciate immediately the implications of the news.

With few exceptions, everyone seemed to be equally taken aback by the abrupt termination of hostilities. Even as the atomic bombs fell on Hiroshima and Nagasaki, plans were well along for a two-pronged invasion of the Japanese homeland. The course of the war had demonstrated that the closer the U.S. troops approached Japan proper, the stiffer the resistance became. With the appalling casualties of Iwo Jima and Okinawa only too clearly in mind, it required little imagination to visualize the bloodshed such an invasion would entail.

Even before V-J Day became a reality with the signing of peace terms in Tokyo Harbor, an unpleasant phenomenon began to manifest itself. It rapidly became apparent that almost everybody in wartime service wanted out, immediately if not sooner. And they made their wants known with mounting strength. Servicemen all over the U.S., Europe and the Pacific held mass meetings and drew up petitions to Congress, while uncounted thousands wrote home to Mom to increase the pressure. Marines played a negligible, if not non-existent, part in this disgraceful business. Not that they didn't want to get out as much as anyone. But somehow their *esprit de corps* and pride of service deterred them from making public spectacles of themselves which might reflect on their Corps.

These demonstrations came as no surprise. Something of the sort had happened in the aftermath of every war in U.S. history. And Congress, succumbing to the pressure of public opinion, cooperated wholeheartedly in getting veterans off the government payroll as quickly as possible. As a result, the armed forces began to shrink at a rate that appeared successively phenomenal, then alarming. The situation in the Pacific differed from any the nation had ever faced before. Russia and China remained unknown quantities. There was serious doubt as to how Japan, which had fought so long and so fanatically, would accept forcible armed occupation. Sporadic resistance continued on many of the captured islands and Japanese garrisons remained on many others that had been by-passed. Rabaul alone contained more than 45,000 unscathed troops.

Here was a potentially explosive situation which called for the presence of strong forces on the scene. In the face of such a need, the U.S. forces were becoming dangerously diminished. That the crisis passed was much more the result of good luck than good judgment on the part of those responsible for the decision.

According to the demobilization schedule, Marine combat strength was to be reduced from six divisions to two. The two, of course, would be the original ones, the 1st and 2d. The others would be deactivated by the most expeditious means.

The 4th Division was the first to go. It had by far the largest percentage of personnel due for imminent rotation. In fact, except for recent replacements, virtually the entire division was scheduled for rotation in the near future. Thus, it appeared most practical to bring it back as a unit and deactivate it as such. This was accomplished by November 1945, the wartime men being discharged, the regulars and those wishing to volunteer for regular service being transferred elsewhere.

The other divisions, in a sense, were largely disbanded in the field. The 1st and 2d Divisions, slated for occupation duty, both contained sizable numbers of troops scheduled for return and discharge. A wholesale reshuffling resulted. Regulars from the 3d, 5th and 6th Divisions were transferred to the 1st and 2d Divisions as replacements for those who were to be discharged. The dischargees, in turn, were transferred to the division from which their replacements came and sent back to the States. The two divisions remaining in the field were obliged to absorb large increments of men from those returning to the U.S.

In what seemed the amazingly short span of time between October 1, 1945 and July 1, 1946, the Marine Corps was cut from its peak strength of 485,113 to 150,318. By the end of 1946, the Corps had reached its permanent strength level of 100,000. This remaining body was difficult to classify. It certainly was not the "Old Corps" in which "it was never like this."

With equal certainty it was not the wartime Marine Corps. It was made up predominantly of regulars, many of whom were former reservists who had chosen to make the service a career and had integrated into the regular establishment. There were also a few reservists who chose to retain that status who continued on, or were called back to active duty, to fill certain special billets. The post-war Marine Corps had a great deal of reorganizing and self-examining to do in order to determine its character and its destiny.

The Reserve presented particularly difficult problems of its own, having emerged from the war in a state bordering on chaos. Prior to World War II the Marine Corps Reserve had been established as an organization similar to the National Guard. Units were organized, essentially along the lines of regular Marine units, in such localities as local interest warranted. The Reserve units held regularly scheduled evening drill sessions, and participated in field training each summer at various Marine Corps bases. The Marine Corps furnished uniforms and arms, and detailed regular officers to supervise training. Marine Reservists received standard pay in accordance with their rank and participation.

The Marine Corps Reserve program had traveled a rocky road. A Corps which lacked experience in handling other than volunteer regular troops had much to learn in dealing with problems peculiar to a volunteer reserve. The Marine Corps had no armories of its own and was forced to depend upon the cooperation of the Navy and National Guard in order to obtain part-time facilities to carry out its reserve drill program. Furthermore, the regulars, from privates to top rank officers had to be inculcated with an understanding and tolerance for what many persisted in considering a bunch of impostors, masquerading in the Marine uniform and capitalizing on prestige they had done nothing to deserve. When appropriations ran short, the first thought was to cut the allotment of the reserve. In the early 1930s, Reservists who had joined in good faith found their drill pay taken away from them and no ammunition provided for rifle range practice, one of the greatest inducements to enlistments.

But if the Reserve did not exactly thrive, or measure up to the hopes of most, it continued to exist and to grow slowly. At the outset it was made up largely of former Marines, a situation which continued in the officer and top non-commissioned officer ratings for some time to come. With that curious characteristic of small, closely knit organizations, its morale thrived on adversity. Its value to the Marine Corps' expansion problem in World War II is well attested by the fact that it contributed 23 battalions and 13 air squadrons to the wartime Corps.

These pre-war organized units had passed out of existence with the wholesale mobilization of the Reserve in 1940. Now, with the war over, many survivors of these units were anxious to have them reactivated, and new ones organized. This was eventually effected. These units, en masse, were designated the Organized Reserve, subject to immediate call to active duty in the case of a national emergency.

But there remained a huge, somewhat amorphous mass whose status was obscure. This consisted of people, both commissioned and enlisted, who had joined up "for the duration," in a reserve status. Many of them desired to retain at least a tenuous connection with the Marine Corps, but for a variety of reasons did not wish to join the Organized Reserve. To take advantage of this large pool of experienced manpower, a category designated the Volunteer Reserve was established. At the outset all a man had to do was signify his desire to belong in order to be enrolled. Headquarters corresponded with such people and issued occasional directives. When an individual failed to answer his correspondence, his interest was considered unsatisfactory and he was dropped from the rolls. Later the Marine Corps set up an undemanding system of voluntary training whereby reservists in this category could earn points toward reserve retirement.

While the Marine Corps was still in the throes of reorganization, it suddenly found itself once more fighting for its life on the home front. For the tenth time in its 170-year history, determined attempts were being made to abolish the Corps. As had happened before, certain misguided and powerful groups were busily engaged in a program to convince Congress that the days of the Marine Corps' usefulness to the nation were past. The ensuing struggle ended with far different results than the Marine Corps' adversaries had confidently envisioned. The smoke of battle finally cleared to find the Marine Corps with its specific roles and functions enacted into law by the National Security Act of 1947.

Rather than abolishing the Marine Corps, its enemies had succeeded in bringing about an Act of Congress which re-emphasized the Corps' vital role in the Armed Forces of the United States. The Act specifies, in part: "The United States Marine Corps, within the Department of the Navy, shall include land combat and service forces, and such aviation as may be organic therein. The Marine Corps shall be organized, trained, and equipped to provide fleet marine forces of combined arms, together with supporting air components. . . . It shall be the duty of the Marine Corps to develop, in cooperation with the Army and the Air Force, those phases of amphibious operations which pertains to tactics, techniques and equipment employed by landing forces. In addition, the Marine Corps . . . shall perform such other duties as the President may direct: Provided, that such additional duties shall not detract from nor interfere with operations for which the Marine Corps is primarily organized. . . ."

With this significant battle behind them, the Marines once more turned their attention to matters with which they were now charged by the law.

There were two main points on which everybody concerned was in complete agreement. First, the traditional concept of the force-in-readiness must be maintained. Second, the amphibious techniques, so laboriously developed and so dramatically demonstrated as one of the great tactical innovations of modern warfare, must not only be maintained but improved and elaborated upon. It was along these basic lines that the Marine Corps set about rebuilding.

From a tactical standpoint, the Marine Corps found itself in a position similar to that it had occupied in the early 1920s. With the advent of the atomic bomb, the critics were quick to point out that the value of the amphibious doctrine the Marines had labored so long and hard to perfect had vanished in the ominous mushroom cloud that rose above the ashes of Hiroshima. Many of the world's most renowned military leaders gloomily uttered profound opinions that there was no defense against atomic warfare.

Again Marine Corps officers disagreed with the pessimistic convictions prevailing in military circles. It was a familiar tune, one they had heard before under a different title—Gallipoli. The lyrics then had been that an amphibious assault could never be launched against modern defensive weapons. The greatest war in history had just proven the validity of the Marines' disagreement with that universal and erroneous conclusion. "The Bomb," the Marines contended, all-powerful though it might be, was just another weapon. Since the beginning of warfare the challenge of any new weapon had been met by creating new tactics and techniques. The answer to the newest weapon presumably lay in the same direction. It was only a matter of finding it.

As the Marine Corps planners saw the problem, it concerned two major considerations. First, the proven concept of a highly concentrated assault force moving against a relatively small landing area was no longer valid. Nuclear weapons had irrevocably banished such tactics to the scrap heap of history. Second, accepted amphibious tactics, by virtue of the methods employed to transport troops, were limited to two dimensions, frontal and flanking attack.

The obvious answer to the first problem, they felt, lay in dispersion. The tactical third dimension they were seeking appeared to lie in vertical attack. Because they required prepared landing areas, conventional aircraft were out of the question as a means of transportation. What was needed was an aircraft that could land and take off in almost any conceivable terrain. The only aircraft capable of meeting this requirement was the helicopter, as yet still very much in the experimental stage. But pioneering in new vehicles was a familiar task to the Marines. Both the landing craft and amphibious tractors that had carried them to the beachheads of World War II had been perfected largely as the result of their efforts.

To develop the new doctrine, an experimental helicopter squadron was organized at the Marine Corps Schools in Quantico in 1947. Just as fourteen short years before, staff officers began to burn the midnight oil, compiling a new manual that embraced a radical concept of warfare.

As it emerged, the Marines' theory of vertical envelopment envisioned helicopter-borne assault forces, launched from fast aircraft carriers far out at sea. Thus, from widely dispersed bases, capable of taking evasive action against atomic attack, the landing force could be concentrated quickly against an objective. In effect, the concept provided for the projection of amphibious assault deep inland, without the necessity for direct assault against hostile shorelines. Experimental work was immediately begun to evaluate the soundness of the new concept, and to work out the techniques of employment. As the work progressed, and doctrine began to emerge, the opportunity for Marines to again test their theories in the laboratory of war was rapidly approaching.

As the gray dawn of June 25, 1950, began to spread across the mist enshrouded paddies of central Korea, 10 divisions of the North Korean People's Army smashed across the 38th Parallel and roared southward. Within three days the Republic of Korea's capital city of Seoul had fallen to the invaders. Pausing only to regroup, the North Koreans moved swiftly southward, smashing the ineffectual defensive efforts of the badly shattered forces of the Korean Republic. Across the breadth of the land refugees choked the narrow, crooked roads with endless streams of humanity that wound their twisting way southward. War had come to the ancient "Land of The Morning Calm."

On June 27, the Security Council of the United Nations, meeting in New York, proclaimed the North Korean's attack a breach of world peace, and requested member nations to aid the Republic of Korea in repelling the invasion. On the same day, the United States formally announced it was giving military aid to South Korea. Two days later President Harry S. Truman authorized the sending of U.S. forces to Korea.

American troops closest to the battle area were the 7th, 24th and 25th Infantry Divisions and the 1st Cavalry Division, comprising the U.S. Eighth Army's occupation forces in Japan. All units stood at approximately 70 per cent of normal strength, and all suffered from the common occupation malady of poor training. A further detriment to their combat efficiency was the serious shortages of arms and equipment that plagued all four divisions. It was a poorly equipped and unprepared Army that found itself rudely snatched from the easy life of occupation duty to face the crushing advance of the North Korean People's Army.

The call for the Marines came from General Douglas MacArthur on July 2, the same day advance elements of the Army's 24th Division flew out of Japan into Korea and a war that was to become the fourth largest in U.S. history. The supreme Allied commander's dispatch was addressed to the Joint Chiefs of Staff. "Request immediate assignment Marine Regimental Combat Team and supporting Air Group for duty this command . . . MacArthur."

As they had been for 171 years, the Marines were ready— what there were of them. Peacetime economy measures had whittled the Corps down to a lean 74,000, "scattered from hell to breakfast," as one observer accurately commented. The Fleet Marine Force Pacific, amounted to 11,853 troops, the bulk of which were carried on the rolls of the greatly understrength 1st Marine Division and the 1st Marine Aircraft Wing, both stationed in California.

Within five days of MacArthur's request, the 1st Provisional Brigade, built around the 5th Marines and Marine Aircraft

Group 33, had been formed at Camp Pendleton. Five hectic days and sleepless nights later the 6,500 Marines cleared San Diego Harbor, the dockside parting words of the Commandant still ringing in their ears. "You boys clean this up in a couple of months, or I'll be over to see you!" General Clifton B. Cates had growled. Rare are the instances in the Corps' long history when Marines have disobeyed their Commandant's orders. This was to be one of them.

During the long, slow voyage across the Pacific every ship of the Brigade's convoy maintained a prominently displayed situation map of the Korean War. As the radio reports outlining the course of the day's action were received, the front lines were carefully plotted. With each passing day the staggered line of blue and red symbols representing the U.N. perimeter moved closer and closer to the southern tip of the Korean peninsula. At mid-Pacific the betting in the troop compartments was even money that the defenders would be driven into the sea before the convoy arrived. A few days later only an easy mark would make the same bet without getting odds. By the end of July the maps showed a pitifully small 80 by 50 mile corner of southeastern Korea being held by the U.N. forces.

When the Brigade sailed from California, it had been MacArthur's intention to use it for amphibious landings behind the enemy. He reasoned that a Marine Regimental Combat Team tearing up the North Korean's rear areas would greatly reduce the pressure on his rapidly retreating defensive forces. The Marines were still eight days at sea when the situation became so desperate that the plans for their employment were changed. The North Koreans, sweeping around the left flank of the U.N. defenders, reached the southern coast to completely encircle South Korea's principal port of Pusan. The Marines were now sorely needed to plug the gaps in the rapidly crumbling Pusan Perimeter.

The Brigade Commander, Brigadier General Edward A. Craig, had flown to Korea in advance of the Brigade to familiarize himself with the situation by first hand observation. He was waiting on the dock when the first ship bearing his Marines nosed into its berth in the center of Pusan's teeming waterfront. Calling his unit commanders together, the General briefly outlined the grim tactical situation. As to the Brigade's mission he wasted few words. ". . . The Pusan Perimeter is like a weakened dike, and we will be used to plug holes in it as they open. It will be costly fighting against a numerically superior enemy."

The General paused, evidently reflecting upon a full month of withdrawal by the U.S. Eighth Army. His calm, gray eyes flicked briefly over the serious faces of his assembled officers. It seemed that his normally ramrod-straight body stiffened even slightly more. "Gentlemen," he said quietly. "Marines have never lost a battle. This Brigade will not be the first to establish such a precedent."

The First Marine Provisional Brigade established several precedents—at least as far as the Korean War was concerned. The first occurred at Chindong-ni, 50 miles west of Pusan, where they relieved the 25th Division's badly chewed-up 27th Regiment. In the early morning darkness of August 7, the Marines celebrated the eighth anniversary of their landing on Guadalcanal by rudely introducing themselves to elements of the North Korean People's Army. The formalities took place when the North Koreans launched a pre-dawn attack against positions held by a battalion of the 5th Marines. Hurling back the enemy assault, the Marines immediately counter-attacked and captured an enemy held hill mass. As the company commander of the assault company directed his platoons to their defensive areas he paused to speak to his gunnery sergeant.

"Must be a hell of a shock to the Gooks to lose a piece of ground for a change!" he said.

The sergeant grinned at his commanding officer. "They may not know it yet, Skipper," he replied, squirting a stream of tobacco juice in the general direction of the enemy. "But they're going to find out this war is just getting started!"

Making good the sergeant's prophecy, the Brigade jumped off in a counter offensive two days later. Smashing through the

North Korean 6th Division, the hard-hitting Marines plunged toward Chinju, enemy headquarters for the southwestern sector. By nightfall of the third day they were dug in on the hills above Changchon, 26 miles deep in enemy territory.

The order from Eighth Army Headquarters to withdraw hit the Brigade Command Post like an incoming artillery shell. Withdraw! With a 26-mile advance behind them and a disorganized enemy retreating before them? "What the hell kind of a war was this?" the Marines asked themselves incredulously. The answer, like the question, was one with which they would soon become familiar. The weakened dike that guarded the Pusan Perimeter had sprung a leak. The Marines were needed to plug the hole.

The puncture had occurred to the north where the western boundary of the perimeter had been established along the natural barrier formed by the Naktong River. West of the village of Yongsan, the river forms a big loop, known to the Koreans as "the Big Bend of The Naktong." Bounded by the river on three sides and on the east by a long, deep valley, the peninsula of land which fills the loop is an isolated fortress of mountains. It was here that the North Korean 4th Division, strongly supported by artillery and armor, had driven a deep salient into the U.N. perimeter. By the 10th of August, they had overrun the entire area, and were pushing on toward Yongsan.

Beyond Yongsan lay the main axis of communications and the supply route which linked Pusan with U.N. forces to the north. Over a period of five desperate days, three Army regiments had launched three counter-attacks against the North Koreans, each time encountering a stone wall of resistance.

The withdrawal order to the Marines in the south had contained instructions for the Brigade to report to the town of Miryang, just east of Yongsan. Here the battle-grimed Marines had their first hot meal since arriving in Korea, and enjoyed the unaccustomed luxury of a peaceful night's sleep. Among the several visitors who called at the Marines' bivouac was a British military observer. Whatever else this officer's brief visit may have accomplished, his daily report to the British command in Tokyo the next day left little doubt as to what it had done for his morale. It read: "The situation is critical and Miryang may be lost. The enemy have driven a division-sized salient across the Naktong. More will cross the river tonight. If Miryang is lost Taegu becomes untenable and we will be faced with a withdrawal from Korea. I am heartened that the Marine Brigade will move against the Naktong salient tomorrow. They are faced with impossible odds, and I have no valid reason to substantiate it, but I have a feeling they will halt the enemy."

"I realize my expression of hope is unsound, but these Marines have the swagger, confidence and hardness that must have been in Stonewall Jackson's Army of the Shenandoah. They remind me of the Coldstreams at Dunkerque. Upon this thin line of reasoning, I cling to the hope of victory."

The Marine attack jumped off on the morning of August 17. The objective was an ugly sprawling spine of terrain called "No Name Ridge." Splashing across the stinking rice paddies, the assault companies were met by a withering hail of machine gun and mortar fire. Overhead Marine Corsairs roared down on the objective, their chattering wing guns merging with the din of battle below. From behind the charging troops, the howitzers of the Brigade artillery thundered across the valley to send their screaming projectiles crashing down upon the enemy.

As the day wore on and the casualties began to mount, the Marines slowly clawed their way toward the crest of the ridge. By nightfall the northern end of the ridge had been torn from the enemy. Throughout the night the battle raged on as the determined enemy hurled desperate counter-attacks against the small sector held by the Marines.

At dawn the Marines renewed their ferocious attack, smashing one enemy position after another. Shortly after noon the 1st Brigade stood alone on "No Name Ridge."

With the loss of the dominating terrain, the North Koreans began a hasty withdrawal toward the Naktong. Sweeping down off the ridges, the Marines pressed swiftly on, turning the retreat into a panic-stricken rout. Swarms of fleeing North Koreans flung themselves into the river in an effort to escape. Soon the river was choked with swimming, wading enemy, scrambling for the safety of the opposite shore. Marine artillery and air turned the rout into a slaughter unparalleled in the Korean War. When the booming guns finally fell silent the Naktong had become a river of blood, and the 4th North Korean Division was no more.

It was at the Battle of the Naktong that the Marines learned that they were something of an enigma to the enemy. Among the few prisoners taken in the fight was a North Korean major. During the course of his interrogation, the prisoner was frankly curious about his captors. He stated that his unit had received a report concerning a strange U.N. battle force of "men with yellow legs" who had recently appeared in the south. The report had said that these new troops were easily identifiable by the camouflage covers they wore over their helmets, and their khaki-colored, canvas leggings. All units were ordered to make every effort to learn what country the strange "yellow legs" were from.

When it came to determining what country any individual was from, the North Koreans had a tremendous advantage over the U.N. troops. One of the biggest problems throughout the Korean War was the constant infiltration of U.N. lines. In every battle area swarms of refugees, lugging their worldly possessions in a huge cloth-wrapped bundle, moved constantly toward the rear. A favorite trick of the North Korean infiltrators was to dress themselves in civilian clothing, conceal their weapons in innocent-appearing cloth bundles, and move into the rear areas with the refugees. Since all Koreans look alike to an American, the only way to spot such infiltrators was to search each refugee, a virtually impossible task. It came as somewhat of a disappointing shock to intelligence officers to learn that all Koreans look more or less alike to another Korean. When one of the Marine officers asked his native interpreter how he was able to distinguish a North Korean from a South Korean, he was told that it really was quite simple. The North Koreans wore different uniforms, the interpreter explained.

In the science of battlefield tactics, the North Koreans stood in a class by themselves. Their standard assault against a defended position demonstrated the classic Oriental disregard for the value of human life. The attack was generally made by three or four successive waves of troops. The first wave invariably was made up of young men who obviously had received very little training. Although all were armed with rifles, very few ever fired them. Their function was to attempt to overrun the enemy position by sheer momentum. Such troops were easily stopped before they reached the position by a well concentrated volume of heavy fire, the exact outcome expected by the North Korean tacticians. A second, and sometimes third wave, attacked in a similar manner, with the same results. Then, with most of the ready ammunition in the battle position expended, a fourth wave of battle-hardened veterans made the main attack. With ammunition reserves well depleted, or completely exhausted, the defenders were often forced to evacuate the position.

But the tactic that topped them all was known as the "refugee attack." It was one that every defender prayed would not be launched against his position. The North Koreans would gather hundreds of refugees together. Then, carefully placing the small children and women in front, they would drive the mob at bayonet point headlong into a battle position. Mingled with the refugees were the leading elements of the enemy's frontal assault which followed directly on the heels of the stampeding civilians. Even the most calloused veteran could never bring himself to open fire on women and children. Most would reluctantly admit that as a battle tactic it was highly successful. But no one ever argued the universal conviction that it was "a hell of a way to fight a war."

With the Pusan Perimeter once more secure along the Naktong, the battle-weary Marines were ordered to return to the southern sector. Going into bivouac as reserve for the 25th Infantry Division, the Brigade took advantage of the opportunity to replenish their equipment and catch up on some long overdue rest. On August 29th, they fell out in formation to receive a distinguished visitor, the President of the Republic of Korea, Syngman Rhee. He made a short speech to the assembled troops, thanking them for what they had done. "You Marines brought hope to my people," he said. "You brought us victory when all we had known was defeat. . . ." Three days after the presidential visit came the order to move north again—there had been another breakthrough.

The intelligence boys had seen it coming the last few days in August. All along the front were signs that the North Koreans were massing for an all-out effort to smash through the Pusan Perimeter. It was only a question of when and where. When, turned out to be the early morning hours of the first day of September. The answer to the second question had a disgustingly familiar ring to a lot of Marines. It was a place called the Big Bend of the Naktong.

On their second trip across the river, the enemy had come prepared to stay. Elements of four North Korean divisions had been identified in the area. In the 11 days since the Brigade had departed, the enemy had recaptured all the original terrain, plus an additional four miles. It was a bad situation the Marines found upon their arrival on September 2. It looked a lot worse the following morning when they began to deploy to their attack positions. During the night the Army lines from which the Marines were to launch their counter-attack had collapsed. As a result, the Brigade's battalions had to retake one thousand yards of enemy territory before they reached their line of departure.

The Brigade gave a repeat performance at the Second Battle of the Naktong. This time it was the 9th North Korean Division that disintegrated before the Marines' savage attack. At the end of three days they had driven the enemy back five and a half miles, recaptured hundreds of pieces of American ordnance and equipment, and left the countryside littered with enough North Korean arms, tanks and vehicles to equip a small army. Even a North Korean paymaster had been caught in the sweeping tide of their advance, much to the delight of the Marines who continued

the attack, their pockets bulging with fantastic sums of worth-
less currency.

On the cold, drizzling afternoon of September 5th they re-
ceived the word they had been waiting for. ". . . COMMENC-
ING AT 2400 5 SEPT BRIG. MOVES BY RAIL AND
MOTOR TO STAGING AREA PUSAN FOR FURTHER
OPERATIONS AGAINST THE ENEMY . . . CONCEAL
FROM THE ENEMY ACTIVITIES CONNECTED WITH
YOUR WITHDRAWAL . . ." From now on someone else
would have to plug the holes in the dike. The Marines had ur-
gent business elsewhere.

While the 1st Provisional Brigade was charging up and down
the Pusan Perimeter, the Marine Corps was making an all-out
effort to bring its 1st Division up to wartime strength. Mac-
Arthur's third request for a Marine division to be sent to Korea
had been granted by the Joint Chiefs of Staff. On July 25, the
1st Marine Division received orders to expand to full war strength
and a new commanding general, Major General Oliver P. Smith.
Between July 31 and August 10, the division joined 6,800 troops
from the 2d Marine Division, and 4,500 other regulars from
posts and stations all over the world. The remainder came from
the Minute Men of 1950—the Organized Reserves.

MacArthur's strategy called for an amphibious landing to be
made deep behind the enemy. He reasoned that such an attack,
coupled with a simultaneous drive by the Eighth Army northward
out of the Pusan Perimeter would place the enemy forces between a tactical "hammer and anvil." Faced with an attack on
two fronts, the North Koreans would have no choice but to
divide their forces to meet both threats.

The site selected for the landing was Inchon, half way up the
west coast of the six hundred-mile Korean Peninsula, and seaport
for Seoul, South Korea's capital, nineteen miles to the east.
Through Seoul, main terminus for Korea's north-south railroads
and highways, passed the principal supply routes of the North
Korean forces massed along the Pusan Perimeter. The objective
of the amphibious attack was to cut these vital supply lines.

Strategically, and tactically, Inchon was the ideal place to make a landing. From a hydrographic standpoint, it was one of the worst sites ever assigned to an amphibious landing force. Boasting some of the most extreme tidal conditions in the world, the port of Inchon in surrounded by miles of oozing mud flats at low tide. Only at maximum tide does the sea level rise the necessary thirty-five feet to completely inundate the vast area of muck. An added obstacle is the high stone sea wall which bounds the port's waterfront in the only area where the landings could be made. Since the maximum high tides occur only a few times each year, the landing would have to be made during one of those infrequent periods. The tide tables indicated the right time to be mid-September, the height of the typhoon season.

Staging out of Pusan, the Brigade joined the 1st Division convoy ploughing through the Yellow Sea. On September 13, the Brigade was officially deactivated, its units reverting to the division.

D-Day was September 15. For the preceding five days, the carrier-based planes and warships of the U.S. Seventh Fleet blasted the harbor and Inchon's waterfront. At first light the 3d Battalion, 5th Marines, stormed ashore on the island of Wolmi-do, joined to Inchon by an 800-yard causeway. By noon the battalion had completed mopping up the island, eliminating the enemy position which flanked the approaches to the main landing site at Inchon. Perched on the commanding hills of Wolmi-do, the 3d Battalion watched the landing craft bearing the 1st Marines and the other two-thirds of their own regiment churn ashore on the late afternoon tide.

Throwing up scaling ladders, the first wave of the 5th Marines swarmed over the sea wall and plunged into Inchon against moderately light resistance.

On the southern outskirts of town, the 1st Marines, obscured by fog and the smoke of the pre-landing bombardment, clanked ashore in their waddling Amtracks. By midnight, after some sharp fighting, both regiments had secured their assigned objectives, ending the critical phase of the Inchon landing.

The exploitation of the beachhead began at 6:30 the next morning. Jumping off in the attack, the Marines were happily surprised to learn that the bulk of the defending forces had withdrawn toward Seoul during the night. Moving swiftly east astride the Inchon-Seoul highway, the division pressed inland. On the northern flank the 5th Marines, throwing back two heavy North Korean counter-attacks, overran Kimpo Airfield two days after the landing. By the evening of September 19, they were dug in on the south bank of the Han River.

It had been heavier going for the 1st Marines to the south. In their zone of advance lay the industrial suburb of Yongdungpo, directly across the river from the outskirts of Seoul. The North Koreans had no intention of giving up Yongdungpo. "If Yongdungpo is lost, Seoul will also fall," the North Korean military leaders had prophesied. They were right, but it took the 1st Marines three days cf bitter fighting to decide the issue at Yongdungpo, and smash through the city to the banks of the Han.

The 1st Marine Division had made their landing at Inchon as the spearhead of the recently formed U.S. X Corps, which also included the Army's 7th Infantry Division. At the time of the landing, the Marine division was more accurately two-thirds of a division. Its third regiment, the 7th Marines, was still six days sailing time away when D-Day arrived. Thus, the division's fighting strength received a welcome boost on September 21 when the 7th Marines and its accompanying artillery battalion arrived at Inchon.

By this time the 5th Marines had already crossed the Han River and were moving southeast toward the rugged jumble of hills which towered between them and Seoul, some seven miles away. It was across the natural barrier of these hills that the North Korean commander had placed two of his best units to guard the northeastern approaches to the city. His orders to the North Korean Brigade and the 78th Independent Regiment had been explicit. They were to deny the commanding terrain to the enemy at all costs.

The 5th Marines began their assault of the jutting heights on September 22. For two long and bloody days the Marines hurled attack after attack against the six thousand defenders, slowly and relentlessly tearing one position after another from the determined enemy. By nightfall of the 24th the exhausted Marines occupied the crest of the hill mass. For the defenders it had literally been a fight to the death.

Crossing the Han behind the 5th Marines, the newly arrived 7th Marines pushed westward along a ridge line to the north of Seoul. Theirs was the dual mission of protecting the exposed left flank and rear of the 5th Marines attacking to the southeast, and cutting the enemy escape routes to the north.

To the south the 1st Marines crossed the Han to deploy through the outskirts of Seoul. Still farther to the south, the 32d Regiment of the 7th Infantry Division, ferried across the river in borrowed Marine Amtracks, prepared to attack the high ground to the south of the city. The stage was set for the assault on Seoul.

The attack roared forward on the morning of September 25. The city streets were a strange battleground to Marines, more accustomed to the jungles of the Pacific and the rice paddies of southern Korea. From sand-bagged emplacements at the intersections of Korea's largest city, enemy machine guns raked the cobbled streets. From the bomb-blasted and artillery shattered office buildings and shops unseen North Korean snipers took their toll of the advancing Marines. But the Marines were taking a bigger toll of the enemy. Working from building to building, they rooted the defenders from the rubble with flame throwers and hand grenades, moving slowly into the heart of the city. On into the night the battle raged, the actors of the macabre drama bathed in the flickering red glow of burning buildings.

It went on for two days, the Marines inching closer and closer to the far side of the city. On the afternoon of the 27th, the North Korean resistance suddenly collapsed, the survivors fleeing for the hills to the west of the city. The battle for Seoul was over.

The liberation ceremonies were held in the Government Palace on the 29th, three months and four days after the North Korean People's Army had launched their invasion against South Korea.

With the successful conclusion of the Inchon-Seoul operation, the backbone of the North Korean Army had been broken. Caught between the rapidly advancing Eighth Army pushing northward out of the Pusan Perimeter and the X Corps moving eastward from Seoul, the enemy's scattered forces fled toward North Korea.

As is customary after a campaign, the Marines' Commanding General sent a message of congratulations to his troops. The final paragraph read: "I fully appreciate, and I am sure the American people now fully appreciate and realize, that only well-trained and determined troops, completely devoted to duty, could have accomplished what the 1st Marine Division did in Korea. You have established your place in history. . . ." Neither the General, nor his troops, had any inkling that these words were to become far more meaningful in the not too distant future. For the 1st Marine Division, the great epic of the Korean War was yet to be written on the pages of history.

By early October, with the bulk of the North Korean forces either destroyed or dispersed, the United Nations command looked forward to a speedy conclusion of the Korean War. When the North Koreans chose to ignore the surrender ultimatum handed them by General MacArthur, the decision was made to destroy the enemy, as the first step in accomplishing the unification of Korea. Toward this end, MacArthur obtained permission to conduct military operations north of the 38th Parallel.

The plan called for the Eighth Army in the west to make the main effort against Pyongyang, the capital of North Korea. In conjunction with the Eighth Army's drive, the X Corps was to make an amphibious envelopment on the east coast. Advancing westward toward Pyongyang, across the narrow waist of Korea, they were to effect a link-up with the Eighth Army and trap the North Korean forces withdrawing from the south.

The 1st Marine Division sailed out of Inchon on October 12, bound for an amphibious assault on Wonsan on the northeast coast of Korea. It was probably the most embarrassing landing ever made by Marines. While they were en route around the southern tip of the peninsula, the 1st Republic of Korea Corps overran Wonsan and sped northward. Much to their everlasting chagrin, the Marines landed to find that Bob Hope and his USO troupe had given a performance at Wonsan airfield three days before their arrival.

The X Corps operations plan had undergone considerable revamping since the Marines had departed Inchon. The unexpected lightness of North Korean resistance, to both the Eighth Army advance in western Korea and that of I ROK Corps in the east, had produced great optimism in the high command. There was much talk, widely echoed by the world's press, of "on to the Yalu" and "home by Christmas." It sounded fine on the stateside radio news; and it looked fine in the newspaper clippings the men got from home. But there was considerably less optimism among those whose reading was confined mainly to the operations map of the 1st Marine Division.

The new X Corps plan envisioned a three-pronged advance to the Yalu River which forms the border between North Korea and Manchuria. The I ROK Corps had been assigned to the right flank, the 7th Infantry Division to the center, and the 1st Marine Division to the left flank. The 3d Infantry Division formed the Corps reserve.

The Marines began their "advance to the Yalu" at Hamhung, seventy miles north of Wonsan, with considerable misgivings. The division had been assigned a sector of responsibility two hundred miles long and forty miles wide, an area which required at least a corps. A source of great apprehension was the 80-mile gap which separated the division's left flank from the Eighth Army to the west. On November 2 concern deepened when a reconnaissance patrol returned with a Chinese prisoner who confirmed the long prevalent rumors that great numbers of Chinese Communist Forces were moving into North Korea from Manchuria. According to the prisoner, three Chinese divisions were already operating in the Chosen Reservoir area which lay within the Marines' zone of action.

The division commander, General Smith, indicated his dissatisfaction with the situation in a letter to the Commandant of the Marine Corps on November 15. The General wrote: "So far our MSR [Main Supply Route] north of Hamhung has not been molested, but there is evidence that this situation will not continue. . . . Someone in high authority will have to make up his mind as to what our goal is. My mission is still to advance to the border. The Eighth Army, eighty miles to the southwest, will not attack until the 20th. Manifestly, we should not push on without regard to the Eighth Army. We would simply get farther out on a limb. . . . I doubt the feasibility of supplying troops in this area during the winter, or providing for the evacuation of the sick and wounded. . . ." In concluding his letter, General Smith indicated his grave concern over "the prospect of stringing out a Marine division along a single mountain road for 120 air miles." Though he didn't mention it directly, the General's thoughts may well have dwelt briefly on the ancient proverb of the Asian warriors, "He who embarks upon a winter campaign in the land of the Mongols courts disaster."

Thanksgiving found the 5th and 7th Marines on the western side of Chosen Reservoir, preparing to advance out of the mountain valley of Yudam-ni. To the southeast, the forward element of the division command post and a battalion of the 1st Marines occupied Hagaru-ri at the southern tip of the reservoir. Between lay 14 miles of narrow, snow-covered road climbing its tortuous way through the steep headwalls of Taktong Pass, 4,000 feet above the valley floor. Still farther south, the other two battalions of the 1st Marines were dug in on the frozen slopes of Koto-ri. Below them lay Funchilin Pass, gateway to the high plateau of the Tobaksan Mountain range which cradles the Chosen Reservoir. Behind them stretched the winding 78-mile life line of the division, the Main Supply Route to the port of Hamhung.

Winter, in all its bitterness, comes early to the high country of northern Korea. As the pitch black night of November 27 dropped like a blanket over Yudam-ni, the temperature plummeted to 20 degrees below zero. Huddled in their battle positions high on the frozen ridges, the Marines peered into the night, cursing the soul-searing cold that numbed their bodies and froze their weapons. Beyond the perimeter, in the frigid darkness of the hidden valleys, Red Chinese by the tens of thousands moved silently into their attack positions. The time had come for the annihilation of the 1st Marine Division. Just before midnight the Chinese slammed shut the gate.

The enemy's main effort was made against the two regiments at Yudam-ni. While two divisions crashed against the perimeter, another cut the road just south of the valley. Farther to the south five more Chinese divisions moved into blocking positions across the MSR and launched simultaneous attacks against Hagaru-ri and Koto-ri.

The enemy had come a long way for their mission. While the 1st Marine Division had been at sea between Inchon and Wonsan, the Chinese command had been unable to determine in just what area they might expect the next Marine attack. As soon as the Marines had been positively identified as being on the northeast coast, the critical area on the Chinese situation maps was hurriedly changed from the Eighth Army front to the X Corps front. The Chinese Communist Forces' 9th Army Group, which included twelve divisions among its three corps, was immediately withdrawn from the Eighth Army sector and ordered to the east. Under forced march, over the rough mountain trails of northern Korea, they moved more than 160 miles in twelve days.

Commanded by battle-wise General Sung Shih-lun, a veteran of over twenty years combat experience in China's wars, the 9th Army Group had one primary objective—to destroy the Marine division. The reasoning behind the mission was clearly evident in Sung's final message to his troops before they moved into their attack positions. It began, "Soon we will meet the

American Marines in battle. We will destroy them. When they are defeated the enemy army will collapse. . . ."

Surrounded by eight Chinese divisions, the 1st Marine Division began its epic advance to the sea. The raw savagery of the breakout of the 5th and 7th Marines from Yudam-ni defies description. They have tried, those who set down the chronicles of history. The war correspondents, writing of the "trapped Marine Division facing annihilation" tried too. They wrote with shining words, of courage and valor, and the indomitable spirit of the unconquerable men who battled their way out of the white hell of Chosen, bringing their dead with them. But they told only a part of the story. The rest, for which they had no words, was written in the glazed, staring eyes and on the gaunt, haggard faces of those who trudged the endless frozen road of eternity that led to Hagaru.

The Marines came out fighting, gathering their scattered, entrapped units as they came. Smashing through the encircling enemy hordes times without number, they fought their way over the ice-bound ridges and along the deep winding valleys that lay below. From Hagaru, across the bitter, wind whipped plateau to Koto-ri and down the twisting, snow-choked Funchilin Pass they moved inexorably toward the sea. It took them thirteen agonizing days to reach the waiting ships at Hamhung. Behind them, in uncounted thousands, lay the frozen bodies of those who had come to destroy them.

"A battle unparalleled in U.S. military history," *Time* magazine reported to the waiting world. "It had some of the aspects of Bataan, some of Anzio, some of Dunkirk, some of Valley Forge. . . ."

The undeclared war of Communist China against the United Nations produced some abrupt policy changes on the high levels of government. The decision was made that U.N. forces would not strike against enemy bases in Chinese territory. It was the only way, the policy makers said, to avoid World War III. From the military standpoint, it also precluded any possibility of winning the Korean War.

It was a strange war, one of the most frustrating ever fought by American military men. Gaining ground was a secondary consideration. The strategy involved inflicting maximum losses on the enemy, while attempting to minimize the losses of U.N. forces. As a consequence, the fighting seesawed back and forth across the 38th Parallel. For the Marines amphibious operations were a thing of the past. They spent the remainder of the war in the alien occupation of land mass warfare as a part of the Eighth Army.

On January 10 the 1st Marine Division moved out of Eighth Army reserve where they had been sent to re-equip and receive replacements after the Chosen Reservoir battle. Their new area of operations was the Pohangdong-Andong sector of south-eastern Korea. The objective was the destruction of a North Korean guerrilla division which was operating with considerable success in the 1,600-square-mile area. Forming guerrilla units of their own, which they dubbed "Rice Paddy Patrols," the Marines began tracking down the enemy. By early February they had inflicted casualties of over 60 per cent on the North Korean division, and the survivors had disappeared from the area.

In the latter part of February the Marines were on the move again, this time into central Korea where they came under the operational control of IX Corps. Spearheading "Operation Ripper," the division led the U.N. advance on the east central front. By April IX Corps had advanced to the Hwachon Reservoir. On the night of the 22d the long expected Chinese counter offensive smashed into the leading elements of the Corps. At dawn the Marines found themselves in the uncomfortable position of defending the Corps sector with both flanks exposed. Under the onslaught of the Chinese attack, the divisions on either side of the Marines had retreated during the night. In the face of the enemy counter offensive, a general withdrawal of the Eighth Army was ordered, a maneuver euphemistically referred to as "rolling with the punch." There was to be a great deal of "rolling with the punch" before the Korean War came to an end.

In late June the enemy began to propose that some sort of truce might be in order, and suggested peace meetings to discuss this possibility. The peace talks were widely reported by the world press as being purely a matter of political maneuvering. A more thorough examination of the factors involved might have led observers to the solid conclusion that the peace talks also constituted a shrewd tactical maneuver on the part of the enemy. It was obvious that the constant pressure exerted by the U.N. forces was beginning to have a telling effect on the Chinese. Although they were far from being defeated, by the middle of the summer they were sacrificing North Korean units, wholesale, to cover their own withdrawal north of the 38th Parallel. The peace talks gave them a much needed breathing spell, and a golden opportunity to regroup their forces.

Having accomplished their purpose, both tactically and from the standpoint of political propaganda, the enemy broke off the peace negotiations in August on the pretext that U.N. aircraft had attacked the neutral conference area at Kaesong. A month later the 1st Marine Division made front page headlines and tactical history in the "Punchbowl" area of east central Korea.

The Korean War had caught up with the Marines' helicopter program less than three years after its inception. The Brigade used helicopters in combat for the first time in the Pusan Perimeter. These, however, were small aircraft and were employed primarily for aerial reconnaissance, casualty evacuation and rescue work. In September of 1951, the arrival of a helicopter transport squadron equipped with 10-place aircraft provided the means of making a real test of the new concept. The assignment to occupy the key terrain in an isolated area of the jumbled mountains east of the Punchbowl provided the opportunity the Marines had been waiting for.

The objective lay in a section so remote that it required at least nine hours to reach on foot. Utilizing their aerial assault craft, the Marines landed 224 fully equipped combat troops, and 17,772 pounds of cargo on the objective in four hours. Topping

off the operation with a neat flourish, one of the helicopters laid
eight miles of telephone wire to the regimental command post in
fourteen minutes. The first helicopter-borne landing of a combat
unit in history had been an outstanding success. Three weeks
later a similar operation was successfully completed with an
entire battalion. From that time on, the Marines' "Whirlybirds"
became a familiar sight shuttling across Korea's battlefields.

The winter of 1951-1952 saw little close-in action, with
activity on both sides confined mainly to localized raids and
patrol skirmishes. In March, after seven months in the Punchbowl
area, the Marines again moved west to take over the left flank
of the Eighth Army. Now a part of I Corps, the division occupied
a blocking position across the ancient invasion route to Seoul
used by Genghis Khan some seven centuries before.

The last year and a half of the war in Korea was reminiscent
of the trench warfare of World War I. The big difference was
that the job of the Marines in Korea was to defend, instead of
to attack. It became a war of patrol actions, bunker life and
artillery barrages. It was a war of contrasts. While the casualties slowly mounted along the outposts line, troops one valley
to the rear practiced close-order drill and received classroom
instruction.

During the Spring of 1953 such military objectives as Outposts Reno, Vegas and Carson splashed across the front pages
of the newspapers back home. These three hills, which commanded the key terrain of the western front, saw some of the
bitterest hand-to-hand fighting of the entire war. There were
similar actions at Bunker Hill, Dagmar and among the jutting,
rocky crags of the ridge known as The Hook, while the Communist peace negotiators played their game of political chess
during the endless truce conferences at Panmunjon. The cumulative casualty report issued in June carried the names of 136,862
Americans. Of that number, 24,386 had been killed in action
or died as the result of wounds.

The war that nobody won dragged wearily to a close on July

27, 1953. Though combat operations had ceased, the Marines were destined to spend an additional two years "sitting and waiting" on the battle-scarred hills of Korea. In April of 1955 they were finally relieved from their defensive positions along the demilitarized zone that separated North and South Korea.

★ ★ ★ ★ ★

15

Aftermath

T HE MARINE CORPS emerged from the Korean War with the greatest peacetime strength in its history. The startling suddenness of the war, and MacArthur's immediate request for Marines, had emphasized the importance of maintaining the Corps as a ready striking force. This vital need in the nation's defense had been reflected in Public Law 416, which was passed by Congress in 1952. As an amendment to the National Security Act, the law specifies that the Marine Corps be maintained at a strength of not less than three combat divisions and three aircraft wings.

With the passage of this legislation, the Corps lost little time in reactivating the 3d Marine Division which had been disbanded at the end of World War II. Using the 3d Marine Brigade as a nucleus, the division was reformed at Camp Pendleton, California, in January, 1952. Due to the great demand for personnel to fill the replacement needs of the 1st Division fighting in Korea, it required the better part of the year to bring the new division up to full strength. By the end of 1952, however, this had been accomplished and the division had attained a high degree of combat readiness as the result of a greatly intensified training program. In August of the next year, the division was sent to Japan to reinforce the United Nations forces in the Far East.

Following the cessation of hostilities, the Marine Corps redeployed its combat potential to more strategic locations to better fulfill its role as the nation's amphibious force-in-readiness. Recalled from Korea in 1955, the 1st Division moved into Camp Pendleton, California. Together with the 3d Marine Aircraft Wing, stationed at near-by El Toro, it forms the Marine Corps' West Coast air-ground combat team.

By 1956, the bulk of the 3d Division had completed movement from Japan to its permanent base on Okinawa. Reinforced by the 1st Marine Aircraft Wing, in Japan, the division is strategically poised for immediate deployment to any area of the Far East.

In the Central Pacific, a regiment of the 3d Division and air elements of the 1st Wing have been combined to form the 1st Marine Brigade, stationed in the Hawaiian Islands.

The Corps' East Coast air-ground combat team, made up of the 2d Marine Division and 3d Marine Aircraft Wing, occupies adjacent bases at Camp Lejeune and Cherry Point, North Carolina, respectively.

To the casual observer, it would appear that the post-Korean, peacetime Marine Corps—housed in comfortable barracks on permanent home bases, diligently engaged in endless cycles of monotonous training exercises—is a far cry from the stirring life "in the old Corps." To the more discerning onlooker, the general pattern of the Corps' activities since the Korean War bears the accustomed stamp of familiarity. Many a salty old-timer in the ranks, most of whom have less than a nodding acquaintance with classical Greek authors, will attest to Plutarch's proverbial observation that history repeats itself.

In February, 1955, Communist Chinese forces seized the offshore island of Ichiang, one of the many islands dotting the northern approach to Formosa Strait. The objective of this tactical move was to render an adjacent group of islands, known as the Tachens and occupied by Chinese Nationalists, completely indefensible. As far as attaining their objective was concerned, the Communist Chinese were eminently successful. The move also unwittingly succeeded in precipitating one of the shortest Marine Corps operations on record—a bloodless campaign which lasted less than a week.

When Nationalist attempts to evacuate the Tachen Islands were blocked by Communist forces, Marine troops from the 3d Division, then stationed in Japan, were hurriedly rushed to the scene. In six days of around-the-clock activity, 25,000 Nationalist civilians and troops were safely evacuated from four islands of the Tachens. Demolition experts, combing the islands for any form of military installations or structures which might be of value to the Communists, soon reduced them to rubble. The brief operation, according to the *New York Times*, "was the most forthright action against Communism since the Korean War."

Three months later the Marines were on their way to North Viet Nam, this time in answer to a call for help from the Vietnamese and French governments. Dubbing themselves the "Far East Rescue Squad," the Marines plunged into another evacuation operation similar to that of the Tachen Islands. When the statisticians finally tallied up the results, the record indicated that more than 300,000 refugees; 68,000 tons of cargo; and some 8,000 assorted vehicles had been safely snatched from the invading Communist Viet-Minh.

With one successful operation after another duly reported by a highly complimentary press, the Marines' stature as the nation's trouble-shooters continued to increase. Then, on the dark Sunday night of April 8, 1956, at Parris Island, South Carolina, fate and a drill instructor who had been drinking on duty united in a tragic episode that rocked the very foundations of the Corps.

Deciding that the recruits in his charge needed a little "toughening up," the overzealous sergeant ordered his platoon out on an unauthorized night march. When the route of march brought them to the swampy edge of a treacherous tidal stream which bounds the area, the drill instructor impetuously ordered the men to continue on into the swiftly flowing water. Suddenly, the darkness was pierced by frantic cries for help. Some of the men were non-swimmers, others were able to swim but very little. Those who were more at home in the water tried desperately to reach their stricken companions. Buffeted by the treacherous current, struggling agaisnt the weight of their packs, helmets and slung rifles, others scrambled for the safety of the muddy bank.

Panic filled the night.

And in the swirling waters of Ribbon Creek six men drowned.

The obvious results of the ensuing investigation and subsequent court-martial of the drill instructor were two-fold. For the first time in a long and proud history public confidence in the Marine Corps was badly shaken. The second result was a complete overhaul of recruit training methods, dictated largely by an indignant public who, blinded by the emotion-packed torrent of national publicity, never bothered to analyze the simple facts of the tragic episode.

For those who had worn the uniform long enough to understand the Corps as a way of life, the less obvious results which never rose to the surface were far more basic—far more vital. For them the issue was crystal clear. A man had erred in his judgment. He had failed in his duty to insure, to the best of his ability, the safety and well-being of fellow Marines entrusted to his care. And because he had failed, six men died.

For those who knew and understood these incontrovertible facts there was only bewilderment that the true issue never clearly emerged from the confusing storm of controversy that raged over the incident.

Why was a training system and a military philosophy which had been the envy of professional fighting men throughout the world for almost 200 years suddenly on public trial, simply because one of its members had failed?

For this question there was no answer. As the weeks passed, they watched in growing wonderment the blundering course of a side-show court-martial being tried in public print—a trial which, for some strange and unfathomable reason, appeared to purposely evade or minimize the fundamental issue. As they watched the savage, and to them unjust, indictment of one of their most cherished institutions, many were assailed by the fearful realization that they were witnessing the eroding destruction of a sacred belief—loyalty to the Corps and what it stands for. For them, now, there was doubt—a doubt that lingers still.

This was the real tragedy of Ribbon Creek. But tragedy gives little pause to time and the relentless current of ever-changing human concern. By October of the same year the eyes of the world were focused on a new crisis. Egypt seized the Suez Canal, and the rapid development of events flared briefly into open hostilities. With the lives of U. S. residents endangered by the conflict, a Marine battalion engaged in a training exercise on the island of Crete was rushed to Egypt. While British and French planes bombed adjacent Egyptian airfields, the Marines evacuated some 1,500 American nationals and citizens of 32 other countries from the beleaguered city of Alexandria.

On May 13, 1958, a Communist inspired mob in Caracas, Venezuela, attacked the automobile of U. S. Vice-President Richard E. Nixon during a good-will tour. Within a matter of hours, a Marine battalion was once again on its way to Latin America— this time to insure the safety of the Vice-President of the United States. The reason was perhaps different, but the routine of sudden movement toward another emergency in that particular area of the world had nostalgic overtones for the old-timers involved.

The fact that Marine units had remained constantly afloat with the U. S. Sixth Fleet in the Mediterranean escaped the notice of most Americans until the summer of 1958. The sudden headlines of the Lebanon crisis focused international attention on Marine activities in that country during July. Facing the threat of a *coup d'état* against his pro-West government, President Chamoun appealed to the United States for troops to protect his nation. Once again the Marines were called upon to fill the familiar role of an instrument of U. S. foreign policy. In mid-July, the quickly formed 2d Provisional Marine Force, consisting of four battalion landing teams, splashed ashore on the beaches of Lebanon—the words of their briefing officers still ringing in their ears. One of the company commanders explained the situation to his men this way:

"If the Navy can get us there on time, we'll hit the beach at fifteen hundred this afternoon. The target is Beirut. Some of you have been there and know what the country looks like.

"For the rest of you, Lebanon is a small country which occupies a strip, about one-hundred and twenty miles long and thirty to thirty-five miles wide, along the eastern shore of the Mediterranean. It has a population of a little over a million and a half; mostly Arabs, Armenians and Turks.

"Many of the people speak English. The two common languages, however, are Arabic and French.

"Almost one-third of the population lives in Beirut, which is the capital of Lebanon and its chief port. The only other city of any size is Tripoli.

"For over two months now a state of rebellion has existed in the country.

"Without boring you with a lot of political history, this revolt has been whipped up by Lebanese rebels—with plenty of outside help.

"As of yesterday, the rebels have taken over control of most of the Syrian border area; a section in the heart of Beirut, known as the 'Basta'; and some parts of the city of Tripoli.

"Since the Lebanese Army, counting all hands, adds up to a few hundred more troops than a Marine division, the Lebanese government has asked the United States for help.

"The word was passed from Washington at zero four hundred this morning. We're the closest U.S. combat troops to Lebanon—and that means we're it."

The captain paused, gazing reflectively at the sea of faces that stared up at him.

"And now I'm going to give you the weirdest order ever issued in the history of the Corps. . . ."

Another pause.

"Don't shoot until you are being shot at."

Promptly at 3:00 P.M. the first wave of Amtracks pitched

through the surf and began to waddle up the gently sloping beach toward Beirut's International Airport, a few hundred yards inland. The heart of the city lay some six miles to the northeast.

One company, riding their LVTs, moved across the airfield and piled out to establish a perimeter on the far side. Two companies, moving through the surf from their LCVPs, fanned out to cover the flanks.

Long before darkness fell, the International Airport, largest in the Middle East, was back in business. While Marines manned their sandbagged emplacements along the edges of the runways, and sentries patrolled the modern terminal building, giant international passenger planes roared skyward toward their global destinations.

The first night was a quiet one. Quiet, that is, if you did not take into account the humming clouds of giant mosquitoes that descended with the coming darkness on the hapless Marines. Quiet, if you could ignore the curious Lebanese citizens who stumbled around the positions, never dreaming that crashing through the underbrush in front of a Marine outpost is a standing invitation to sudden death.

The next morning a battalion boarded their LVTs and roared into Beirut to occupy their second objective. Mission: to secure the bridges guarding the northern approaches to the city and establish control of port facilities.

By now the routine was pretty well established. Religiously following their strange orders, the troops expended a lot of effort and will power in what for them was an unheard-of pastime—staying out of trouble.

It called for some doing.

Down in Beirut's dock area a group of Marines watched a ragged peddler, lugging a huge basket of soft drinks, approach them.

"You like buy cold drink, yes?" he whined in broken English, as he lowered the heavy basket to the pavement. "You wait. I go get ice. Come back quick, yes?"

He turned and scurried down the street.

Less than a minute after the Arab disappeared around the corner, the basket exploded with a thunderous WHOOOM, scattering jagged shards of glass in all directions.

For several seconds following the explosion there was a deathly silence. Then, from behind a huge packing crate—a good safe distance away—a camouflage-helmeted head popped into view.

Sharp blue eyes scanned the street.

"Okay, you guys, Abdul has shot his wad."

Emerging from their various hiding places, the Marines sauntered over to inspect the still smoldering remains of the bomb.

"Must be the Arabic version of the Molotov cocktail, huh?" one of them commented.

"Yeah," grunted a corporal. "These gooks must think we're a bunch of 'boots' to fall for an old gag like that!"

Out on the perimeter the troops manning the outposts fought the mosquitoes; temperatures that often hit 100 in the shade; and that age-old enemy of all military men—boredom.

As soon as darkness fell, they knew they could count on a little excitement. The "Ollies," as they called the rebels, would come out of the olive groves to begin their nightly harassing tactics.

Some nights it was firecrackers, strung along the barbed wire surrounding the outposts. Other nights the tormentors contented themselves with roaming the near-by hills, screaming and howling like banshees.

Several times they rounded up burros and stampeded the braying animals into the Marines' positions. It was a very effective maneuver for setting off the carefully placed trip flares.

But the trick that showed real ingenuity, and earned the grudging admiration of the Marines, was the "wild dog" attack. Creeping up as close as they dared, the rebels would hurl large chunks of raw meat into the Marine positions. Within a few minutes the whole area would be covered with packs of wild dogs, snapping and snarling at each other as they fought over the food.

"Those dogfights," one observer comments, "were really something to see—and hear!"

On July 31, Lebanon elected a new president and the tension

eased. Yet it was the middle of August before the Marines started home.

In the long chronicles of war, the landing in Lebanon is set down as one of the strangest chapters of all. To *L'Orient,* the most influential newspaper in the Middle East, the affair had this significance: "The United States Marines have demonstrated how Western troops can penetrate a country as friends, and come away without losing that standing. . . ."

Though they take justifiable pride in this accolade, Marines draw their own conclusions as to the significance of their brief sojourn in Lebanon. From their viewpoint, it was basically added verification of an unshakable conviction of long standing—one they often give voice to with a quote from Rudyard Kipling. "It is not the big stick that counts; it is the liftable stick."

As the 1950s gave way to a new decade, Marines renewed their acquaintance with Southeast Asia. In 1959, and again in 1960–61, as Communist-inspired civil war came to Laos, the hidden trails of the deep jungle again knew the familiar tread of Marine combat boots.

In the late summer of 1959 the Corps suddenly found itself back in the rescue business. Marine Helicopter Squadron 261, operating from the *USS Thetis Bay,* sped to Taiwan to perform a week-long mercy mission. During the emergency, caused by the worst floods in the island's history, the "whirlybirds" flew almost a thousand missions, lifting two million pounds of relief supplies to stricken areas and evacuating hundreds of refugees.

The operation marked a vital milestone for the Marine Corps. It had been conducted with the aid of an LPH—an entirely new breed of ship which the Marines had fought to see become a reality for many years. LPH is the official designation for Landing Platform Helicopter, a ship designed specifically to support the Corps' doctrine of vertical assault. As the world's first assault helicopter transport, the *Thetis Bay* (a converted jeep-class aircraft carrier of World War II vintage) was the "guinea pig" for a unique fleet which today boasts eight ships. The *Valley Forge, Princeton* and *Boxer* are converted *Essex*-class carriers. The *USS*

Iwo Jima, launched in October 1960, was the first LPH to be constructed from the keel up for her special mission. She was followed by the *USS Okinawa* in 1961, the *USS Guadalcanal* in 1963 and the *USS Guam* in 1964.

Among the historic dates profusely sprinkled throughout the proud record of the Corps, none shines more brightly than February 20, 1962. On that sun-filled Tuesday morning a freckle-faced Marine thundered into the heavens atop a giant Atlas rocket to become the first American in space. With the epic flight of his *Friendship Seven* capsule, Lieutenant Colonel John H. Glenn, Jr., a 20-year veteran of Marine aviation, launched the United States into the era of space travel.

Later in the spring of 1962, three thousand combat ready Marines landed in Thailand. As it had been so many times in the past, their mission was to protect the territorial integrity of a small, pro-Western country against the threatening forces of an ubiquitous enemy.

In much the same fashion, Marines moved into Viet Nam in 1962—where many of them still remain. There in the steaming jungle swamps and across the copper-brown mud flats of the sprawling Mekong delta country they carry on the frustrating struggle of guerrilla warfare against three stanchly allied foes— time, the river and the Viet Cong.

It was during October of the same year that the nation—and the world—learned that Communist intercontinental missiles had been emplaced only ninety miles from the mainland of America. Cuba had become a launching pad. The eastern half of the United States was the target.

Long before the news was publicly announced, Navy and Marine Corps units moved quietly into southern Florida and the Caribbean air stations to bolster U. S. air defense capabilities.

From their air bases at El Toro, California, and Cherry Point, North Carolina, 1st and 2d Marine Division "ready battalions," units on around-the-clock stand-by for emergencies, were airlifted to the U. S. Naval Base at Guantanamo Bay. The battalion from the West Coast had reported "prepared to move" less than five hours after receiving the order to embark. Six hours after lift-off they were standing on Cuban soil. It would be difficult to find a more striking example of the by-word that has long since become a part of the Marines' creed—readiness.

In the era of the "cold war," the Marine Corps has found itself in the unique position of maintaining its traditional combat readiness in not one, but two types of warfare. Military thinking in the United States is divided as to just what the nature of the warfare of the future will be. One school of thought subscribes to the thesis that the next great war will be fought with nuclear weapons.

On the opposite side of the argument are those who are convinced that a stalemate has been reached among the nations of the world insofar as nuclear warfare is concerned. This school of thought holds that wars of the future will be "brush fire," limited wars, fought solely with conventional weapons.

To still others, including Marine Corps planners and strategists, this controversy is interesting, thought-provoking—and largely academic. The answer to the argument, they contend, obviously lies somewhere in the uncertain future. It is an answer that only time and the unpredictable course of ultimate events will provide.

But amid the clatter and clamor of the vociferous debate, certain factors are unmistakably apparent. To chart a course for the future on the certainty of nuclear conflict, while conventional warfare remains an eminent possibility, involves a completely unacceptable risk. On the other hand, the assumption that a war of the future will be one completely devoid of nuclear weapons is much too naïve for realistic military thinkers. The only sensible solution, they maintain, is to be prepared for either eventuality: a course of action the Marine Corps wholeheartedly champions.

The continual refinement of the vertical assault concept as the tactical answer to nuclear warfare has produced some radical changes in the appearance of Marine combat units. The modern doctrine for amphibious operations, which envisions deep penetration of enemy territory by helicopter-borne assault forces, emphasizes speed, mobility, flexibility and the wide dispersal of battalion-sized units. As a result of years of painstaking research and development in new weapons and equipment, the streamlined, nuclear-age Marine division is 10 per cent smaller, considerably lighter and carries far greater fire power than its Korean War ancestor.

Armed with the weapons of modern warfare, the Marine Corps of the Atomic Age faces the challenges of the future. As it has been throughout almost two centuries, the true measure of its ability to meet these challenges lies not in the number of its battalions nor in the instruments of war with which they ply their trade.

It is to be found in the glowing record of those who have bequeathed to it an untarnished legacy of military achievement—the priceless heritage of a proud band of men.

Selected Bibliography

Allen, Gardner W., *A Naval History of The American Revolution,* Houghton Mifflin, 2 vols., Boston, 1913.

Arthur, R. A. and Cohlmia, Kenneth, *The Third Marine Division,* Infantry Journal Press, Washington, D.C., 1948.

Bartley, Whitman S., *Iwo Jima: Amphibious Epic,* Historical Branch, Headquarters, U.S. Marine Corps, GPO, Washington, D.C., 1954.

Bayler, Walter L. J., *The Last Man Off Wake Island,* Bobbs-Merill, New York, 1942.

Blankfort, Michael, *The Big Yankee,* Brown, Boston, 1947.

Boggs, Charles W. Jr., *Marine Aviation in The Philippines,* Historical Branch, Headquarters, U.S. Marine Corps, GPO, Washington, D.C., 1951.

Cass, Bevan G. (ed) *The History of The Sixth Marine Division,* Infantry Journal Press, Washington, D.C., 1948.

Catlin, Albertus W., *With The Help Of God And A Few Marines,* Doubleday, Page, New York, 1919.

Clark, George R. and others, *A Short History of the United States Navy,* Lippincott, Philadelphia, 1939.

Collum, Richard S., *History of the United States Marine Corps,* Hamersly, New York, 1903.

Conner, H. M., *The Spearhead,* Infantry Journal Press, Washington, D.C., 1950.

Craige, John H., *What the Citizen Should Know About the Marines,* Norton, New York, 1914.

Davis, Burke, *Marine,* Little, Brown and Company, Boston, 1962.

DeChant, John A., *Devilbirds,* Harper, New York, 1947.

Devereux, James P. S., *The Story of Wake Island,* Lippincott, New York, 1947.

Fehrenbach, T. R., *This Kind of War,* The Macmillan Company, New York, 1963.

Feldt, Eric A., *The Coastwatchers,* Oxford University Press, New York, 1946.

Fuchida, Mitsuo and Okumiya, Masatake, *Midway: The Battle That Doomed Japan.* U.S. Naval Institute, Annapolis, 1955.

Geer, Andrew, *Reckless, Pride Of The Marines,* Harper, New York, 1955.

————, *The New Breed,* Harper, New York, 1952.

Griffith, Samuel B. II, *The Battle For Guadalcanal,* J. B. Lippincott Co., New York, 1963.

Harbord, James G., *Leaves From A War Diary,* Dodd, Mead, New York, 1925.

Heinl, R. D. Jr., and Crown, J. A., *The Marshalls: Increasing The Tempo,* Historical Branch, Headquarters, U.S. Marine Corps, GPO, Washington, D.C., 1954.

Heinl, R. D. Jr., *The Defense Of Wake,* Historical Branch, Headquarters, U.S. Marine Corps, GPO, Washington, D.C., 1947.

———, *Marines At Midway,* Historical Branch, Headquarters, U.S. Marine Corps, GPO, Washington, D.C., 1948.

———, *Soldiers of the Sea,* U.S. Naval Institute, Annapolis, Maryland, 1962.

Hoffman, Carl W., *Saipan: The Beginning Of The End,* Historical Branch, Headquarters, U.S. Marine Corps, GPO, Washington, D.C., 1950.

———, *The Seizure Of Tinian,* Historical Branch, Headquarters, U.S. Marine Corps, GPO, Washington, D.C., 1951.

Hough, Frank O., *The Assault On Peleliu,* Historical Branch, Headquarters, U.S. Marine Corps, GPO, Washington, D.C., 1950.

———, *The Campaign Of New Britain,* Historical Branch, Headquarters, U.S. Marine Corps, GPO, Washington, D.C., 1952.

———, *The Island War,* Lippincott, New York, 1947.

———, Ludwig, V. E. and Shaw, H. I., *Pearl Harbor To Guadalcanal,* —History of U.S. Marine Corps Operations In World War II, vol. I, Historical Branch, Headquarters, U.S. Marine Corps, GPO, Washington, D.C., 1958.

Hunt, George P., *The Story of The U.S. Marines,* Random House, New York, 1951.

Isley, Jeter A. and Crowl, Philip A., *The U.S. Marines and Amphibious War,* Princeton Univ. Press, 1951.

Johnston, R. W., *Follow Me,* Random House, New York, 1948.

Josephy, A. M. Jr., *The Long And The Short And The Tall,* Knopf, New York, 1946.

Karig, Walter and others, *Battle Report: The War In Korea,* Rinehart, New York, 1952.

Knox, D. W., *A History Of The United States Navy,* Putnam's, New York, 1948.

Leckie, Robert, *Helmet For My Pillow,* Random House, New York, 1957.

———, *March To Glory,* World Publishing Company, New York, 1960.

———, *Strong Men Armed,* Random House, New York, 1962.

———, *Conflict,* G. P. Putnam's Sons, New York, 1962.

Lejeune, John A., *The Reminiscenses Of A Marine,* Dorrance, Philadelphia, 1930.

Lewis, Charles L., *Famous American Marines,* Page, Boston, 1950.

Lodge, O. R., *The Recapture Of Guam,* Historical Branch, Headquarters, U.S. Marine Corps, GPO, Washington, D.C., 1954.

Mahan, Alfred T., *Sea Power In Its Relation To the War Of 1812*, Little, Brown, Boston, 1905.

McCahill, William P., *First To Fight*, McKay, Philadelphia, 1942.

McCrocklin, J. W. (ed), *Garde d'Haiti 1915–1934*, Naval Institute Proceedings, Annapolis, 1956.

McMillan, George, *The Old Breed*, Infantry Journal Press, Washington, D.C., 1949.

Merillat, H. L., *The Island*, Houghton Mifflin, Boston, 1944.

Metcalf, Clyde H., *A History Of The United States Marine Corps.*, Putman's, New York, 1939.

——, *The Marine Corps Reader*, Putnam's, New York, 1944.

Monks, John, Jr., *A Ribbon And A Star*, Holt, New York, 1945.

Montross, Lynn and Canzona, Nicholas A., *The Inchon-Seoul Operation —U.S. Marine Operations in Korea, 1950–1953*, vol. II, Historical Branch, Headquarters, U.S. Marine Corps, GPO, Washington, D.C., 1955.

——, *The Chosen Reservoir Campaign—U.S. Marine Operations In Korea, 1950–1953*, vol. III, Historical Branch, Headquarters, U.S. Marine Corps, GPO, Washington, D.C., 1957.

——, *The Pusan Perimeter—U.S. Marine Operations In Korea, 1950– 1953*, vol. I, Historical Branch, Headquarters, U.S. Marine Corps, GPO, Washington, D.C., 1954.

——, Kuokka, H. D., and Hicks, N. W., *The East Central Front—U.S. Marine Operations in Korea*, vol. IV, Historical Branch, Headquarters, U.S. Marine Corps, GPO, Washington, D.C., 1962.

Montross, Lynn, *Cavalry Of the Sky*, Harper, New York, 1954.

Morison, Samuel Eliot, *History Of United States Naval Operations In World War II*, 14 vols., Little Brown, Boston, 1947.

Nichols, Charles S. Jr., and Shaw, Henry I. Jr., *Okinawa: Victory In The Pacific*, Historical Branch, Headquarters, U. S. Marine Corps, GPO, Washington, D.C., 1955.

O'Sheel, Patrick and Cook, Gene (eds.) *Semper Fidelis*, Sloane, New York, 1947.

Pierce, Philip N., "Forgotten Glory," *Marine Corps Gazette*, January 1948.

——, "The Seven Years War," *Marine Corps Gazette*, September, 1948.

——, "Tell It To The Marines," *Marine Corps Gazette*, May 1952.

——, "Force in Readiness," *Marine Corps Gazette*, November, 1959.

——, "The Unsolved Mystery of Pete Ellis," *Marine Corps Gazette*, February, 1962.

——, "Holocaust At Pearl," "King of La Gonave," "The Hill" and "Lebanon," in Karl Schuon (ed), *The Leathernecks*, Franklin Watts, Inc., New York, 1963.

—— and Schuon, Karl, *John H. Glenn: Astronaut*, Franklin Watts, Inc., New York, 1962.

Potter, E. B. (ed) *The United States And World Sea Power*, Prentice-Hall, Boston, 1955.

Pratt, Fletcher, *The Marines War*, Sloane, New York, 1948.

————, *The Compact History of the United States Navy*, Hawthorn Books, New York, 1957.

Proehl, C. W. (ed.) *The Fourth Marine Division In World War II*, Infantry Journal Press, Washington, D.C., 1946.

Rankin, Robert H., *Uniforms of the Sea Services*, U.S. Naval Institute, Annapolis, Maryland, 1962.

Rentz, John N., *Marines In The Central Solomons*, Historical Branch, Headquarters, U.S. Marine Corps, GPO, Washington, D.C., 1952.

————, *Bougainville And The Northern Solomons*, Historical Branch, Headquarters, U.S. Marine Corps, GPO, Washington, D.C., 1948.

Richmond, Sir Herbert, *The Navy As An Instrument Of Policy*, Cambridge University Press, London, 1953.

Roosevelt, Theodore, *The Naval War Of 1812*, Putnam's, New York, 1889.

Russ, Martin, *The Last Parallel*, Rinehart, New York, 1957.

Russell, W. H., "The Genesis of FMF Doctrine," *Marine Corps Gazette*, April–July 1951.

Semper Fidelis, Marine Corps Combat Correspondents, Sloane, New York, 1947.

Sherrod, Robert, *Tarawa: The Story Of A Battle*, Duell, Sloan and Pearce, New York, 1944.

————, *History Of Marine Corps Aviation In World War II*, Combat Forces Press, Washington, D.C., 1952.

————, *On To Westward*, Duell, Sloan and Pearce, New York, 1945.

Schuon, Karl, *U.S. Marine Corps Biographical Dictionary*, Franklin Watts, Inc., New York, 1963.

———— and Smith, Earl, *Marines and What They Do*, Franklin Watts, Inc., New York, 1962.

Smith, Justin H., *The War With Mexico*, MacMillan, New York, 1919.

Smith, Holland M. and Finch, Percy, *Coral and Brass*, Scribner's, New York, 1949.

Stockman, James R., *The Battle For Tarawa*, Historical Branch, Headquarters, U.S. Marine Corps, GPO, Washington, D.C., 1947.

The U.S. Marines on Iwo Jima, Marine Combat Writers, Infantry Journal Press, Washington, D.C., 1945.

Thomas, Lowell, *Old Gimlet Eye*, Farrar and Rinehart, New York, 1933.

Thomas, R. C. W., *The War In Korea*, Gale and Polden, Aldershot, England, 1954.

Tregaskis, Richard, *Guadalcanal Diary*, Random House, New York, 1943.

Uncommon Valor, Marine Combat Correspondents, Infantry Journal Press, Washington, D.C., 1946.

Wilson, Earl J. and others, *Betio Beachhead*, Putnam's, New York, 1945.

Wise, Frederic M., *A Marine Tells It To You*, Sears, New York, 1929.

Index

THE AUTHORS AND THEIR BOOK

LIEUTENANT COLONEL PHILIP N. PIERCE, UNITED STATES MA-
RINE CORPS RETIRED, *was born in Gardiner, Maine on September
20, 1917. He was graduated from the University of Maine in
1942 with a B.A. in Journalism and enlisted in the Marines.
Within five months he was commissioned a Second Lieutenant.
During World War II he saw action in the Pacific at Saipan, Tinian, Iwo Jima and the Marshall Islands, receiving combat decora-
tions for service at Saipan and Iwo Jima. From 1945 to 1948 he
was Chief of the Press Branch at Marine Corps Headquarters in
Washington, D.C. He was with the First Provisional Marine Brigade in Korea a month after the conflict began. Returning from
Korea he was assigned to teach at the Marine Corps Schools
(Quantico, Virginia) and later at the Naval Amphibious Base
(Coronado, California). From 1958 until his retirement from active duty in 1962, he served successively as Deputy Director of
Information and Director of Media at Marine Corps Headquar-
ters in Washington. The holder of 12 combat decorations and ci-
tations, Colonel Pierce is one of the Marines' best-known authors.
His magazine work has appeared in national publications in the
United States, Canada, Mexico, Britain and Europe. He has written for radio and television, and is a contributor to* Encyclopaedia
Britannica, Encyclopedia Americana *and* World Scope Encyclopedia. *He is the author of several military texts and co-author of*
John H. Glenn: Astronaut *(Franklin Watts, 1962), a book club
selection, and* The Leathernecks *(Franklin Watts, 1963).*

The late LIEUTENANT COLONEL FRANK O. HOUGH, UNITED
STATES MARINE CORPS RETIRED, *was born on June 4, 1899 in
Rochester, N.Y. He ran away from prep school at seventeen to enlist in the Marines, falsifying his age to enter. After World War I
he returned to school. He graduated from Brown University in*

(1924), a member of Phi Beta Kappa. He then worked as a newspaperman, an advertising copywriter, a free-lance writer and a Brown University English instructor. In 1942 he re-entered the Marine Corps as a reserve officer and served with the First Marine Division in action at New Guinea, New Britain and Peleliu. He received a combat decoration for his service at Peleliu. He retired from the Marine Corps in 1947. On May 15, 1958 he died at San Miguel, Mexico. His works include The Assault on Peleliu (*Marine Corps Historical Branch, 1952*), The Campaign of New Britain (*Marine Corps Historical Branch, 1952*), The Island War (*Lippincott, 1947*), *and* Pearl Harbor to Guadalcanal (*Marine Corps Historical Branch, 1958*).

THE COMPACT HISTORY OF THE UNITED STATES MARINE CORPS, *New and Revised Edition (Hawthorn, 1964) was completely manufactured by American Book-Stratford Press, New York City. The text type is Times Roman, originally designed by Stanley Morison for use by* The Times *of London. Gil Walker drew the illustrations for the text and endpapers.*

A HAWTHORN BOOK